OUR LIFE IN GOD'S LIGHT

Our Life in God's Light

ESSAYS BY HUGH T. KERR

EDITED BY JOHN M. MULDER

THE WESTMINSTER PRESS

PHILADELPHIA

Scripture quotations from the Revised Standard Version
of the Bible are copyrighted 1946, 1952, © 1971, 1973
by the Division of Christian Education of the National
Council of the Churches of Christ in the U.S.A., and are
used by permission.

Book Design by Dorothy Alden Smith

First edition

Published by The Westminster Press ®
Philadelphia, Pennsylvania

PRINTED IN THE UNITED STATES OF AMERICA

9 8 7 6 5 4 3 2 1

Library of Congress Cataloging in Publication Data

Kerr, Hugh Thomson, 1909–
    Our life in God's light.

    "Bibliography: the writings of Hugh T. Kerr": p.
    1. Theology—Addresses, essays, lectures.   2. Kerr,
Hugh Thomson, 1909–   —Addresses, essays,
lectures.
3. Theology today—Addresses, essays, lectures.
4. Kerr, Hugh Thomson, 1909–   —Bibliography.
I.   Mulder, John M., 1946–   II.   Title.
BR50.K39   230   78-24089
ISBN 0-664-21372-3
ISBN 0-664-24235-9 pbk.

Contents

ACKNOWLEDGMENTS

It has been a singular honor and privilege for me to be involved in the editing of these essays by Hugh T. Kerr for publication, and I want to express my gratitude to several others who helped make the volume possible. James I. McCord gave enthusiastic support to the project from its inception and provided his own tribute to Tim Kerr's contributions to THEOLOGY TODAY and Princeton Theological Seminary. John A. Mackay, who had the vision to launch the journal during the bleak days of World War II, graciously offered his essay and much encouragement in the process of preparation. F. W. Dillistone eagerly accepted an invitation to assess Tim Kerr's impact on contemporary theology and the life of the church; his superb introduction provides a fitting framework for Tim's essays and editorials. Rose Rickert, the Business Manager of THEOLOGY TODAY, and Trudy Pettichord, her assistant, gave valuable assistance at several points. Elsie Anne McKee devoted hours of diligent labor to compiling the bibliography, and Elizabeth A. Meirs' secretarial skills were indispensable.

The volume itself would have been inconceivable without the cooperation of Tim himself. Initially embarrassed and shy about resurrecting his essays for publication again, he has looked over the entire text and helped at many stages of the preparation. I have had the good fortune to work with him on THEOLOGY TODAY for a decade, and in this project and in every other, I have always felt his willingness to see others as colleagues and co-workers in a common enterprise. The book is only a small way of expressing my gratitude and the indebtedness of his readers and students for what he has taught them and who he is.

It is also gratifying to see this volume appear under the imprint of The Westminster Press, which shared its paper allotment with THEOLOGY TODAY during World War II so the journal could begin publication, and which published Tim Kerr's first book, *A Compend of the Institutes of the Christian Religion by John Calvin* (1939), a volume that this year celebrates its own fortieth anniversary of being in print. The staff of the Press has sustained and guided this present volume to completion, mitigating the many problems that arise in the process from manuscript to printed book.

The following selections are reprinted as they appeared in THEOLOGY TODAY. Potentially confusing anachronisms have been deleted for the sake of clarity, but each essay is substantively untouched. The conventions of English style have evolved over the years at THEOLOGY TODAY. The title of this volume, the essays themselves, and the editing of them reflect Tim Kerr's desire to communicate "our life in God's light," and not simply "the life of man in the light of God."

JOHN M. MULDER

PREFACES
AND
INTRODUCTION

PREFACE

The Journalist as Evangelist

By John M. Mulder

In one of his frequent bouts of frustration with the Danish press, Søren Kierkegaard exploded: "The lowest depth to which a person can sink before God is defined by the word 'journalist.' If I were a father and had a daughter who was seduced, I should not despair over her; I would hope for her salvation. But if I had a son who became a journalist and continued to remain one for five years, I would give him up."

I do not know what the reaction of Hugh T. Kerr, Sr., was to the journalistic efforts of his son—first with his "Over-Seas Letters" to *The Presbyterian Banner* in the 1930's, then as the editor of *The Register* at Louisville Presbyterian Theological Seminary, and subsequently as Associate Editor (1944–1951) and Editor (1951–   ) of THEOLOGY TODAY. It seems likely that the elder Kerr took a somewhat more tolerant and sanguine view of his son's interests, for both were contributors to Vol. I, No. 1, of THEOLOGY TODAY. But Kierkegaard's fulminations suggest the precarious lot of journalists and editors. Scourged by authors and disparaged by readers, they rarely receive sufficient credit for undertaking the onerous task of trying to perceive what is new and make sense of it for others.

What is at first glance extraordinary about Tim Kerr's venture into journalism is his perseverance and tenacity over more than four decades, thirty-five years of which have been in association with THEOLOGY TODAY. During that time he has made an indelible imprint on theological inquiry in the twentieth century and established THEOLOGY TODAY as the most widely circulated and influential quarterly journal of theologi-

15

cal thought in the United States. With only one year's respite, he has remained faithful to the vocation of journalist and editor, despite the incessant demands of deadlines and a full teaching load at Princeton Theological Seminary.

His own literary production during these decades, as evidenced by the bibliography in this volume, is staggering. Books, articles, reviews, and poetry flowed from his pen, and in contrast to the specialization that plagues all areas of contemporary academic life, Tim Kerr's writings testify to the wide scope of his interests, his intellectual courage in venturing out into many fields, and his refusal to be confined by the scholastic guilds. The thirty-five selections that comprise this book are only a sample of his writings for THEOLOGY TODAY; they fail to include much of his commentary on developments in theology, church, and society that made the column "Theological Table-Talk" a valuable guide for thousands of readers. Still less does this collection reflect his writings for other publications or those contained in his several books.

In addition, virtually all of the thirty-five volumes of THEOLOGY TODAY contain the hidden, but unmistakable evidence of Tim Kerr's stylistic and editing skills, and even anonymous authorship. Frequently I have seen hefty manuscripts go off to the printer with the first five pages crossed out and the penciled instruction on page six: "Start here." Or, there are the cases of manuscripts of dubious literary grace and clumsy construction that emerge from the editor's typewriter with a directness and lucidity that confound the author. His correspondence with contributors could well serve as a manual for any writer. With a combination of encouragement and trenchant criticism, he has frequently reminded them of the basics of effective communication: "Get to the point; don't run in place." "To whom are you writing? Remember your audience." "Don't be timid; readers are interested in what *you* have to say, not the interminable rehashing of what everyone else said."

Equally important, Tim Kerr's leadership of THEOLOGY TODAY has been marked by a fidelity to the title of the journal as well as its motto: to be both a contemporary journal of theological thinking and a forum for careful reflection on the transient character of "our life in God's light." In thirty-five years, THEOLOGY TODAY has charted every major movement in the church and theology—from neo-orthodoxy through the theologies of revolution, hope, and liberation. In no case did the journal or the editor capitulate to any one trend; instead, Tim Kerr's response has been sympathetic and yet critical, measuring each with an irenic eye and hoping to see in every new expression a contribution to the renewal of the church and its proclamation of the gospel. His emotional and intellectual ballast during these confusing and perplexing times in theology has been his own grounding in the Reformed tradition and the biblical message. As he has written, "The Reformers were not concerned with the novel but with the gospel, not innovation but re-formation. To them was given new insight into old truth, and that is why Luther and Calvin and the many Reformation creeds took their stand upon the Scriptures and the revelation of what God had done in Jesus Christ."

Animating Tim Kerr's entire career, as I have briefly witnessed it, has been a vision of what it means to be an evangelist —a proclaimer of God's good news to the world. I encountered him first as my teacher, introducing me to "Classic Systems of Theology" with perceptive lectures, intriguing questions, and an evident concern for the class members as human beings. His wit and humor enlivened what we all found difficult and made the inaccessible reaches of the tradition somewhat closer at hand. The inevitable abstractions of theology were never allowed to be treated as mere intellectual toys, unrelated to life or the church. For Tim Kerr as editor and journalist, the life of the mind has always been the life of faith, and the life of faith has been the activity of the Spirit in human relationship and community.

The apostle Paul has written, "But how are people to call upon him in whom they have not believed? And how are they to believe in him of whom they have never heard? And how are they to hear without a preacher? And how can people preach unless they are sent? As it is written, 'How beautiful are the feet of those who preach good news!' But they have not all obeyed the gospel; for Isaiah says, 'Lord, who has believed what he has heard from us?' So faith comes from what is heard, and what is heard comes by the preaching of Christ" (Rom. 10:14–17).

Tim Kerr's career has been an evangelistic calling in the truest sense—a literate, coherent presentation and distribution of the gospel of Jesus Christ to a broken world. It is hoped that through this collection of his essays, written over the past several years, the reader will be able to see again how all preaching, written or oral, despite its occasional character, may have the enduring quality that evangelism and preaching have when blessed by the Holy Spirit.

The Editor as Teacher

By James I. McCord

The well-known quarterly journal THEOLOGY TODAY is the lengthened shadow of two editors, John A. Mackay and Hugh T. Kerr. John Mackay was the creative spirit who brought the journal into being in the tumultuous spring of 1944. It was a major achievement in his lifelong ambition to restore theology to its rightful place in religion and culture. From the beginning of this journalistic enterprise, as a young professor of doctrinal theology on the Princeton Theological Seminary faculty, Hugh Kerr was the founder's indispensable associate and ally. With the end of World War II, and the growing duties of a seminary president, the editor's mantle fell on the assistant's shoulders, and for more than three decades it has been apparent to a growing readership that the person and the position were tailored for each other.

What are the strengths that characterize a great editor? A deep knowledge of and commitment to a *living* tradition is certainly one. Tim Kerr, as most of his friends and colleagues call him, brings to his editorial task the fruits of historical research in the classic Christian tradition and especially in the Reformers, Luther and Calvin. He has continued to represent the "Reformed" position in the widest, most catholic sense of the term, as John Mackay himself understood the label, and to reach out and engage virtually every dimension of culture and human inquiry from this perspective. Tradition is more than the dead weight of the past. It is the ongoing, living embodiment of the whole life and thought of the people of God as this process has been nurtured and corrected by the Holy

19

Spirit. This has enabled the editor to maintain for the journal a steady course through the stormy seas of recent history, as one theological skiff after another has capsized, and the entire theological landscape has often seemed a shambles. Throughout his career as editor, Tim Kerr has sought to see *all* human life in *God's* light, and to demonstrate the reality and vitality of theological existence and critical reflection.

Another mark of a great editor is the ability to sense trends as they develop, but not to take them with ultimate seriousness. THEOLOGY TODAY was designed to be a literary, not a technical, journal, to illuminate new ideas as they develop, to include articles dealing with disciplines cognate to theology, and to attract as its readers intelligent lay people as well as members of the clergy and teachers of religion. To preside over such a broad undertaking demands constant vigilance of the cultural scene. While carrying a full load in teaching and committee work on the Princeton Seminary faculty, Tim Kerr managed to stay in touch with books and articles, sermons and lectures, as they appeared, and these trends were reflected in editorials and in the feature section known as "Theological Table-Talk." But it is one thing to be sensitive and alert to what is going on, and another to be merely "trendy." The latter has never been a problem for THEOLOGY TODAY because of a wise editor who has been able to keep things in perspective, perhaps because he was teaching and editorializing at the same time.

A third quality to be found in a great editor is concern for literary clarity and style. Under Tim Kerr's guidance, THEOLOGY TODAY has remained over the years both fresh and clear, demonstrating that theological lore need not be stylistically unbecoming. This has involved giving careful scrutiny to innumerable manuscripts, solicited and unsolicited, through the years, revising and revamping, and often virtually rewriting them. This has been accomplished with amazing patience, unerring skill, and with the approval of hosts of writers and authors.

Tim Kerr, it must be said, has done far more than preside over the destiny of an influential theological journal, important and time-consuming as that is. His own contributions to theological thought are found throughout each volume in editorials, articles, reviews, and in "Theological Table-Talk." One is impressed in rereading this substantial corpus of theological literature with the catholicity of the author's interests and the wide range of issues to which he brings theological insight and criticism. These issues are as varied as worship, ecology, language, preaching, story, arts, education, and the nature of dialogue and communication. Each editorial and essay bears eloquent witness to the author's conviction that theology is not a dismal science, remote and aloof, but a joyous one, relevant to human life in all its dimensions of aspiration and striving.

Any tribute to Hugh T. Kerr would be incomplete that does not mention his distinguished career on the Princeton Theological Seminary faculty. Here he was an unrivaled leader, meriting and securing the respect of his colleagues. He was often asked to chair some of the most important faculty committees. He headed the group that drew up the faculty's by-laws; chaired the curriculum review committee that ended the era of a program of study that was virtually frozen by required courses; initiated, with John Mackay and a few others, dialogue with Princeton University regarding doctoral programs; sat with outside accrediting associations; and served several terms as chairman of the department of theology. His manner or style was seldom assertive—at times it appeared even diffident—but he was always prepared, and ready to speak a decisive word when the occasion called for it. A gentleman at all times, still he never suffered fools gladly. His early retirement from active teaching to give full time to the affairs of THEOLOGY TODAY deprived the faculty of its most effective antidote to undue loquacity.

In the classroom, as I have reason to know, Tim Kerr was never routine. His courses tended to be adventures in understanding and creativity. He was far more interested in learning than in schooling, in something happening in the life of the student than in transmitting a body of information. Term projects might be the usual research paper, but they also included producing films, or writing and directing plays. He was in constant search of new and more effective methodologies, and spent one of his sabbaticals visiting schools and colleges to study experiments in learning. Several articles and editorials in THEOLOGY TODAY reflect this interest. During the chaotic years of the late 1960's and early 1970's, he remained close to students, earned their respect, and was a major factor in helping a groping generation work through the problems occasioned by continuing racism and the war in Vietnam. My own strong impression is that he retired from teaching when his influence was at its peak.

As one who has worked with Tim Kerr, as faculty and editorial colleague, for nearly two decades, it is a joy to salute him publicly and to pay tribute to his brilliant career. It gives us all confidence to know that his vigor and freshness remain undiminished and that he will continue to oversee the affairs of THEOLOGY TODAY for years to come. This is the best guarantee that the theological enterprise will be monitored and enriched by one of the keenest minds and most sensitive spirits of this generation.

On the Road

By John A. Mackay

My first encounter with Hugh T. Kerr was on a Pennsylvania highway. It occurred quite casually in the summer season some forty years ago. We chanced to be rambling at the time in recreational mood in opposite directions. We stopped along the road, greeted one another, and entered into conversation. He was then on the faculty at Louisville Theological Seminary, and I had been for some years president of Princeton Seminary.

In the course of our conversation I was thrilled to discover that this young man was the son of a distinguished Presbyterian minister in Pittsburgh, Pennsylvania—a gentleman whom I had come to know personally and to admire greatly. It was but natural that I should later become interested in receiving further information regarding Tim Kerr, who devoted several years to academic work in Scotland, where he received his doctorate from Edinburgh University, and in Germany, where he studied at Tübingen University.

In 1940 I had been president of Princeton Seminary for four years. It was in that year that the incumbent of the Benjamin B. Warfield chair of theology passed away. With the favorable consent of the Seminary faculty, and the full approval of the Board of Trustees, I invited Tim Kerr to become his successor. This he did, becoming a most popular teacher.

That was also the time when I made the decision that the hour had arrived to bring to birth a journal that would give relevancy and status across wide frontiers to the study of religious ultimates, to truths concerning God and man and their

23

relationship. It was then and in that context that THEOLOGY TODAY came into being.

My first words as founder and initial editor of THEOLOGY TODAY were these. It is an appropriate moment to repeat them:

Why this adventure in journalism? a chorus of voices ask. When the earth quivers beneath the flail of total war, when battles mount in fury around the globe, when the most momentous year in modern history is running its course, why should a new journal be issued? The answer is simple. Theology is never irrelevant, nor should it ever be insensitive to the affairs of men, least of all in days like these. In a period of confusion and crisis, when tomorrow is being born in the travailing womb of today, theology is the most important study in which men can engage, as they make their pilgrimage from one era to another, and from this world to the world to come.

Now is the time of all times to be concerned about the living God, for His changeless being, and for His redemptive purpose for mankind. For what is theology in its ultimate meaning, but earnest thinking about God, carried on in the light of God and designed to help men to be God-like in their character and God-centered in their behavior.

As the years go by, and as problems multiply, I feel increasingly that one of the most important decisions I made during those presidential years at Princeton Seminary was to ask Hugh Kerr to follow in my steps as editor of THEOLOGY TODAY. The first issue appeared in April 1944. I was editor and Tim Kerr assistant editor. In a couple of years he assumed the chief editorial responsibility. Because of my increasing involvement in the development of the Seminary, I delegated to Tim the major task of producing the new theological journal. And this he has continued to do, with amazing energy, marvelous dexterity, and abounding wisdom.

From data now available it would appear that THEOLOGY TODAY has a wider circulation than any other quarterly theological journal in our time. Its readers live in some eighty countries around the globe. Each issue goes to some ten thousand subscribers.

Now as I approach nonogenarian status, having lived and

served in three cultures (the Celtic, the Hispanic, and the North American), I do not exaggerate when I say that one of my most treasured relationships across the years has been with Princeton Theological Seminary and especially with the journal THEOLOGY TODAY. And of course I cannot think of this publication without giving centrality to my beloved friend and colleague Hugh Kerr.

Thank you, Tim, for your comradeship and cooperation across the years. How much you have meant to me, and also to your students, to your colleagues, and to the readers of THEOLOGY TODAY around the globe. You have a wide clientele of grateful folk who thank God for your contribution to religious thought in our confused but aspiring generation. In the years of your official retirement which has now come, in your home on that lovely hillside overlooking Princeton, may you continue to give creative expression both through pen and personality to what it means to be a Christian theologian today.

Let me conclude this tribute with a very personal note. My lifelong partner, Jane, who was privileged to be your hostess on many occasions in Springdale, our Princeton home, joins me in conveying to you and to your beloved spouse, Dorothy, our most affectionate greetings and remembrances. Our earnest prayer and abiding hope is this: May the living Christ, who through the years of our earthly pilgrimage has been central in the personal experience and theological thinking of us all, be our Guide and Guardian on life's road till traveling days are done.

The Editor as Pilgrim

By F. W. Dillistone

An editor's job is surely one of the most arduous and demanding that anyone can undertake. It is comparable to that of a tightrope walker. On the one side there is the pull of special interests: on the other side the attraction of a wide popular appeal.

I would not say that Hugh T. Kerr has sat in the editor's chair over the past thirty-five years but rather that he has lived on the tightrope of Christian journalism, holding THEOLOGY TODAY as his balancing pole. No one, I think, could accuse the journal of propagating extremes, yet it has never, in my judgment, become a mere guardian of the *status quo*. It has never tried to become highbrow, and yet it has never become theologically flaccid. Above all, perhaps, it has tried to be faithful to all that is meant by our classic Christian heritage, while remaining constantly aware of its responsibility to reinterpret that Christian heritage within our rapidly changing modern world. For thirty-five years, Tim has never let up. First as assistant editor (and mostly behind the scenes), then as editor (planning the quarterly issues and writing a long series of editorials), he has carried the journal steadily forward and shows no signs of faltering in the great adventure.

I

I regard my own association with THEOLOGY TODAY as one of the happiest episodes of my life. In 1931, I went out to India

to work in a theological seminary and there gained the friendship of John Wick Bowman, principal of the United Theological College of Saharanpur. Ten years later, he had returned to
America, and I was in Canada. He invited me to join the team
which was then beginning work on the *Westminster Study
Bible* under the leadership of a group of scholars, including
John A. Mackay. This in turn led to an invitation from Dr.
Mackay to join the Editorial Council of THEOLOGY TODAY. My
first visit to Princeton was in the company of Donald Coggan,
who is today Archbishop of Canterbury. My friendship with
Tim Kerr, therefore, dates back to the earliest meetings of the
Editorial Council in Princeton.

The publication of the first number in April 1944 was a
notable event. I still prize my own copy. Dr. Mackay set out
the aims of the journal in his own inimitable way. The heroic
Joseph Hromádka expressed his faith in resurrection, "which
starts at the bottom of the human abyss." H. Richard Niebuhr,
with his customary incisiveness, probed the meaning of "otherworldliness." Paul Minear voiced the need for a "confessional
New Testament theology"—a need which his own labors over
the past thirty-five years have done so much to meet. I had the
privilege of writing about the gospel and made special reference to the work of C. H. Dodd, little thinking that I should
one day write his biography. (*C. H. Dodd: Interpreter of the
New Testament,* Eerdmans, 1977.)

II

I want to glance back at some of the editorials to see if they
reveal any recurrent themes. Without question the first theme
in time and in importance has been "the gospel." After assuming full responsibility as editor, Tim Kerr's first words to his
readers were:

The gospel is unexpected good news. . . . It was because in Christ
the unexpected had happened that saints, apostles, prophets, martyrs

expected the gospel to turn the world upside down. . . . The living spark of Christian faith is extinguished when the unexpected becomes the traditionally accepted. . . . If in the church the flame of sheer audacity for God's sake is quenched by chill conformity or the inertia of convention, judgment is nearer than we think.

Three years later he returned to the same theme under the striking title "Touching the Untouchable": "The gospel is the good news that God is in touch with us. God is not aloof or remote from us. God deliberately identifies with sick, sinful humanity." He then turned, as he has often done since, to the realms of symbolism and Christian art, pointing out that one of the earliest forms used for suggesting the presence and power of God was the hand. This in turn led him to italicize what he clearly regarded as central in his own interpretation of the gospel: "*Christ himself may thus be likened to the finger of God in touch with humanity, and the church—which is his body—is truly the church as it identifies itself by contact with the sick, the sinful and the untouchable.*" He concluded the article with a lovely reference to the epitaph applied to Goldsmith in Westminster Abbey ("He touched nothing that he did not adorn"), and he added, "It is true of the touch of our Lord and it has the force of an ultimatum for his church today."

This challenge to the church leads us at once to a second theme which constantly appears among the editor's concerns. He has throughout the years been a teacher in a theological seminary, and he has never forgotten his responsibility to his students and to the ministry to which they are committing themselves. In his first editorial, after exulting in the unexpectedness and the potency of the good news contained in the gospel, he moved at once to "the place and purpose of the ministry today." The editorial deplored the rising emphasis on professionalism: learning techniques and establishing programs rather than opening the mind to the new that continues to come through Christ and the gospel. He urged that pastors must be in touch with people where they really are. "This means that the minister must be willing to touch what are often taken to be unconventional and untouchable problems of human life." Relevance is a key word, and yet relevance must never be allowed to detract from the distinctiveness of revelation. Here is another example of the tightrope walker, confident that the mystery of the ages has been revealed in Christ, and yet deeply conscious of the fact that the good news often seems to have no connection with the problems and perplexities of people in their ordinary daily lives.

In another attempt to face this problem in more detail, he picked up the vocabulary of the advertising world with the intriguing title "Hard or Soft Sell." Is the gospel to be communicated by means of a strategy of concentrating on one phrase or promise or prescription and repeating it as loudly and as frequently as possible? Or is the strategy rather to be that of indirect communication, subtle suggestiveness transmitted with the maximum of charm? Clearly neither is satisfactory, if only because the gospel is not a patent medicine or a packet of cereal. Nevertheless, there is an obvious difference between the two approaches, and the editorial leans toward the second option rather than the first. Don't try to tell all! Don't make too many claims! Above all, don't clobber with clichés; be creative and imaginative! I think that in this editorial Tim came as near to defining his own responsibility and strategy as anywhere in his writing. No clichés, no stereotypes, no reissue of obsolete coinage. "Creative imagination must be summoned and enlisted in the cause. Not in order to be tricky or devious or esoteric. Not in order to say a new thing but to say an old thing in a new way." Finally, in striking fashion the editorial contrasted the "steel-like traditionalism," the isolation of the "verbal cliché-curtain" with the "interesting, colorful, exciting" new translation of the gospel by creative and imaginative minds. But he recognized all too well that there is widespread resistance to change and that the business of translation is "dreadfully hard work," costly, the way of the cross.

III

In many ways 1957 was a boom year. Europe was recovering, America was prospering, standards of living were rising, and the churches seemed, outwardly at least, to be flourishing. One writer recently described 1957 as a "brief golden age for scholars," and this was soon to be followed by an expansion of higher education on an unprecedented scale. Ecumenically, too, there had been progress in the decade since the Amsterdam meeting of the World Council of Churches in 1948, and this was to reach a notable climax in the Assembly planned to be held in 1961 on Asian soil in New Delhi.

In the field of theology there were differing perspectives and differing methods of approach, but the Bible retained its place as the final court of appeal and as the unique medium through which the divine Word was communicated. The reign of the giants was not yet over; the works of Barth, Bultmann, Tillich, Niebuhr, and Rahner were eagerly read, and ecumenical understanding seemed still to be growing. THEOLOGY TODAY had from the beginning opened its pages to articles dealing with church order, liturgical developments, and ministerial training, all within the context of the church on the way to unity. So far, the main emphasis had been upon the articulation of a strong biblical theology centered in the *kerygma* and upon the setting forth of a doctrine of the church which would be constructive and unifying rather than denominational or divisive.

The journal had not been unaware of developments in the thought and life of society at large. It had, for example, provided room for a careful summary of Arnold Toynbee's multivolume *A Study of History*. It had printed a remarkable article by Reinhold Niebuhr on "The Tyranny of Science." It had made a feature of "The Church in the World," and Tim Kerr in his "Theological Table-Talk" had touched on a number of interests appearing in secular quarters. But on the whole, I think it is fair to say that the first half of the past thirty-five years witnessed a time of relative stability, with the central affirmations of the Christian faith reinforced by the work of biblical scholars and church historians, and with the general structures of church and ministry gaining wider understanding and acceptance, even though there might be differences about detailed points of order. It was acknowledged that there must be openness to change, but change could still be relatively slow and held under control.

But by 1960 there were signs not only that the world was changing but that the pace of change was quickening. In 1959 there is a reference in THEOLOGY TODAY to the "TV Age" which was then already upon us. The Space Age was about to dawn. Microconductivity, making possible the amazing developments in transistor radios and computers, was a further technological development. And what has been called the foremost scientific discovery of this century, the structure of the genetic code, was soon to lead to hitherto undreamed-of possibilities. All these had some bearing on the nature and function of communication, and whatever else a journal may or may not do, it must communicate or it will quickly die. It may, of course, decide to concentrate all its attention upon a limited audience, familiar with a traditional or a specialized vocabulary, and so confine its efforts to bolstering the tradition and confirming the devotees of particular language forms. But the motto of THEOLOGY TODAY has been human life in the light of God. In the issue of January 1961, the question was raised, "Where do we go from here?" and at a meeting of the Editorial Council in Princeton in April of the same year the editor produced a comprehensive memorandum, looking back on the past seventeen years and looking forward to a policy for the future.

It is an impressive document. Not without some pride it claims that THEOLOGY TODAY is the most widely circulated religious quarterly in the world (as it continues to be). Its subscribers are primarily pastors and ministers of all denominations in urban, rural, metropolitan, and suburban areas. But the editor finds no cause for complacency. New ideas are needed for the changing world. Articles must probe important current questions aggressively. And then, there are paragraphs which reveal much about the editor's own labors and concerns:

> It is the Editor's lot to read hundreds of well-intentioned articles, essays, sermons, digests of theses, addresses to clerical clubs, etc., most of which are dull beyond imagining.
>
> What we need today are hard-hitting articles, growing out of deep conviction, by authors who have something to say and are not afraid of taking a stand, unfurling a banner, going out on a limb, engaging in critical controversy. We don't want any mere pulse-takers, crepe-hangers, comparative analysts, viewers-with-alarm, anti-institutionalists.
>
> We are looking for ideas—new ideas or old ideas newly minted, fresh concepts and novel ways of expressing them, wide-awake awareness of the new age in which we are living, coupled with the expectancy and exhilaration which only the gospel can provide.

Awareness and expectancy have, I suggest, been keynotes of Tim Kerr's fulfillment of his own task since that time.

IV

The memorandum presented new proposals of a practical kind that for one reason or another (probably mainly financial) have not been realized. But the more general proposals about books to be reviewed, about widening the range of attention to the arts—literature, painting, drama—and for a radical criticism of traditional forms both in theology and in the communal life of the church have, under his guidance, borne fruit in keeping the journal as alive and interesting and relevant as any other responsible organ in Christendom today.

A survey of the issues during the decade 1960–1970 reveals how faithfully the editor sought (using the language of an earlier editorial) to "keep in touch" with movements in theology and also with movements in the world which stood in need of theological appraisal. It was during this decade that theologians took seriously the immensely important problems of language raised by philosophers. If the central concern of Christianity is the communication of the gospel, it cannot afford to bypass questions about the nature and function of language, about symbols and concepts, about interpretation and meaning. The significant term "hermeneutics" began to appear in the journal, and readers were informed about language-events, speech-events, the new hermeneutic, models, dialogue, and so on.

What a decade it was! And Editor Kerr was not slow to react to it, although he always kept his cool and did not allow himself to lose sight of the dialectic which he had established in the 1950's between the old and the new. In 1963 the London *Observer* carried the now famous headline, "Our image of God must go," and John Robinson's book *Honest to God* was launched on its way. Within a few months Paul van Buren's American counterpart, *The Secular Meaning of the Gospel,* was issuing a similar challenge to traditional ways of doing theology. Robinson then began to apply his new thinking to the moral situation, but in this field it was America's turn to produce the best-seller. In 1966 Joseph Fletcher's *Situation Ethics* made its sensational appearance, and the "new morality" was discussed not simply in academic circles but in diverse quarters and in many tongues.

Meanwhile THEOLOGY TODAY was opening its pages to discussions on the nuclear dilemma, problems of the inner city, revolutionary challenges to church and society, and the black experience. In 1967 Tim Kerr spoke out forthrightly on his own position regarding the war in Vietnam, and student protests did not pass unnoticed. Finally, there was the need to come to terms with the "death of God" theologians, all of whom had at one time or another made contributions to THEOLOGY TODAY. It was a stirring and a tense decade. No wonder that at the end of it the editor handed over his responsibility for a year, during which he went off on a well-earned academic leave to study teaching methodology and theological education.

V

After the sensations and turmoil of the 1960's the theological scene in the 1970's has, I think, so far been quieter. But this does not imply any absence of major problems, and Tim Kerr, refreshed by his sabbatical, has tackled them with renewed zeal. On his return he wrote a charming editorial entitled "Still Running" (reminding me of John Wain's autobiography *Sprightly Running*). He quoted an inspired translation from *The Jerusalem Bible:* "I am still running, trying to capture the prize for which Christ Jesus captured me." "One thing seems sure," he affirmed, "we must keep moving forward." So the pace has quickened, the sweep of the vision has widened, and THEOLOGY TODAY has, I believe, enjoyed over the past eight years its finest period yet. The journal has focused attention on just about every subject of importance and has remained faithful to its motto of viewing everything "in the light of God."

What have been some of the pressing issues since 1970? In politics, it has surely been the question mark overshadowing the democratic ideal. When belief wanes, when mass communications become ever more technically efficient, when the sense of responsibility within well-defined communities becomes ever more tenuous, can democracy survive? In morals, the nature of justice, the relationship between the sexes, genetic determinism, and the legitimacy of violence have all become pressing problems; and THEOLOGY TODAY has not avoided helping its readers, either by articles or by reviews of books, to see that the Christian ethic is still relevant. Perhaps the most dramatic issues have been the advances in technology, the mechanics of which seem to be beyond the comprehension of the layperson, and yet the results of which in practical living have become all too obvious. Again the journal has tried to find connections between theology and technology, although it must be admitted that this is one side of the theological enterprise where so far there is little evidence of any *rapprochement.* The postulates and methods of the two disciplines are so different from one another that it becomes all too easy for each to operate within its own separate field.

In religion generally, the most notable change has been the increasing awareness, among a wide public, of the existence of great religious systems other than Christianity, of great social systems which contain features of a quasi-religious kind, and of the growing number of cults which bear some resemblance to traditional Christianity. The facility of travel, movements of populations from one area to another, and the dissemination of information through the mass media have brought about a situation where "religion" has become a blanket term, including a vast variety of ideas and practices; and this term functions in an environment where it is tempting to assume that no criterion of truth or even of moral value any longer exists. The sociology of religion has become an increasingly important subject, and THEOLOGY TODAY has tried to give guidance within this exceedingly complex area.

Tim Kerr has long been deeply interested in the arts. From his first contribution to THEOLOGY TODAY, "The Human Problem in Contemporary Thought," with its reference to Rodin, right on to the splendid number in April 1977 on religion and the arts, with his own fascinating commentary on "Treasures of Tutankhamun," Tim has seized every opportunity to acquaint his readers with significant developments in drama, film, the novel, poetry, and the visual arts. I doubt if any religious journal has a more honorable record in this respect. He has at the same time explored issues in the philosophy of art, particularly the nature and significance of symbols and the problems of form and content. Perhaps even more helpfully for the pastor in the parish, he has kept his eye on the art forms which have made the greatest popular appeal and has tried to assess their value as probes into the meaning of human existence.

In theology generally, the journal seems to me to have given perceptive coverage of all the major subjects of interest and debate over the past ten years. In this field, there has been a new confidence that some form of natural theology, whether

Teilhardian or Whiteheadian, is possible. Black theology and liberation theology have been fervently advocated. Biblical theology has been subjected to new criticism. Moltmann and Pannenberg and Küng have all made outstanding contributions to theological understanding through their books. No reader of THEOLOGY TODAY could complain that any of these developments has been ignored or treated with anything but careful evaluation. In one respect, indeed, I think that the editor made a truly creative contribution to a subject which has aroused increasing interest not only in theological but also in literary circles. I refer to the July 1975 issue on narrative theology. A brilliant editorial by Tim led his readers to share his own excitement about "story and narrative in theology"; a fine team of experts in various fields drew out the importance of the story form for the task of doing theology today. Somehow the editor has kept his ear to the ground or his sails to the wind and has alerted his readers to the new patterns of thought and action most worthy of attention in the rapidly changing scene today.

VI

In this introduction, I have concentrated mainly on Tim's work as editor. Besides this, however, he has never ceased to reflect upon the task of theological education in which he has been directly concerned over the past forty years. He has registered his thinking through editorials, through his "Theological Table-Talk," and through articles which grew out of his experiences during his study-leave. He has also recorded the results of practical classroom experiments. His total output in this area constitutes, I suggest, as incisive and constructive a consideration of ministerial training as can be found anywhere in recent literature. He does not hesitate to criticize, even to satirize, and yet this is never done in a negative or destructive way. His discussions of the student as person, of lifelong learning, and of the classroom as community go to the heart of the matter, and his extended article on "Education in General and Theological Education" deserves the consideration of all who hold any kind of teaching responsibility in the Christian church today.

Let me try to sum up. I can imagine few more difficult tasks than that of an editor. One of them has written about the tempo of his mind being "haunted by the next job and conditioned by the habit of writing for immediate consumption." There is always the pressure of the deadline. There is always the risk of causing offense by criticism or by the process of selecting what articles to print. An editor must give a firm lead and at the same time keep a tight rein on the use of the journal for displaying merely personal ideas. An editor must establish a recognizable tradition and yet always be ready to introduce change, and must be able to spot the particular object of current interest, while exercising the widest possible catholicity in judgment.

How well a paragraph in Robert McAfee Brown's letter to Hans Küng in the July 1977 issue fits Tim Kerr!

I particularly appreciate your openness not only to the tradition in the broadest sense, but also the world around you; you listen to the nuances of the secular world, drawing on other academic disciplines, hearing the novelists, the dramatists, the musicians (everyone from Mozart to *Hair*) and letting the historians, skeptics, and sociologists speak their word to you. Maybe the politicians and economists don't get the attention they deserve, but that is my personal dissent only. You have written in a way that demands that they return the compliment and listen to you as carefully as you have listened to them.

Dare I add the scientists to the politicians and economists so far as THEOLOGY TODAY is concerned? To draw them in isn't easy, but the power and prestige of science are without parallel in the contemporary world, and it is an area that the journal may well want to explore in future issues.

Later in his letter, Brown raised a question about Küng's book which seems pertinent to Tim Kerr's achievement. He praised Küng's crucial theological work on church structure and the role of Scripture, what may be called the "inner ecclesial struggles of the church to reform and purify itself." He asked Küng now to turn more of his attention in an outward direction, to the church in the world. So far as I can judge, the first half of the past thirty-five years of THEOLOGY TODAY saw a fine concentration on the gospel and the church, seeking to speak positively about message and its communication on the one hand, about community and its unification on the other. Tim's achievement (as if anticipating Brown's advice) has been to turn attention during the second half, and especially over the past eight years, to the Christian's relation to world problems and world movements in the arts, in ethics, in politics, in philosophy, in the social sciences. This has made THEOLOGY TODAY a journal which is relevant, instructive, and in the best sense entertaining.

I have not mentioned humor—always an important ingredient in a successful journal. Lewis Chamberlain, with his amusing but winsome "Rev. Albert Flaugh," has been a real "find"; and Tim's own editorial, "Not like They Used To," produced plenty of fun, with wise reflections as well. Humor after all is intimately concerned with redressing balance. The Editor of THEOLOGY TODAY has never given any impression that life consists in a safe middle-of-the-road policy along a straight track. Perhaps the tightrope balancing act with which I began is not the proper simile. At least it can be said that through all the pressures of the past thirty-five years Tim has gone ahead, cheerfully and purposefully, avoiding extremes on either side, supported by colleagues and readers, encouraged by the knowledge that from the editor's chair he can regularly address a wide and thoughtful audience who could easily disappear if not satisfied with the fare provided.

I personally am deeply grateful for all that THEOLOGY TODAY has meant to me and for Tim's continuing friendship, even though we have been able to meet only on rare occasions. I salute him from across the water with admiration and affection and wish him many years still of sprightly running in his editorship. In the famous words of Harry Lauder, "Keep right on to the end of the road!" Or, more subtly, of T. S. Eliot, "Not fare well, But fare forward."

I
A CRITICAL THEOLOGY

Revelation
and Relevancy

For the unbeliever the gospel is—quite simply—irrelevant, whereas for the believer it is of all things the most relevant.

The purpose of Christian witness and proclamation, consequently, would appear to be to make relevant the seemingly irrelevant.

From all sides today there is heard the plea for relevance. Religious publishers seek to commend their books by emphasizing their relevance. The following are random but typical phrases culled from current advertisements: "His practical approach to the Bible . . ."; "This book is significant for its pointing up of the many parallels to today's situation . . ."; "Sermons which clearly relate the parables of Jesus to the people, morals, and psychology of America in the atomic age . . ."; "How the Christian gospel illuminates the significance of our everyday lives . . ."; "This new book gives a clear exposition of the ethical and religious ideas found in the Old Testament and discusses their relevance to modern thought."

Preachers, theologians, teachers, counselors, missionaries, evangelists, church workers—all are drawn into the quest for relevance. Perhaps that is why there is so much topical preaching today. Perhaps this passion for the relevant lies behind Bultmann's "demythologizing" and Tillich's "method of correlation" and is one reason why so much attention has been given these two controversial thinkers. A "successful" church, we say, is one which ministers to the needs of all groups and

Theology Today, X (1953), 143–149.

is related to the total life of the community. The crucial test of the ecumenical movement in the coming years, we hear, will be whether or not it can take hold at the grass roots level.

I

Now it may be argued that the contemporary concern for relevance finds justification in Scripture itself, that there is, indeed, a correspondence between revelation and relevance. Is not revelation a kind of divine accommodation to human existence? Are not the media of revelation related to the historical and human situation? Is not Christ himself, the Word become flesh, the supreme illustration of the relevance of revelation? Are not his teachings, his self-identification with sinful humanity, his atoning death, and his glorious resurrection which brought life and immortality to light—are not all these evidences of the relevance of the Christian faith? If we have been created in the image of God, if in Christ the Almighty has condescended to "become like we are so that we may become like he is"—then may we not confidently boast that Christianity has the answers to all our problems? Must we not conclude, therefore, that if the gospel seems irrelevant to some, the reason is not because that's the way it is, but because that's the way we've made it?

Can we not then say that all our restlessness of mind and spirit, all our quests for peace and security, all our hopes for meaning for ourselves, for history, and for the world, all the ultimate questions of life, are met and answered in the Christian revelation, and that the gospel is the only really relevant message for our day?

II

But consider this stubborn fact—namely, that the revelation itself is frequently presented to us in Scripture and in Christ from a very different point of view. Revelation, to be sure, means the disclosing and uncovering of what has been hidden (Rom. 16:25), but it is also true that "the revelation of the mystery" is only appropriated by faith. Jesus was the incarnate Word, but he was crucified by those who accused him of blasphemy. His miracles attested his claim to be the Son of God, but for many they were only signs and wonders. When Nicodemus was told that he must be born again, he asked in bewilderment, "How can this be?" When Jesus informed his disciples that he must suffer and die, Peter (who had just asserted that Jesus was the Christ, the Son of the living God) blurted out, "God forbid, Lord!" And when he spoke to them of eating and drinking his flesh and blood, his disciples retorted, "This is a hard saying; who can listen to it?"

When the apostle to the gentiles referred to the cross, he said it was "folly to those who are perishing," that God had made "foolish the wisdom of the world," and that "it pleased God through the folly of what we preach to save those who believe." The revelation, says Paul, is "a secret and hidden wisdom" and is not perfectly self-evident for all to see and understand. "The unspiritual man simply cannot accept the matters which the Spirit deals with—*they just don't make sense to him,* for, after all, you must be spiritual to see spiritual things" (I Cor. 2:14, Phillips; italics supplied).

Consideration of such texts makes us hesitate to equate revelation with relevance. We must now ask what we mean by "relevant"—relevant to what, for whom, how? Is the gospel relevant in the sense that it *corresponds* with our needs and questions? Or is the gospel relevant in the sense that it *contradicts* our aspirations, ambitions, and riddles in such a way as to redefine ultimate questions? On the one hand, if we insist upon the *correspondence* we may unwittingly reduce the originality of the gospel by identifying it with some ulterior or human-made ideal; on the other hand, if we accent the *contradiction,* how then do we communicate the gospel as good news? The one temptation is as perilous as the other, and there is plenty of evidence that we in our day have yielded to both.

III

In our eagerness to evangelize, we may actually distort the gospel by identifying it with a program or ideology which is already acceptable. Thus the distinctiveness of the Christian faith appears either as religious or biblical confirmation of what on other grounds is already regarded as true and good, or as deepened or heightened insight into whatever is generally taken to be true and good in itself. It is possible, thus, to correlate Christianity with slavery, white supremacy, capitalism, nationalism, fascism—in fact, with anything which at the moment is taken to be a good. But this is to make the gospel relevant at the cost of its own integrity. In a significant and untypical sermon published in 1937 under the title "The Church Must Go Beyond Modernism," Harry Emerson Fosdick warned his congregation that "we cannot harmonize Christ himself with modern culture. What Christ does to modern culture is to challenge it." And since 1937 we have further reason to beware of the peril of harmonizing the gospel with the *status quo*, whether it be National Socialism, the American way of life, South African apartheid, or the communist agrarian revolution.

At a lower but no less important level, we may make the gospel relevant to individual and personal life, with its problems and anxieties, in such a way as to pervert its character by peddling it as a patent medicine cure-all. It is not uncommon to meet those in business who believe that it is possible (and economically profitable) to put the Golden Rule, or the Beatitudes, or the Sermon on the Mount into the structure of commercial life. There are many unsuspecting men and women who become interested in the Christian faith because they hope it will insulate them against the woes and hurts of life.

The danger here is that disillusionment is always just around the corner. There is no New Testament warrant for holding that faith or devotion will spare us the agonies and tragedies of existence. In urging others to follow in the footsteps of Jesus, let us not forget that his steps led to Calvary. Speaking of the influence of Christ, Otto Dibelius of the East Zone in Berlin said: "He has not made life easy for me. On the contrary. It would have been more comfortable to be without him than to live with him. He puts burdens on the soul, which one would rather let pass by unheeded."

But if it is possible to distort the gospel by harmonizing and adapting it to existing ideologies, it is also possible to isolate the gospel in such a way that its message becomes esoteric and cryptic, and as such is deliberately denied relevance. To insist upon the "scandal" of Christianity in such a way as to suggest that preaching, for example, must be foolish (which is not what Paul said), is to deny the sovereignty of God, the incarnation of Christ, and the freedom of the Holy Spirit. Bushnell was speaking for our day as well as his own when he said, "Nothing makes infidels more surely than the spinning, splitting, nerveless refinements of theology." To the laity, theologians frequently seem to be an embattled secret learned society, quibbling among themselves about irrelevant matters, making the simple difficult, and doing their best to detach the gospel from life. A recent traveler to central Africa, reporting on his visit to a small native theological seminary, asked one of the students what he was studying in theology. The reply was, "Tomorrow the textbook assignment is on the incommunicable attributes of God." This is as good an illustration as any of how irrelevant theology can get. A cloistered theology, no less than a cloistered virtue, can hardly speak to our day.

IV

What then is the proper relation between revelation and relevance? It is clear that we are dealing here with a basic and perennial issue of faith and life, and one that defies a simple solution. But the recognition of the issue is itself a first step toward a constructive approach to the problem. Neither facile identification nor radical discontinuity seems adequate. To make the gospel relevant *according to our views of relevance* is

to manipulate God's revelation to suit ourselves—but then we
do not allow *God* to speak *to* us in *God's* own way. To intimate
that the gospel is irrelevant is to deny to God the sovereign
freedom to be revealed as God pleases. We must go on to say,
regardless of the paradox or dialectic involved, that revelation
is relevant, but that the norm of relevance is not to be located
in the world or in us but in God. This is the force of the familiar
lines in the hymn by William Cowper, who, according to
legend, was moved in "a mysterious way" to abandon an attempt at suicide:

> Blind unbelief is sure to err,
>   And scan His work in vain;
> God is His own Interpreter,
>   And He will make it plain.

This is also the significance of the large number of passages
in the Gospels where Jesus' replies to his questioners take the
form of reinterpreting and recasting the questions themselves.
It has often been noted that he had a way of avoiding direct
answers to specific questions, especially those which were cal-
culated to trick or trap him. But the point is not that he refused
to answer, but that his answer required a complete reorientation of the question and the spirit in which it was asked. That
is why his answers came as a radical reversal of what might be
expected. Thus, there is relevance in his words, but it is a
relevance that turns our norms and standards upside down.
This would certainly not prevent us from applying the revelation of God in Christ to all and every human area and need,
but the relevance of revelation, simply because it is *God's* word
and not ours, will overturn and transpose all our questions,
anxieties, and problems.

V

It would be instructive to pursue the relation between revelation and relevance with regard to a whole series of contemporary issues, but by way of illustration let us look briefly at one

single and highly controversial matter. The Second Assembly of the World Council of Churches, meeting in Evanston, Illinois, in 1954, has chosen as the theme of the conference—"Jesus Christ the Crucified and Risen Lord, the only hope of the Church and the world." The exact formulation of the theme awaits further definition, but the Christian hope—or what is known as the doctrine of eschatology—is the proposed subject for discussion. Now, there have been many voices raised in opposition to this theme precisely on the ground that it is irrelevant. To become involved in apocalyptic questions about the end of the world and the return of Christ—so the argument runs—is to preclude the possibility of speaking a relevant word to a distracted world.

There is justification for this protest to the extent that eschatological reflection may and often has resulted in an other-worldliness that virtually makes the gospel irrelevant. There is also the danger that the diversity of interpretation on these matters may disrupt and fracture that unity of the churches which has already been achieved. But if that is a possibility, and if it is true that no controversial matter dare be raised in ecumenical conclave, then it must be said that the ties that bind us together are tenuous indeed.

But is eschatology so irrelevant after all? The two preliminary reports on the theme which have been issued—a third one will be prepared this summer—make the point that the Christian hope is a very relevant topic for such a day as ours. They do so not merely because of the world's anxiety but on quite specifically biblical grounds. In the last generation there has been a revolution in biblical and theological thinking about eschatology. What was once regarded as an appendix to the Christian faith is now seen to be integral and determinative.

We are just beginning to catch up with Schweitzer's insistence that the eschatological element in the gospel cannot be avoided without radically disrupting its meaning. It has, of course, been avoided, and the plea can be made that only in this way can the gospel be made relevant. But then let us be clear what we are doing—we are using standards of relevance which are our own and not the Bible's. Furthermore, it is not historically true that eschatological concern makes for otherworldliness. To stand passively on a hilltop waiting for Christ's return is an aberration of the Christian hope for which there is no biblical warrant. But whenever the church has taken seriously the full-orbed biblical eschatology, which involves the here as well as the hereafter, the new life in Christ as well as the hope of the resurrection, the revelation of God has come with peculiar and overwhelming relevance.

What the Christian hope implies for the question of individual destiny, for the meaning of history, and for the rise and fall of nations may not be in accordance with our wishes and dreams, for the biblical eschatology may reverse and upset the hopes of the world in revealing the awful and ultimate relevance of God's judgment and purpose.

Dead Dilemmas
and Living Paradoxes

It is the claim of the gospel that in Christ "the old has passed away . . . the new has come" (II Cor. 5:17). The *New* Testament has much to say about the new person, the new creation, the new commandment, a new name, a new garment, a new and living way, a new song, a new spirit, a new hope, new heavens and a new earth. To the seer on the Isle of Patmos came the fortifying and enlivening words, "Behold, I make all things new" (Rev. 21:5).

I

The newness of the gospel was, of course, not unrelated to what had gone before, to the old, in other words. If the early Christians and their opponents recognized an element of novelty about the gospel, they also were constantly reminded that this was in the nature of fulfillment and not repudiation of what had gone before. Still, to have lived in those days would have surely been to sense the re-creative, dynamic power of the gospel to transcend and go beyond the impasses and stalemates of a religious tradition that had degenerated into a stultifying and barren traditionalism.

A wholly new dimension of God's will and purpose had been disclosed in Jesus Christ, and nothing astonished his contemporaries so much as the way he defied inherited, sacrosanct traditions as he announced and developed new doctrine which

THEOLOGY TODAY, XIV (1957), 449–454.

nevertheless was rooted and grounded in the old ways and beliefs. "You have a fine way," he said, "of rejecting the commandment of God, in order to keep your tradition!" When he was confronted with the questions and puzzles and riddles of the day, on which even the experts were divided, he frequently redirected the whole discussion by asking a new and quite unexpected question. If someone should ask, with reference to the tedious debate on definition, "Who is my neighbor?"— Jesus answers in a parable and asks another question, "Which of these three, do you think, proved neighbor to the man who fell among the robbers?"

Presumably this re-creative potential is not limited to the New Testament but is, or ought to be, the continuing character and trademark of the Christian faith in every age. This, indeed, would provide an instructive clue and criterion to the study of church history; for we can say that the church is really the church when it is not only open to the new possibilities of the gospel in the world but actually goes out of its way to encourage and promote such possibilities. We are today at least partially aware of this, and that is why we speak so much of the revival, renewal, witness, and mission of the church. Even our contemporary interest in tradition is oriented in this direction. The special committee of the Faith and Order Commission of the World Council of Churches and Albert C. Outler's exciting book, *The Christian Tradition and the Unity We Seek*, interpret the *paradosis* as something to be handed on or over to succeeding generations, not for its own sake or as an end in itself, but in order to prod and remind the church of its current responsibilities.

Yet at the same time it is all too clear that in all too many respects the church seems hobbled and hindered by its own native resistance to change, by the sheer inertia of inherited custom, by the temptation to look backward rather than forward, by the perpetuating of a dead—rather than a living— tradition. Can it be said truthfully of us today in our church life and preaching, in our religious teaching and theology, that "the old has passed away . . . the new has come"? We have all heard sermons, and listened to lectures, and read articles in religious journals which bore no contemporary copyright whatever, which could have been preached and proclaimed and written twenty-five to fifty years ago without any considerable modification in structure or message. Preachers and teachers are sometimes surprised to discover that their congregations and students couldn't care less for what is being declared to them as of first importance. The reason is not only that we continue to raise dead questions no one is asking, but that we are unaware of the live questions that are being asked.

II

Speaking of the lack of creative new movements in current philosophy, Susanne K. Langer, in her stimulating book, *Philosophy in a New Key,* says, "If we would have new knowledge, we must get us a whole world of new questions." And it has often been observed that our age needs not only new answers and solutions to the old problems but new ways of asking questions and raising issues so that the old may become new. This is certainly as true of theology as of philosophy. We may highlight this by saying that we need in our day to distinguish between dead dilemmas and living paradoxes.

A dilemma (literally, "two assumptions") suggests two (or more) alternatives involving a choice which is never easy to make because neither option seems to be adequate or satisfactory. Hence we speak of being on the horns (either of which can impale) of a dilemma, of being between Scylla and Charybdis (that useful rhetorical pair), of Hobson's choice (which is no choice), of falling between two stools (because they are so far apart), of shuttling from pillar to post (aimlessly like a drunk), of being caught in a cross fire (as liable to be killed by one's friends as one's foes), and so forth.

Such literary figures are not commonly found in theological textbooks, but they give expression to a common device for representing basic problems and issues in theology. Indeed it would be possible and perhaps instructive to outline the history

of doctrine with reference to such alternatives, the trademark
of which would be the sign for *versus*. Thus, one could speak
of the Hebrew-Christian tradition vs. the Greco-Roman, of
Athens vs. Jerusalem, of Arianism vs. Athanasianism, of Nes-
torianism vs. Eutychianism, of Augustine vs. Pelagius, of scholasticism vs. mysticism, of realism vs. nominalism, of justification by faith vs. justification by works, of Luther vs. Zwingli,
of predestination vs. freedom, of Calvinism vs. Arminianism,
of puritanism vs. episcopacy, and so on, and on, and on.

Now it must be said that many of the questions raised in
these alternatives were live issues at one time or another, and
some are still with us and perhaps others need to be revived in
our day. But it is also true that this approach tends to divide
too neatly into two extremes matters of great importance that
defy such easy categorizing. In any case, the modern mood
adopts a "plague on both your houses" attitude regarding many
of these traditional options. And it is simply a fact, for good
or ill, that many of the older theological and ecclesiastical issues
which once divided denominations no longer exert any real
influence or power. It has been said that, on the whole, our age
is not in the mood for the kind of heresy hunts which we
associate with past generations. That may mean we are merely
tolerant in a complacent, indifferent way. But it may also mean
that, like army generals, old controversies do not die, they just
fade away.

III

A paradox (literally, "contrary to opinion") suggests a statement or point of view at odds with common sense and popular,
prevalent opinion, which nevertheless is deserving of serious
attention since it may be true. A paradox tends to be in conflict
with preconceived notions of what is reasonable or possible. (It
is only by extension of this basic meaning of the word that we
sometimes speak of a paradox as being self-contradictory or
absurd.) Thus paradox implies conflict, tension, dialectic, and
as a rational (not irrational) device it seeks to draw attention

to ideas and truths which might otherwise be obscured or neglected. So Kierkegaard says that "paradox is not a concession but a category of thought," and Tillich asserts that "the paradox is a new reality and not a logical riddle." A dead dilemma differs from a live paradox not only because of the distinction of the qualifying adjectives but because a dilemma offers a choice falsely put, whereas a paradox asserts what is contradictory to received opinion, but which nevertheless may be true.

According to this distinction, it would be easy to show that the Bible is on the side of paradox rather than dilemma. Whether we take the Old Testament prophets, or the Beatitudes, or the Judgment scene recorded in Matthew 25, or Paul's assertion in II Cor. 4:8–11, we are in the atmosphere of paradox. So, too, in Christian thought whether we follow Tertullian, Augustine, Luther, Pascal, Kierkegaard, Chesterton, Barth, or Niebuhr, the paradox of theology is transformed into the doxology of faith. The gospel as contrary to human *doxa* (opinion) is seen to be the *doxa* (glory) of God.

We can illustrate the difference between dead dilemmas and living paradoxes by referring to the shift of emphases in recent years regarding certain basic theological problems. For example, it now seems clear that the long-standing debate on reason vs. revelation is often nothing more than a dead dilemma when presented in a theological context of a bygone age which was worried by questions we no longer ask in quite the same way. The older dispute seldom gets off the ground these days, partly because the terminology itself is ambiguous, and partly because philosophy and biblical studies have immeasurably widened our understanding of both reason and revelation.

The dilemma of myth vs. history, suggesting legend or fancy as over against concrete fact, has been completely redirected in our day by a deeper psychological appreciation of myth, by our reluctance to define history in exclusively objective terms, and by such biblical experiments as "demythologizing" and "remythologizing."

Christology has often taken the form of a dilemma by posing

a choice between a Christ who was either human or divine. But Christology, surely, is the paramount evangelical paradox, affirming that "God was in Christ"—contrary to human opinion as to such a possibility. And today, as the late Donald Baillie has so lucidly shown, we want no mere historicism and no more docetism.

Again, that ancient and hardy dualism between sacred and secular, so monotonously rehearsed in pulpit and so complacently approved by pew, has been scrutinized anew in our day by those who boldly relate the incarnation to the contemporary problems of church and society, by those who sense the "religious" message of existential, even atheistic, literature and art, by those who affirm that the church is the body of Christ while taking seriously the division of its members.

IV

Whether we translate the gospel into living paradoxes or not, the responsibility for proclaiming the meaning of God in Christ in ever new and fresh ways is laid upon us. In the area of biblical studies, stimulating insights and perspectives on the gospel have already been given to us. It is no accident that this new biblical theology is now being challenged to produce, to transform and reform, to communicate. This will require of us in our preaching, teaching, and witness more than the discovery of techniques and devices. It will demand a whole new set of questions, not only about our estrangement from others, the world, and God, but also about the faith that "God was in Christ reconciling the world to himself." This supreme affirmation, be it noted, follows in Paul's argument directly after the words with which we began—"The old has passed away . . . the new has come." If we are to make this true of our day in every realm of life and thought, we must humbly but courageously undertake "the ministry of reconciliation."

Time
for a Critical Theology

Twenty years is not a long span of time as theology counts time. It seems only yesterday when, with fear and trembling but with boldness, the first issue of THEOLOGY TODAY appeared—in the midst of a war, in spite of a paper shortage, and in the face of dire predictions that this was no time to launch a new theological quarterly. But recent and newborn as it may seem to some, the beginnings of THEOLOGY TODAY now belong to the past. Theologically speaking, what was important and significant twenty years ago belongs to yesterday. And so the first thing that must be said on this journal's twentieth anniversary is that yesterday's theology can never be theology today.

I

Birthday celebrations usually provoke both nostalgia for the past and anticipation of the future. Theologically, the recent past may seem good and much of its promise as yet unfulfilled today. Certainly theological scholarship twenty years ago produced a substantial consensus. Much of today's practical theology (preaching, religious education, evangelism, congregational life, worship, social witness) has not yet caught up with the dominant theological emphases of two decades ago. But it is not likely ever to catch up, for in the meantime theology in 1964 has moved on from where it

THEOLOGY TODAY, XX (1964), 461–466.

was in 1954 and certainly from where it was in 1944. *Nothing* is quite the same at the end of this short generation, not even the problems.

The restoration of theology in the past generation, the revival of biblical studies, the centrality of Christology, the ecumenical renewal of the church, the recognition of the church's obligation to be in, if not of, the world—these comprise the theological trust funds of the recent past which have been bequeathed to our generation. And as is so often the case in other matters, gratitude in the present generation seems a lost virtue.

But in the meantime and simultaneously, philosophical analysis has irritated us into examining our high-sounding theological language, demythologizing has forced us to take a good second look at the *kerygma*, behavioral scientists have magnified in stereo the noise of our solemn assemblies, theologians with a minor in art erase the line between sacred and secular, nonpastoral ministers seek new forms of the church, and—to go the limit—if God is not dead and buried, at least we must be scrupulously honest even if this means talking in riddles or keeping silent.

This all adds up to a dilemma: never has there been such a theological consensus about the fundamentals of the Bible, Christ, the church, and the world; yet never so much confusion as to what to do about it or what it means. Yesterday's hardwon victories which, for example, unified the scattered fragments of the biblical message and enthroned Christology as theological sovereign, give today's thinkers little cause for rejoicing.

Anniversaries, we said, should anticipate the future and not merely recall the past, whether to praise it or to bury it. Whatever shape today's and tomorrow's theology may take, two programmatic principles may be hazarded. First, the times call for an interpretation of the *function* of theology as a critical discipline; and second, the *perspective* of theology must be open enough to take in a multiplicity or pluralism of possibilities.

II

The proposition regarding the *function* of theology needs to be raised simply because there has been a radical shift in understanding what theology is and what it does. Traditionally, professionally, and, still, popularly, theology is defined as involving a system or structure of doctrinal beliefs. To "do" theology, under this definition, is to analyze, interpret, organize, and, possibly, restructure the doctrines under observation. But important as this theological function may be even for today's doctrinally illiterate generation, current theological thinking is much less substantive in its results and much more critical in its intention.

Theology today is not so much a structure or content as it is a way of thinking. It is not so much an end product as a tool for fashioning raw material. It is not so much a deposit of the faith as cerebral activity.

If a structureless theology seems a contradiction, we may be reminded of two analogous developments in our midst. One is what has been happening to philosophy. Those who were reared in either the classical Greek or modern Kantian traditions may well feel that contemporary linguistic analysis is structureless to the point where philosophical content evaporates entirely. Philosophers today are not concerned to establish or evaluate systems; they are concerned to think critically and clearly about the language they use, the propositions they make, the statements they utter.

The second contentless illustration is in contemporary art forms of many kinds. Today's painter, sculptor, dramatist, or movie director is particularly anxious to give expression to an experience which may or may not be reciprocated by anyone else. If you ask what it is, the artist will likely ask in return what you think it is, and whether it makes you feel anything intensely.

Whatever obvious limitations philosophical analysis or Fellini's *8 ½,* for example, may present, many today would hold that it is in these reflective, critical areas that fresh ideas and new vitality are to be found. The older forms, the traditional goals, have not been deliberately repudiated or refuted; they have simply been bypassed and outflanked.

What is happening in theology is long overdue. We may recall that there are venerable, respected traditions of biblical criticism, historical criticism, musical criticism, literary criticism. Why not, then, theological criticism? By that we mean not just the criticism of theology by theologians, which is an absorbing intramural pastime for those who have the time, but a critical reflection upon anything and everything from the point of view of biblical message, Christocentrism, or whatever.

Why cannot the consensus of twenty years ago be made to work for us as a critical fulcrum? That would mean taking seriously theological *self-*criticism, but it would also mean that the main function of theology for our day is critique-making without too much regard for "establishments," be they theological, ecclesiastical, or otherwise.

A critical theology, let it be said for those who cherish continuity as well as discontinuity, might well be the fulfillment of one major piece of Reformation unfinished business. How else can the prophetic protest of Protestantism assert itself in our day? Beyond this, a critical theology, taking seriously the revelatory dimension of the gospel, could be our best safeguard against selling out completely to a "religionless Christianity" which is no more distinguishable from secular humanism. *This* issue, precipitated upon our time by Bonhoeffer and the *Honest to God* ruckus, needs our best *critical* attention and not just outright denunciation or easy acceptance.

III

The problem of theological *perspective* is related to the demand for critical theological reflection. Here again philosophy and art may help illuminate the issue. Philosophy today has largely abandoned the verification norm as ultimate, asking of any proposition not whether it can be verified but what in any case it is intended to mean. The contemporary artist, more than ever self-conscious about the multiple levels of symbolism, is not so eager to communicate a single, sweeping idea or feeling but to open up as rich a kaleidoscope as possible.

If much of contemporary theology is to be critical and reflective rather than highly structured, then the perspective which theology adopts will have to be permissive rather than dogmatic, open rather than closed, patient rather than intransigent. For the intention of theological thinking would then be not so much to make judgments between right and wrong theology but to evaluate critically what as a matter of fact passes for theology at whatever level of life and thought.

If the philosopher recognizes many different kinds of truth assertions, and if Genet's *The Blacks,* for example, can be experienced from several levels of symbolism, why cannot theology tolerate a multiplicity of *kerygmatic* possibilities? So far as theological evaluation goes, the clues for our day are located in integrity of feeling and authenticity of expression rather than in uniformity or consistency of content.

We have begun to accept the pluralism of denominations, even of faiths, and perhaps someday of religions. Why should it be so difficult to accept the plurality of theological expression at many levels? Without succumbing to a flat or futile relativism, a pluralistic theological perspective might go a long way in reducing the fruitless tensions between theologian and preacher, clergy and laity, reason and revelation, science and religion, Barth and Tillich, and so on, and on, and on, as if the main task of theology were to set opposites against each other in order to achieve one single solitary sovereign position.

IV

Whatever the theologians decide to do or not to do about their own craft, two new factors on the current scene seem destined to force some issues out into the open. One is the racial revolution through which we are now moving, and the

other is the train of events started in Rome by Pope John
XXIII. Both will deeply affect the future of Christian faith and
life in the next twenty years.

The racial revolution, as is true of all revolutions, means both
the death and abandonment of old traditions and the emancipation of new, perhaps uncontrollable, dynamic forces. For
many in America, and in other parts of the world, the nonwhite
explosion is a cataclysmic threat equal only to nuclear explosion. Even for whites who sympathize with the black liberation
movement, things will never be the same again. As James
Baldwin has put it pointedly, the emerging problem for the
white person is not what to do about the black problem. That
decision no longer rests with white people; they can neither
direct nor hinder the drift of the black revolution. The white
problem is how to live at peace with a bad conscience.

If anything can teach the Christian church in these days
what it means to think and act self-critically, it will be the racial
revolution. Perhaps it is already too late. But it would be a
tragedy of classical proportions if the deep Christian commitment of black people, on the one hand, and the equally profound Christian obligation of the American churches to demonstrate their authenticity, on the other hand—it will be
absolutely fatal if these two factors are not focused creatively
on the present situation. No one can quite see how this is to
be accomplished, if at all. But it will not likely come about
through ecclesiastical pronouncements or well-meaning gradu-
alistic programs.

As in theology, so too here, it is not so much structure and
systems that meet the issues of the day but resolute and daring
critiques of traditional orders no matter how sacrosanct. How
the churches in their thought and in their action meet this
challenge may decide whether Christian theology in the next
generation will experience a radical rebirth or whether for all
practical purposes it will henceforth slip into obsolescence.

The second decisive movement in the contemporary situation which seems certain to affect theology and church life in
the decades to come is the Vatican Council now sitting in

Rome. One of the massive ironies of religious history is being dramatized before our eyes: the Roman Catholic Church is rapidly emerging in the eyes of the world as the symbol of progressive ecclesiastical and theological *reform!*

How far the reform will reach within Romanism remains to be seen. But it is already evident that a totally new chapter is being written in Catholic theology. Since the Reformation of the sixteenth century, Protestantism has imagined itself providentially entrusted with a monopoly on reform. What now? And what about tomorrow?

If Protestant theology, and this will be an even harder lesson for Romanism to learn, can accept creatively the multiform levels of faith and life which enjoy some relative permanence, then a new day for the ecumenical movement will surely dawn. And, looking at the Protestant-inspired World Council of Churches, this may seem to come just in time! If the older competitive, exclusivistic tendencies reassert themselves, the outlook for the Christian witness, both Catholic and Protestant, is grim indeed.

The Open Option

Traditional apologetics has always assumed that Christian faith makes some sort of sense of the whole of reality. Whatever the mysteries of revelation, the paradoxes of thought, or the limitations of language, the basic presupposition of Christian communication is that faith provides a clue of sorts to the riddle of the universe. Without faith that is just what the universe is taken to be—a riddle. With faith, so we argue, meanings are disclosed, patterns emerge, structures develop, and all things work together toward ultimate unity, harmony, and purpose. But it could be argued nowadays, and many suspect, that this traditional assumption about Christian faith making sense does not itself make sense.

I

The contemporary problem in presenting Christian truth-claims is not that older methods have now been proved false, or that Christian faith itself is intellectually untenable, but rather that the traditional assumptive world is no longer convincing. The eager search for tidy meaning-structures that inspire so many sermons, biblical studies, and theological discussions can scarcely commend itself to our present situation. For we have learned, in the name of science, philosophy, psychology, and the arts, to claim less and to take for granted that this is, as William James reminded us many years ago, a pluralistic universe.

THEOLOGY TODAY, XXII (1966), 467–471.

Without supporting these assertions or arguing about them, we may ask what would be involved in presenting the claims of Christianity today if the traditional apologetic assumptions are no longer relevant? How could the Christian go about the business of being a witness for the faith in a time when the whole idea of a meaningful universe is a meaningless assumption? It is a temptation for the Christian apologist to offer some stratagem of intellectual devising in answer to such a radical question. So perhaps the dire predictions about the demise of the church's influence may be assuaged and the obsequies for the death of God indefinitely postponed. But that temptation must be resisted if we are really to take seriously the fractured, multiform situation of today. Really to affirm a pluralistic universe and the irrelevance of all monistic structure-systems that try to make sense of everything under heaven and earth means *not* to search for a new structure. It means that Christians must learn to relax and loosen their grip. It means that everything is up for grabs, that the open option is not only tolerated but happily welcomed, that *any* view is permissible, that truth, reality, nature, as well as gospel, theology, church, are all laid out in bits and pieces, that authentic meaning can be found in any one or more of the integers but not necessarily, or only, in all together in unison. "This is my Father's world" may still be a lyrical affirmation of faith, but "the music of the spheres" is a singularly obsolete way of speaking and hardly supportive of Christian faith. Faith's assertion can no longer assume or imply nature's endorsement; the two affirmations simply don't walk hand in hand.

The new situation in which we find ourselves requires that we abandon altogether traditional apologetic assumptions. The big new problem for Christians is whether they can adopt an attitude that allows for the possibility that the faith is only one option among many. To be so open and permissive may appear to some to betray the Christian claim before it is even stated. But this would only mean that we are operating on an assumptive level which by definition excludes the possibility of a pluralistic universe. It may be that Christian apologists will see that a piecemeal approach can ultimately lead to a monistic conclusion, but today they dare not begin with that conclusion as if it were a major premise which everyone accepts. And it is not a conclusion to which everything must be directed as if the stages along the way were unimportant except as they all interrelate within one clear-cut sequence.

II

If the traditional assumptive world is obsolete simply because it no longer works as it once did and therefore no longer supports Christian truth-claims, we may ask further what kinds of assumptions are possible. Three at least can be advanced.

For one thing, we are moving theologically into an era of the *open option.* This suggests a recognition of truth's multivalence and a denial that there must always be one, single, correct interpretation. In religious affairs, we have already learned to accept this on the level of Protestant denominationalism. The multiplicity of churches which for so long has been decried as the scandal of Protestant proliferation seems less heinous today. Nowadays everyone is ecumenical, including the pope, but at the same time we have learned to live creatively with our differences rather than being embarrassed by them. But so far this mood of coexistence, so obvious in the new development at the Protestant–Roman Catholic level, has scarcely begun to manifest itself at the levels of theology, apologetics, biblical studies, preaching, or missionary strategy. In all these areas we still tend to operate as if everything could be gathered together, neatly or by force if necessary, into a unifying monistic pattern. The only alternative, so we have heard monotonously, runs headlong into the quagmire of relativism and syncretism. But this is more a paper problem than an actual threat.

If multivalence assumes the stature of a premise today, it is partly related to a second contemporary truism that *the meaning of existence is ambiguous* because all attempts to state what it is collide with the absurdity of the human situation. This mood, partly cynical, partly humorous, protests against all the

solemn, traditional meaning-structures that try to isolate the
essence of life, truth, history, and destiny. Grand as the Thomistic system certainly was, its synthesis of Aristotle and
Augustine, of reason and revelation, of philosophy and theology, of virtues and vices, of God and the world, of heaven and
earth claims too much for today. It, and other such structures,
have not been proved false; they are simply being bypassed and
ignored. And one reason is that all such meaning-structures are
unable or unwilling to take account of the absurd, the unhar-
monious, the incongruous. Will some preacher someday dare
to preach the gospel as it illustrates, rather than solves, the
sheer ambiguity of life?

A third elementary assumption in our day relates to the
hunch that *fragments of truth* can be more significant than
truth as a whole. There is an experimental quality to contemporary attitudes about life and the world. Authentic experience,
no matter how fragmentary or dislocated, is more to be desired
than wisdom about the causal connections within the whole
vast complex of reality. This is a protest against all traditional
harmonies and chains-of-being, not because they aren't fascinating in their escalation from one level to another, but because postmodern society thinks that any particular link may
be as important as the chain itself. Tennyson's sentimental
reflection about the "flower in the crannied wall" still makes
sense today not because it holds the secret of "all in all,"
including God and humanity, but because it has its own integrity, meaning, and purpose and ought to be gratefully appreciated as such without being artificially immortalized within
some grandiose divine-human schema.

III

The most difficult difference to grasp, and the most painful
to accept, as between traditional ways of presenting Christian
truth-claims and the contemporary assumptive world in which
we live, lies in the *nondidactic* attitude of our times. To proclaim the gospel has always implied a teaching purpose to the

end that the ignorant may be enlightened, the unbeliever converted, the selfish made to see the errors of their ways, and so on. To be a Christian is to be a disciple, a pupil, a learner, as well as an apostle, a witness, a missioner. So theology, preaching, biblical exposition, religious education, and even social action have usually been motivated in the past not only by conviction about the faith but by an unquestioned evangelistic concern to interpret the meaning of life and the adequacy of the gospel in comprehensive, consistent, meaningful patterns.

But how are we to defend the faith to a generation which sits uncomfortably while being instructed on the moral and religious "lessons" of nature and history? If traditional cosmological and teleological arguments no longer accompany the faith in any convincing way, will the gospel itself become imperiled if these supports are withdrawn? Bultmann argued that the authentic message of the gospel is not necessarily tied to the biblical mythology and that the latter was in fact an obstacle in the way of modern acceptance of the former. May the same be said for the whole gamut of traditional apologetics which sought to commend the Christian faith by demonstrating how unique, monistic, and exclusivistic and therefore how harmonious, unifying, and comprehensive it was?

Increasingly the *theological* problem of our day becomes an *apologetic* problem. The search for doctrinal clarity and consensus seems to many less demanding than the urgency to decide how the gospel can be proclaimed in the open option atmosphere of our day. With all the traditional supports removed, we must learn afresh how to translate the gospel for our day, as William Tyndale did for his in 1525, as a faith that "signyfyth good, mery, glad and ioyfull tydings, that maketh a mannes hert glad, and maketh hym synge, daunce and leepe for ioye."

Theology as Irritant

The yawning gulf that separates our day in things religious and theological from the day before yesterday is often painfully sharpened by a liturgical phrase that arrests devotion and draws attention to itself. So aware are we these days of the imperative for the church to be in the world, for theology to be relevant in the concrete areas of life, for ethics to be related to specific situations, for the Christian to make life more human, that much of our liturgical language and piety seems altogether obsolete.

I

Usually we do not stop to analyze prayers and hymns linguistically, though at times a phrase provokes a discrepancy that cannot be avoided. One such, from a familiar hymn, may serve as an example.

In George Croly's "Spirit of God, Descend Upon My Heart" (1866), there occurs in the fourth stanza the phrase: "Teach me the struggles of the soul to bear." In further explanation of what this involves, the petition continues: "To check the rising doubt, the rebel sigh." The stanza then concludes: "Teach me the patience of unanswered prayer." One reason surely why these verses have sung themselves for a century into the devotion of countless Christians is that in every age we know very well "the struggles of the soul" and the experience of "unanswered prayer."

Theology Today, XXIII (1967), 459–466.

What seems an anachronism today is the suggestion that the spiritual life (the Christian life lived by the Holy Spirit) ought to stifle "the rising doubt, the rebel sigh." This may have been assumed as part of Christian piety in the middle of the nineteenth century when the assurance of salvation was understood as soaring above the lower levels of uncertainty. As in Bunyan's *The Pilgrim's Progress,* the Christian must not be distracted from the steady pursuit of the Celestial City, or, as in the first verse of Croly's hymn, we should pray that the Holy Spirit will "wean it [my heart] from earth."

Whatever may have been true one hundred years ago, today this way of speaking is ludicrously out of date. The piety of the day before yesterday implied a clear distinction between earth and heaven, profane and sacred, this world and the next, secular and spiritual. To be a Christian within these categories meant to move from one to the other, from the lower to the higher, and, having done so, never to look back like Lot's wife, and to pray for strength not to be tempted.

But this runs completely contrary to everything that has been happening during the past fifty years in biblical studies, theology, church appraisal, religious education, evangelism, and missions. Far from petitioning the Holy Spirit to wean us from earth, Christians are praying to be used within the profane structures of secular life. In reflecting upon the temptation of Jesus, what seems significant for us today is not merely that the temptations were real or that Jesus resisted the tempter but that *it was the Spirit* who "drove him out into the wilderness" to be tempted. Again, we feel the urgency today of redefining the church not as the elect fellowship at prayer but as the tenuously committed who sense something askew in the structures of society and who think some protest ought to be made. Least of all do we feel today that Christian life and experience should "check" doubt or dissent. Far from stifling "the rebel sigh," we want in every way to protect, defend, encourage, stimulate, and extend "the principle of protest." Unlike our Reformation forebears, from whom we got the idea, we are as much concerned to turn dissent in upon ourselves as to complain of the abuses of others outside. Even Roman Catholics, or should we say especially Roman Catholics, understand their contemporary assignment as demanding a thoroughgoing revitalization of the traditional establishment. Anyone who has heard or read theologians such as Hans Küng knows how exciting and prophetic this new Catholic inner Reformation can be and how far it separates us from the Counter Reformation and even the Protestant Reformation.

II

The current concern for renewal in the life and work of the church issues in two different, and sometimes conflicting, views of what should be done. The first and certainly at the moment the dominant view translates "renewal" as the continuing development, consolidation, extension, and elaboration of traditions already laid down. If the establishment has become ingrown, insensitive, insecure, so this position maintains, the road to renewal requires the rebuilding of the highways, perhaps the construction of turnpikes, cloverleafs, ramps, bypasses, so that the traffic may move more easily and, it is hoped, unimpeded. It would not take much effort to document current theological trends as mostly of this order. In church architecture, for example, we have moved the furniture around and utilized the new materials primarily in order to extend the accepted image of the church. In biblical studies, the scholars (mostly from Germany once more, as in the nineteenth century) discuss hermeneutics endlessly and whether Bultmann was right or wrong, but the net effect is to capitalize on the results of comparative scholarship and move forward in the continuing quest of a viable kerygmatic perspective (this may even rehabilitate the older quest for the historical Jesus). In theology, the refrain is the same. If Barth, Brunner, and Tillich are less compelling (and less read and studied) than they once were, our present task must surely be the pruning and refining and thus the chastened continuation of doctrinal formulations of the faith. A new creedal manifesto (for example, the United Presbyterian "Confession of '67") may reshuffle the topics and adopt another biblical organizing theme, but in the main the result is a recognizable facsimile of past theological traditions. *Renewal in all these instances comes from within and implies continuity.*

The second, and highly contested and controversial, translation of "renewal" implies total restructuring rather than continued development. *Renewal in this sense means outside pressure and radical discontinuity.* If the former view finds its inspiration within its own ever-renewable tradition (phoenix-like), the second view shows little confidence in reformation-from-within and seeks its norms and pointers from "secular" insights. If we use the traffic figure, the second view we are trying to describe would regard all attempts to solve the jam by constructing superhighways as merely palliative, like putting a Band-Aid on a cancer. The traffic problem will not be solved by building better roads or by making safer cars. The really important question for tomorrow is: "What will replace the internal combustion car of today?" As Marshall McLuhan insists (in *Understanding Media*) the "mechanical bride," as he calls the motorcar, "will go the way of the horse." The wheel is becoming obsolete and is on the way out as surely as the cuspidor was doomed "when the lady typist arrived on the business scene." Changing the figure, McLuhan reiterates his aggravating thesis: "it is the framework itself that changes with new technology, and not just the picture within the frame." (This is what is meant by saying that "the medium is the message.")

Suppose the traditional notion of the church building, for example, as sacred-space-set-apart must now be completely scrapped in order to reconceptualize what it is the church must be in society today? Suppose instead of hunting for hermeneutical presuppositions by which to expound the gospel, we take seriously (to invoke McLuhan again) the end of the "Gutenberg Galaxy" with its written, verbal, linear, repeatable, homogeneous, assembly-line pretensions so that the Bible can be seen for what it once was, namely, an oral, scribal, tribal, *memoriter*-oriented, *multiple*-meaning resource? Suppose in theology we abandon altogether the notion that it is important, even if it were possible, to organize or elucidate Christian "truth," and concentrate instead on raising itchy, gadfly questions about what people are doing and why?

These two roughly sketched views of renewal, however we evaluate them, are often violently in conflict with each other. All those who identify with the developmental view feel threatened, and a little exasperated, by the radical renewers. All those who identify with the total restructuring view know well enough their own minority status but feel frustrated by the administrator and caretaker mystique that talks about reform but perpetuates the establishment.

III

It would be ridiculous to adjudicate between these two as if any useful purpose could be served by declaring one right and the other wrong. Many of us would want to plant a foot firmly in each camp, and we might even maintain that only in this way can a solid stance be secured. But the suggestion that theology be defined as "irritant" is not so farfetched after all, the Christian witness boasting a long pedigree as minority protest movement.

In all the current, and slightly scared, talk about the stalemate in the civil rights program, the white backlash, and black power, we must not lose sight of the substantial witness already made by the protest movement. That is now *history.* In dramatic and often violent ways, the civil rights issue has emerged as a *white* problem. It is not a *black* problem except as the white problem of accepting blacks creates an intolerable social situation for everyone. If federal legislation has achieved what gains have been made *de jure,* the protest movement has punctuated the American conscience *de facto.*

Protest and dissent, especially in theological matters, almost always encounter stiff opposition. Whether any particular kind of dissent is right or wrong, it is a pity that the church tends to resist so readily, for the ability to assimilate ought to be one of the trademarks of Christian faith. Consider the opposition, and the *kind* of opposition, that gets generated against the "death of God" enthusiasts, Bishop James A. Pike, Malcolm Boyd's nightclub prayers, experiments with drama-in-the-church, liturgical jazz, contextual ethics—especially when dealing with sex.

IV

The various types of theology-as-irritant that can be mentioned are not all of equal significance, and indeed many may merely be irritating. But a theology unafraid of the "rising doubt, the rebel sigh" is making an impressive claim for attention these days. The aims of radical renewal movements always seem to weigh heavier on the negative than on the positive side. The advocates of renewal-from-within rightly chafe under a critical bombardment that seeks to obliterate all the old landmarks. And the advocates of gadfly pressure rightly scoff at the timidity of any renewal program that clings to the tried (and in their judgment "tired") patterns of the past. Traditionalists wrongly assume that gadflies reject the classic doctrines of the faith for intellectual reasons, whereas the problem has nothing to do with the truth or falsity (or verification) of dogma but simply with adequacy and "sincerity" (to use Hans Küng's distinction between truth and truthfulness). Radical renewers for their part wrongly despair of the reform-potential latent in established institutions, the most astonishing and unexpected example in our day being the Roman Catholic Church. If we really take our pluralistic society seriously, we must rediscover the *theological* significance of the ancient adage that it takes *all* kinds of people to make up the world. Furthermore, in this psychological age, we ought to guess that the dispute on the outside finds its parallel in each of us on the inside.

V

The big question about the next step ahead cannot be answered by taking a poll. It seems certain that the tension stirred up mainly by the irritators will be with us for a long time and will determine the agenda for theological discussion. It probably will *not* be a doctrinal-theological dispute about the "meaning" of justification or whether God exists or not but rather a critique of forms ancient and modern, evaluated functionally as to their authenticity, honesty, and "sincerity," and *not* according to their historicity, accuracy, or verifiability.

An illustration of how this critical perspective leads to an understanding of the role of theology as irritant may be taken from *Time* magazine's devastating review of the movie *The Bible,* produced by Dino De Laurentiis and directed by John Huston (Oct. 7, 1966, pp. 119f.). We quote only a few sentences:

> Lured by ballyhoo or simple piety into the vast, glittering void of this enterprise—an experience roughly equivalent to being swallowed by a whale—a bored viewer will nonetheless feel twinges of gratitude. After all, it might have been worse. . . .
>
> Most entertaining is a kinetic, eight-minute Creation, astir with turbulent photography. Unfortunately, it is a long way from The Beginning to the end. The Word is interpreted altogether literally, neither revitalized with the logic of drama nor illuminated by the magic of myth. . . .
>
> "God blessed them and said: Multiply," the voice intones, clearing the way for a shot of fuzzy, nuzzling seals and simultaneously raising questions of identity. There is somebody up there, all right, but who? A director, a Deity, or Our Man in Disneyland? . . .
>
> Any characters who are at all respectable converse with a vengeful Deity mainly by lifting eyes skyward, and the pauses throb with crashing drums, heavenly choirs and bird song—everything, in fact, but a bouncing ball to help the audience pray along. Better read The Book.

The significant thing for our discussion here is to ask our two kinds of renewers how they would respond to this criticism, assuming it has some validity. The traditionalists would doubtless note that this is what we should expect from Hollywood which has a talent for vulgarizing the holy. The only way to cope with bad biblical films is to make better ones. Gadflies, however, would observe that something has happened in the last hundred years not only to Hollywood but to biblical studies and theology, rendering such attempts futile and phony from the start.

Perhaps this forces us back to elemental questions. Should movies of the Bible (gospel) be attempted at all? What would a Barthian director do, or a Bultmannian, or a Tillichian, or a Bonhoefferian? If it can't be done at all according to contemporary theological rubrics, what does that mean?

What Use Is Religion?

That there is a causal connection between religious faith and ethical behavior would be regarded by many as elemental and obvious. Faith and commitment, most of us would say, have ethical and moral consequences. To believe is to behave. Christian conviction includes individual and corporate imperatives for living. Though religion can be abused and misused, surely one positive use is to sustain a common morality and an implicative value system.

I

Religious faith, we must also observe, does not automatically assure high ethical obedience. Christians, by and large, are not demonstrably more loving, more tolerant, or more humane than those of other religions or of no religion at all. In the 1930's, when the first *Humanist Manifesto* was issued, a cardinal principle expressed throughout the document was that ethical humanism can be structured without being tied to traditional religious doctrines. The brave conclusion asserted, in the masculinist language of the times, that "Man is at last becoming aware that he alone is responsible for the realization of the world of his dreams, that he has within himself the power for its achievement. He must set intelligence and will to the task."

But in our day, apparently, neither the traditional religious

THEOLOGY TODAY, XXXI (1974), 1–5.

systems of beliefs nor the supposedly self-generating ethical
humanism of a more optimistic time is able to produce a moral
or cultural dream world. It may be that religious faith today,
whether expressed by Christians individually or by churches
corporately, does not give much cause for celebrating the exalted moral behavior that is supposed to issue from religious
conviction. But it is also true that atheists, agnostics, humanists, secularists, or those who are just indifferent to religion in
any form do not give us much assurance that a compassionate
morality and a humane society can emerge of themselves.

In any case, nearly everyone today, religious or not, acknowledges that we live in the midst of moral and ethical chaos. The
whole Watergate miasma has italicized our current dis-ease.
Well-intentioned government public servants, even highly religiously motivated people, can subvert and abuse the democratic process for private and selfish ends. Little expression of
regret or remorse has accompanied these activities over a period of years, except when wrung from subpoenaed witnesses
before a grand jury or a Senate hearing committee. The erosion
of individual moral perception, and the resultant myopia regarding the larger issues of social justice, have shocked and
paralyzed our common life in an unprecedented way.

II

Over the past few months, while ruminating on these matters, several quotations, gathered for other purposes, suddenly
converged on a thesis that seems worth stating. *When the
religious value system that once supported the culture is ignored
or rejected, the moral and ethical value system plunges into
chaos.* When "moral values" are no longer sustained by "religious values," they apparently aren't sustained by anything
else.

Collected for my own teaching purposes, the citations which
follow may be recorded here as a clue to our ethical and moral
disorder.

(a) The first quotation comes from an interview between

William F. Buckley, Jr., and Malcolm Muggeridge, the well-known British author and journalist, and former self-avowed agnostic. Muggeridge says:

Basically what is happening, I think, in the world is [the dominance of] scientific materialism's view of life (that we can by means of science solve all our problems, create for ourselves a happy, fulfilled life by our own efforts), [and] that the Christian religion on which after all our civilization was founded no longer has any real validity. . . . First of all, we'll abolish all sense of a moral order, which is very largely done now, and having abolished all sense of a moral order, it seems to me almost inevitable that every other form of order will likewise disintegrate. . . . In my opinion, we are witnessing the total moral breakdown of a way of life. . . . Chesterton . . . said, "When people don't believe in God, they don't then believe in nothing, they believe in anything." (From the transcript of the *Firing Line* program, "Has America Had It?" Taped in London, Aug. 20, 1973; broadcast on PBS, Sept. 16, 1973, pp. 4–6.)

(b) The second quotation is excerpted from the recent book by Joseph Campbell, *Myths to Live By* (1972). Author of *The Hero with a Thousand Faces* and other works on comparative mythology, Campbell—unlike Muggeridge—could hardly be described as a religious "convert."

Literally read, [religious] symbolic forms have always been—and still are, in fact—the supports of their civilizations, the supports of their moral orders, their cohesion, vitality, and creative powers. With the loss of them, there follows uncertainty, and with uncertainty, disequilibrium, since life . . . requires life-supporting illusions; and where these have been dispelled, there is nothing secure to hold on to, no moral law, nothing firm. . . . There is everywhere in the civilized world a rapidly rising incidence of vice and crime, mental disorders, suicides and dope-addictions, shattered homes, impudent children, violence, murder, and despair. These are facts; I am not inventing them. (*Myths to Live By*, Viking Press, 1972, pp. 10f.)

(c) The third quotation is taken from an interview by Alden Whitman with Erich Fromm, the distinguished author and psychologist, who came to America forty years ago as a refugee from Hitler. A land that once seemed so hopeful to Fromm now seems dominated by a passion for destructiveness. This is the paradox that informs his new book, *The Anatomy of Human Destructiveness.*

There is still a moral residue in America composed of our religious and humane tradition in which the proper goal of society is to serve its members. . . . What is urgent now if we are not to continue on the path of destructiveness and national suicide is a renewal of a sense of general religious values. (*The New York Times,* Dec. 15, 1973, p. 33.)

III

What are we to make of such comments? Well, first off, there are some too-simple inferences to avoid. (1) It won't do to say, no matter how dismal the record appears, that there is *no* corporate morality whatsoever. As Erich Fromm observes, there is "a moral residue in America." The widely circulated and reprinted editorial by Gordon Sinclair, the popular Canadian broadcaster, daring to praise "the Americans" as "generous," implies the same substratum of moral compassion. "When distant cities are hit by earthquakes, it is the United States that hurries to help. So far this spring [June, 1973] 59 American communities have been flattened by tornadoes. Nobody [from other countries] has helped."

(2) Nor will it do to say, as so many are saying, that religion in America is declining and has been generally rejected. If some church statistics are down, others are up. If Episcopalians, Presbyterians, and Methodists wring their hands, Pentecostals, Jehovah's Witnesses, and charismatics of all kinds are lifting theirs in joy and praise. Andrew M. Greeley has made his point that, while the "conventional wisdom" of some sociologists and academics posits a general decline of religion, there are overwhelming empirical data supporting what he calls "the persistence of religion" in America. If it is difficult to find in the established churches, it is out in the open on college campuses and articulated in countless paperbacks on eastern religions, occult rituals, and mystical movements.

(3) Another misleading, and unhelpful, response, also very common today, acknowledges our moral morass but contends that it is no worse than it always has been. If the Committee to Re-Elect the President (CREEP) has been caught handling hot campaign cash, well, the Democrats undoubtedly are also guilty but have avoided detection. In one of her syndicated columns, Ann Landers was asked, "What is this world coming to? . . . I can't remember a time when there was so much hate, killing, and crazy people loose. Can you explain it?" The reply: "There has always been hate, killing, and nutty people on the loose. A country that has grown in population and complexity, as ours has, must expect more of *all* kinds of people—crazies included." Presidential assistant John McLaughlin, a Jesuit, is reported in *Commonweal* as saying that compared to some ecclesiastical skeletons, Watergate is like the "peccadilloes of novice nuns."

(4) Still another simplistic inference, ambiguous because partly true, argues that the complete moral collapse of our society can only be prevented if enough people will turn to religion. Preachers, evangelists, and moralists insist that if more of us were to accept Christ or be more devout in our religious practices, this would not only be good for us but we, then, would be good for others. But it is exceedingly risky to correlate personal religious faith, or the worship experience of believers, with moral and cultural consequences. Apparently, the more convicted people are, religiously, the more intolerant they are of others and the more withdrawn they become from the "outside world" around them. Neither the supporters of Billy Graham nor of Key '73 try to measure the elevation of ethics on the local or national scene as a result of such evangelistic campaigns. President Nixon is a self-professed religious man, as are several of his closest associates. His largest single charitable contribution, according to his income tax returns, was to the Billy Graham Evangelistic Association. This Administration received "a mandate from the people," partly at least, because it was *for* law and order and *against* permissiveness.

IV

Beyond such ambiguities, there are surely more constructive, perhaps programmatic, things to say. We mention only two. *First,* we desperately need in the area of theology a new chapter on the interlocking relation between religion and culture. Reinhold Niebuhr did this for a previous generation, and Paul Tillich bequeathed to us an intriguing formula—"religion is the substance of culture, culture is the form of religion." With our current involvement in the sociology of religion, and with our confusing time of troubles, this seems a providential time to explore afresh religion's investment in the whole implicative human enterprise. This should be something other than a recall to the social gospel or a plea to the churches to become responsible for the practical problems of social justice. *How* this is to be done remains to be seen; *that* it must be done seems obvious.

And, *second,* the correlation between religion and morality needs to be factored into the apologetic and evangelistic claims of the churches. It is not enough to assume that religious devotion results in ethical or compassionate behavior. To quote Tillich again: "The principle of evangelism must be to show to the people outside the church that the symbols in which the life of the church expresses itself are answers to the questions implied in their very existence as human beings."

The Stoic as Heroic

In a time when so many in public life, and in our culture generally, seem to have lost their moral directions, Stoic resignation may be as heroic an ideal as most of us can contemplate. In an age of the nonhero, it may seem the best we can do is to cultivate qualities of imperturbability and stolid aloofness. "Blessed are those who expect nothing," wrote Alexander Pope in the first quarter of the eighteenth century, "because they shall not be disappointed." That is a Stoic beatitude that commends itself to many in our contemporary society. Consider the following random items:

The newly appointed Archbishop of Canterbury, Donald Coggan, speaks of our culture as "a sick society" that cannot become healthy until "it starts living by some rules again." He then went on to say something that would otherwise seem to be a piece of pious banality, except in a time of utter moral chaos such as ours: "There's a lot to be said for the Ten Commandments."

Speaking to Columbia University graduates, President William J. McGill observed, solemnly, "Our country is in the midst of a crisis of moral values. . . . Many writers now seem to assume that American society is rotten to the core."

At the same time, across the street, Margaret Mead, the articulate anthropologist, told Barnard seniors that we "need

THEOLOGY TODAY, XXXI (1974), 183–186.

to redefine our moral values." Since we are "totally without
leadership" where leaders are most expected, it is "more than
ever true" that today we must look to the young for moral
renewal, even though they have good reason to be unmoved by
such appeals.

Apparently, we can't expect much from the older generation, since they have so little reason for hope. Like the elderly
woman who shocked Congressman Edward Mezvinsky of
Iowa, the junior Democrat on the House Judiciary Committee,
when she offered him her philosophy of life: "I'm glad I don't
have long to live, because there really isn't much to live for."

High school students, according to an annual poll conducted
by Rep. Edwin B. Forsythe, of the Sixth (N.J.) Congressional
District, express moods of "worry, uncertainty, disillusionment, and, at times, sarcasm." Almost without exception, students described the recent fuel shortage as "fake, fraud." As
one high schooler put it, "There are too many politicians who
are out just to make money off the people, instead of trying to
help the public."

A survey sponsored by Potomac Associates, Inc., a nonprofit,
foundation-supported organization, reports that "there has
been a pronounced tendency to turn inward," internationally
and domestically, and that more Americans than ever think
they and the country as a whole are "worse off today and with
less hope for the future."

In a less somber vein, Art Buchwald, the columnist, speaking
at the Holy Cross (Massachusetts) commencement, wagered
with the graduates: "If you believe President Nixon knew nothing about Watergate, I invite you to see me after the commencement exercises. I have some lovely swamp land in
Florida I'd like to sell you." And to the seniors at Miami
University (Ohio), he said: "Don't get me wrong about Nixon.
I worship the quicksand he walks on." (Mr. Buchwald, incidentally, returned four thousand dollars in college speaking fees for
scholarship purposes.)

I

Some of these sentiments seem more tilted toward cynicism than Stoicism. If Stoicism adopts an attitude of impassive aloofness to the world ("apathy" in the classical sense), cynicism has nothing but contempt for the world or for values and ideals. It is easy, and sometimes very tempting, to adopt a cynical point-of-viewing, partly because it doesn't cost the believer anything, and it can readily pose as an arch and expansive perspective. But to be a true Stoic means to live one's life with a certain heroic nobility despite the crumbling of culture all around.

Classical Stoicism was itself the product of cultural disintegration in the Greco-Roman world. Initiated by Zeno of Citium, a Phoenician colony in Crete, early Stoicism merged eclectic emphases from both oriental and Semitic sources. Unsystematic but rigorous in its demands for personal rectitude, Stoicism emerged within and spoke to a time of religious, political, and philosophical dissolution not unlike our own day. In Seneca, a contemporary of St. Paul, and in Marcus Aurelius, who sensed the breakdown of his own culture without being aware of the coming Holy Roman Empire, Stoicism paralleled and competed with the gospel of Jesus Christ and the ethics of redemptive, suffering love.

While writing this, I remembered that Reinhold Niebuhr had often spoken appreciatively of Stoic heroism. There are, as I checked it, some twenty references to Stoicism in his *Nature and Destiny of Man.* On one occasion, he correlates the Stoic search for serenity with the word of Jesus, "Be not anxious." And in a well-known sermon on "The Providence of God" (a tape of which I have used in my classes), he argues that, against the Christian temptation to lobby in the courts of the Almighty for special privileges, "there is an element of nobility" in Stoicism, which impassively takes things as they come.

This eloquent sermon, by the way, is reproduced in a new volume of Niebuhr's prayers and casual pieces, *Justice and Mercy* (Harper & Row, 1974), edited by Ursula M. Niebuhr.

And on the page after the frontispiece, Niebuhr's so-called "serenity prayer" (1943) is also reproduced:

God, give us grace to accept with serenity the things that cannot be changed, courage to change the things that should be changed, and the wisdom to distinguish the one from the other.

II

With all its nobility of purpose and heroic restraint, Stoicism has always been clouded with a sense of portending doom, and its mood has always been inevitably glum. Stoic resignation can insulate us against sympathizing with the plight of others less fortunate, but it cannot of itself generate contentment, happiness, or joy. It can steel us against the vagaries and vicissitudes of a disintegrating culture, but it is powerless to save, heal, or re-create.

In his excellent, and still delightfully readable, essay on "St. Paul and Seneca," Lightfoot concludes his largely affirmative evaluation of Stoicism by demonstrating its essential contrast with the Christian ethic.

Though the sterner colors of Stoic morality are frequently toned down in Seneca, still the foundation of his ethical system betrays the repulsive features of his school. His fundamental maxim is not to guide and train nature, but to *overcome* it. The passions and affections are not to be directed, but to be crushed. The wise man, he says, will be clement and gentle, but he will not feel pity, for only old women and girls will be moved by tears; he will not pardon, for pardon is the remission of a deserved penality; he will be strictly and inexorably just. (J.B. Lightfoot's commentary on *Philippians*, 1903, pp. 296–297.)

In the same manner, for Marcus Aurelius, the Stoic virtues are clearly impressive if equally unavailing to salvage a sinking society. In an introductory essay on "The Background out of Which Christianity Came and the Environment Into Which It Was Born," Kenneth Scott Latourette sketches the portrait of a heroic but tragic figure.

In Marcus Aurelius, indeed, one can see the shadow of impending doom. Possessed of a strong sense of public duty, upright, stern in his self-admonitions, living as under the eye of a God who desires righteousness, there seems to have been about him no enthusiasm. . . . He was weighted down by sadness, the burden of empire, and the certain expectation of death. . . . There is no sense of joyous expectation, either for himself, his friends and neighbors, or for the world as a whole. In him can be caught a glimpse of an age which was fearful of approaching demise and was steeling itself to meet it. (Kenneth Scott Latourette, *The First Five Centuries,* Vol. I in *A History of the Expansion of Christianity,* 1937, p. 18.)

III

With this slight review of Stoicism, it may be instructive to turn again to Paul's celebrated address before the Athenians on Mars' Hill in view of the Areopagus (Acts 17:16–34).

Paul's apologetic approach and the content of his argument indicate clearly that he knew the substance of the Stoic philosophy (which he summarizes in vs. 24–26). And like Zeno of Citium, who precipitated oriental and Semitic influences upon classical Greek philosophy, the Apostle to the Gentiles was also an eclectic, a Greek-speaking Jew of Roman citizenship, and a Christian.

The conventional wisdom, when expounding Paul's Mars' Hill address, is to suggest that he failed to persuade his audience on rational grounds and henceforth determined to preach only "Jesus Christ and him crucified" (I Cor. 2:1–6). But there are three other, quite different, comments to make. *First,* however we evaluate the impact of Paul's address, the historical fact remains that Stoicism, with all its Christian parallels and with all its heroic posturing, increasingly dissipated its force until it fizzled out like a spent firecracker.

Second, it is illuminating to remember that the Areopagus was the same court that five hundred years earlier had charged Socrates with corrupting the city youth and for not believing in "the gods of the state" (Plato's *Apology,* 24B; cf. Acts 17:18). The irony of the coincidence is that while Stoicism ran parallel to Christianity, it never substantially intruded on its thought processes, whereas the Platonic-Socratic tradition, with its built-in idealism, became the basic philosophic apparatus for the normative theology of the early church. So in spite of the fact that Stoicism was the existential perspective of the day, reflecting academic and sophisticated ennui over against the collapse of conventional values, religious, political, and philosophical, it was the Platonic-Socratic tradition that impinged its trademark on the emerging Christian culture.

And *third,* we must be careful how we interpret Paul's crucial reference in his address to "Jesus and the resurrection." Too easily Christian apologists have assumed that this kerygmatic intrusion put off the curious but detached Athenians. Perhaps so. It is a daring, and philosophically absurd, idea anywhere, anytime. But it could be that the main difference between Christians and Stoics was not so much particular tenets of belief but the implication of those beliefs on mood and outlook. Both affirmed divine existence and the creation of the world, both acknowledged the commonality of humanity, both argued for an intelligent faith and a life of moral restraint and uprightness, and both believed in life beyond death.

It is easy to say that "Jesus and the resurrection" make the difference, and that is true. But on another level this Christian conviction also implied that because of "Jesus and the resurrection" the classical Stoic attitude of imperturbability was shown up to be essentially hopeless and therefore powerless. In times of confusion, whether in the first or twentieth century, the Stoic can exhibit a certain heroic nobility. The Christian should not scorn or despise that posture, and it may be as much as many today can aspire to; but it cannot take up the cause of the oppressed in our midst, it cannot provoke a mood of expectation, and it cannot bring in the future.

What's the Story?

Everyone who has ever been a student remembers a few former teachers. The more schools attended, the more teachers remembered. "Old Professor Snodgrass, wasn't he a character!" "Remember the day when Ruth Jacobowitz announced that she was . . . ?" "How about the time Henry Cooper came to class with a . . . ?" "Will you ever forget the look on Dr. Frey's face when he . . . ?" Almost anyone can supply words and incidents for the blank spaces.

What students remember most about teachers falls on the side of antics, mannerisms, classroom episodes, and anecdotal trivia. We tend to remember the person rather than the course. We recall vividly certain personality traits but have long ago forgotten what these had to do with what we were supposed to learn. Sometimes we remember only the stories and nothing else.

I

In my own early public school days, the Assistant Principal of Liberty School was a "Miss Faloon." I can't remember anything at all about her or the school except that we sang a verse during recess:

> Miss Faloon went up in a balloon
> And never came down till the fourth of June.

Theology Today, XXXII (1975), 129–132.

In college, old "Geology Scott" was so nearsighted that after the class monitor had checked off the empty seat numbers in "Geology 201," several last-row students always slipped out the back door unnoticed. As the professor droned on, no one was the wiser; certainly not those who copped out.

"Prexy" Patton, who had the distinction of serving as President of both Princeton University and the Theological Seminary, was reported to have asked a seminarian in theology class to explain Calvin's doctrine of double predestination. The student stuttered bravely but soon admitted defeat. "I have read the assignment, Professor, and I did know the answer, but now I've forgotten." To which Patton replied, addressing the whole class: "What a pity! The only person who ever knew the answer cannot now recall it."

Such stories multiply almost endlessly when former classmates meet at reunions, sports events, and on visits back to the old campus. Ephemeral nostalgia, perhaps, but isn't it curious how such isolated tales of former teachers and school days stick in the mind?

We seem to remember the unusual rather than the normal, the oddity rather than the routine, the amusing rather than the solemn, the mythology rather than the chronicle. As to teachers, we remember their influence, not their lectures; their personal quips and cranks, not their scholarship; their embarrassing moments, not their controlled reflections. And it is *only* these teachers we remember at all. The others are long since forgotten and beyond recall. Very learned teachers, no doubt; correct and proper in every way, diligent and demanding about their "disciplines," restrained and invulnerable personally, scholars and pedagogues, surely. But they belong mostly to that long procession of instructors who made school so tedious.

Tedious? Well, maybe one reason we remember best only the amusing, funny, and incidental episodes of our school days is that education was for many of us a very sober business with little to laugh about or enjoy. Like the innocent catechumen in the Scottish kirk who always thought the answer to the first question of the Westminster Shorter Catechism was: "To glorify God and endure him forever." The tyranny of the daily class schedule, the relentless demands of assignments and homework, the constant judgmental supervision—this oppressive experience may well linger in the memory but appear only subconsciously in dreams and nightmares. Several university alumni magazines a year ago were deluged with letters in response to a college graduate who wrote how, many years later, he still dreamed of missing a class, of not being prepared, of taking an exam on material he hadn't studied. All the writers reported similar terrifying fantasies that still plagued them regularly. With so much to be frightened about, it's no wonder we remember with relish the few fun-times in a long educational servitude.

II

If history is "the remembered past," then all such incidental stories, yarns, and episodes are important in lending substance and authenticity to the record. Those of us in the Judeo-Christian tradition, of course, already know all about this. Our religion celebrates the acts and events, often scattered and disconnected, of the remembered past as recorded in the Old Testament and as continued and reinterpreted in the New Testament. "O.T. history," as every Bible student knows, is a jumble of legendary stories, preposterous names, astonishing events, and miraculous happenings. The New Testament is allegedly the story, and the sequel, of the life of Jesus. But it, too, is a skein of many threads, twisted in irregular patterns, even if at the same time we also insist that it is "gospel," that is, "God's spiel." As one of my biblical colleagues put it, speaking of its narrative richness: "It takes a genius to make the Old Testament dull." And the Christ story keeps reappearing in fresh format every year even though we don't get much closer to the historical Jesus.

So it is that today we witness a new appreciation of the place of story and narrative in theology. Especially in an anti-intellectual time when philosophical structures and discursive reason-

ing find few takers, it may be inevitable that the illustrations
in history's textbook are more to be cherished than the text
itself. The scholars among us may be partly to blame. We are
very good, we think, at critical analysis, but there aren't many
biblical scholars who are also known as raconteurs. Theologians
can draw up impressive comparative evaluations of various
positions, but not many provide line drawings or cartoons for
their texts, if indeed they could think of anything to illustrate.
Perhaps seminaries should require courses in story-telling and
yarn-spinning as well as in theology and homiletics. Ministers
who aspire to the role of enabler might be reminded that most
of their older parishioners love to regale any willing listener
with seemingly trivial and endless reminiscences. The older
generation, incidentally, has much in common with the very
young—both like to tell tales and live in a fantasy world of
make-believe.

III

Why do those who advocate "story and narrative in theology" find the notion so fresh and exciting? Perhaps because our
middle-age and middle-century generation somehow forgot
what others before knew by instinct. Perhaps our present time
is emerging as a story-oriented age. Librarians and book publishers tell us that "biography" is making a comeback. Part of
the fascination of Watergate was the continuous unfolding of
new episodes in a true-life mystery stranger than fiction. As we
come to celebrate the Bicentennial, the chances are we will be
more interested in newly remembered bits and pieces from the
past than in principles of freedom, liberty, and justice. We will
find it easier to sketch the illustrations in our history books than
to articulate the ideals we aspire to but cannot attain.

But more influential than anything, perhaps, has been the
story-obsessed and narrative-ridden appetite of the media, especially TV. Every night we are treated to thumbnail biographies of "personalities" on the talk shows. All day long, if we
could endure it, there are soap operas made up of interminable

chapters. In prime evening time, the "sitcoms," the "made-for-TV" films, the serials of mystery, mayhem, and violence—all thrive apparently on the public's fascination with stories, yarns, anecdotes, whodunits, and cliff-hangers.

Well, someone may respond, "Isn't this life? Isn't life itself, every person's life, a story-narrative? Isn't this, then, the best possible reason for recovering for theology what has been lost but rechanneled in other ways?" Some might go even farther and, taken up with the new trend, insist that the story is sufficient unto itself, that the string of episodes remembered *is* history, that the meaning of any biblical narrative "is the narrative itself" (Hans Frei). If this were so, then all that we need today are more and better ways to spellbind our hearers, whoever they are, with scenarios, vignettes, and sagas.

Intriguing perhaps, but too simple. Let us return to my early recollections of teachers and their oddities and quirks. What we recall, even the trivial incidents, are surely important for our own personal history, but no one would suggest that such remembered stories about teachers tell us much about education. The myths and legends of a people make up the pattern of their history, their self-identity, their culture and religion. But unless this store of lore is somehow interpreted and expounded anew for each new generation, the stories will be forgotten or remain only inconsequential items such as we all include in our own version of the teacher's tale. If all we have are the Bible stories, we might have enough, but as a matter of fact the narratives are already embedded in interpretation.

Theology can be enriched, possibly even revived, through the creative imagination of new narrators. But theology is not itself story and cannot exist without some investment in prosaic description, discursive analysis, and reconstructive exposition.

The theologian, inevitably, is the person who strings stories in sequence, who asks about the meaning of the joke, who probes for personal motivations, who reflects about and not only recounts the narrative of faith. In the midst of fun and games, the theologian can look like a spoilsport. Among the storytellers, jokesters, and stand-up comedians with their one-liners and throwaways, the theologian cannot compete. But those of us with ministerial responsibility for articulating and communicating the faith must learn to refine and perfect our own special tools of the trade. If story and narrative can help, so much the better, for today preachers, ministers, and teachers need all the help they can get.

To the question: "What's the story?"—the answer can be in story form. But to the question: "What's the story all about?"—the answer must try to interpret, explain, and apply. Both are needed if we are to tell "the old, old story of Jesus and his love."

Theological Roots

Interpreters of the American cultural scene are intrigued, and no wonder, by the enormous public response to Alex Haley's *Roots*. The book, the author, the theme, the research, the travels, the TV series, and the overflowing and intense involvement of millions—add up to a major social phenomenon.

I

Related to the bicentennial search for national identity, *Roots* is precipitating a rippling quest for personal integrity. People by the thousands are poring over dull census records, old passenger lists, and church baptismal minutes in a surge of genealogical enthusiasm. Dominant symbols of American culture of only a few years ago, such as the Statue of Liberty, Ellis Island, the "melting pot," *E Pluribus Unum*, are being bypassed in an effort to accent ethnic individuality.

Once we assumed that immigrants wanted to forget their past and become assimilated as stereotypical "Americans." Now, third and fourth generation young people, as well as many senior citizens, are returning to their ancestral sites, seeking out long-lost relatives, and digging around here, there, and everywhere for their almost-forgotten and long-undernourished roots.

In many ways, the *Roots* phenomenon cancels out the whole

THEOLOGY TODAY, XXXIV (1977), 239–241.

"now" generation, the existential involvement in the present moment, and the conventional pragmatic American eagerness to be where the action is. Long out of fashion on the college and seminary campus, history and languages may well experience a revival. Archives, civil and church records, lists of names and addresses, tombstone inscriptions, dusty tomes hidden on library shelves—for many people these may, incredibly, compete with the latest paperback and the slickest illustrated magazine.

Of course, we may overrate the current craze. It could be only another fad, a flash in the pan. Time will tell whether *Roots* has actually struck a spark to ignite the human spirit and lift the imagination in new and enduring ways.

II

In any case, what is happening at the present moment in the widespread genealogical quest parallels what some have been saying recently about theology and the religious life. Many of the experiments in the past several years in theology, church programs, liturgical practices, and personal spirituality have deliberately cut loose from historical roots. In all the above areas, we have been pressured by a "now" generation, disdainful of the past, ignorant of traditions, and mawkish about discovering the really real.

In a pertinent, and much quoted, critique of the present church situation in America, James I. McCord has said that we suffer from "collective theological amnesia." We have forgotten our heritage. We languish because a loss of memory obscures our roots, and we hardly know who we are, what we are doing here, or where we are going.

The biblical word of reprimand, as well as of promise, for all deracinated peoples is "remember." "Remember" is one of the heavy words in the Hebrew Scriptures and is spoken especially to exiles in foreign lands. "Hearken to me, you who pursue deliverance, you who seek the Lord; look to the rock from which you were hewn, and to the quarry from which you were digged. Look to Abraham your father and to Sarah who bore you . . ." (Isa. 51:1–2).

III

Now, we can hear the gleeful chorus of conservatives in all fields: "We told you so; in fact, we've been telling you for years, but you don't listen." Well, what they say is true, but it is not the whole truth. The point of genealogical search for roots is not only to uncover the identities of forgotten relatives or to pitch a tent on ancient sites to get the feel of another age. It is as stultifying to live in the past as it is to be swept to and fro by every wind of doctrine. Roots are meant to nourish the branches of the tree, and, in the classic symbolism, what is below the ground corresponds with what is above, as a tree by a quiet lakeshore seems to have a dual, complementary form. As up, so down; as below, so above.

If "remember" is a typical Hebrew covenantal word, perhaps the corresponding Christian concept is "new." The Christian religion is a faith in new beginnings, growing out of ancient roots. So we celebrate the birth of a new child, are baptized into a new name, put on new garments, obey a new commandment, become a new creature, and look forward to a new heaven and a new earth. In this sense, the quest for roots is *in order to* live meaningfully in the present and look forward to the future with hope, promise, and exaltation. As the Apostle put it: "I leave the past behind and with hands outstretched to whatever lies ahead I go straight for the goal . . ." (Phil. 3:13–14, Phillips).

IV

Genealogy, as anyone who has tried it knows, can be very, very hard work. It is not easy to recover the past. Some roads lead nowhere or to a dead end; others can detour our plans or turn up something we don't want to know about. Even when we find what we're looking for, we're not always sure what to do with it. The big names, the important places, the carefully nurtured family tree—that's no problem. But most of us are not pedigreed, and we sit uneasily toward the past unless we can capture a sense of how one generation is linked with another in an ongoing, purposeful progression.

The closing lines of Alex Haley's *Roots,* recounting the burial of his father, are worth quoting:

The Pine Bluff service over, we took Dad to where he had previously told us he wanted to lie—in the Veterans' Cemetery in Little Rock. Following his casket as it was taken to Section 16, we stood and watched Dad lowered into grave No. 1429. Then we whom he had fathered—members of the seventh generation from Kunta Kinte —walked away rapidly, averting our faces from each other, having agreed we wouldn't cry.

So Dad has joined the others up there. I feel that they *do* watch and guide, and I also feel that they join me in the hope that this story of our people can help to alleviate the legacies of the fact that preponderantly the histories have been written by the winners.

Tomorrow via Yesterday

Birthdays, anniversaries, holidays, and national celebrations —such as the Bicentennial—lift us out of the present into the past and prod us to ruminate about the future. In returning to earlier sources of creativity, we hope to replenish lost strength, courage, and vision. Most of our rituals and ceremonies, religious and national, are rehearsals of original creative moments, staged and orchestrated with the expectation that what was once vital may once again inspire and enliven.

This is a deeply rooted biblical principle, and one that is especially characteristic of prophetic religion. "In returning and rest you shall be saved; in quietness and in trust shall be your strength" (Isa. 30:15).

In one of his own fine articles in *A Theological Word Book of the Bible,* Alan Richardson lumps together "Repent, Repentance, Convert, Conversion, Turn, Return." He notes that "'turning' means much more than a mere change of mind, though it includes this; it represents a reorientation of one's whole life and personality, which includes the adoption of a new ethical line of conduct, a forsaking of sin and a turning to righteousness." So "returning and rest" imply remembrance of things past, refreshment at the springs of life, and restoration of purpose.

In whatever ways this biblical principle can be applied to the Bicentennial, and to a presidential election, it offers criteria for surveying the religious scene, yesterday and today. Peter Berger

Theology Today, XXXIII (1976), 196–197.

has done just that in a perceptive essay on "Religion in a Revolutionary Society" (one of the chapters in the symposium *America's Continuing Revolution,* published by the American Enterprise Institute for Public Policy Research, Washington, D.C., 1975).

From the perspective of a sociologist of religion, but also from an avowedly Christian believer's point of view, Berger skillfully compares and contrasts the religious situation of twenty-five years ago and today. When he comes to discerning the signs of the future, he is careful and restrained. He thinks the reported demise of religion, like Mark Twain's obituary, has been exaggerated, and he is convinced of "the intrinsic inability of secularized world views" to answer the really basic human questions.

In a penultimate paragraph, drawing upon his analysis of religion in America and, we may venture, upon his own Christian-biblical commitment, Berger offers two predictive propositions. He states them bluntly, as follows:

> First, any important religious movements in America will emerge out of the Judaeo-Christian tradition rather than from esoterica imported from the Orient. And second, the likelihood that such revitalizing movements remain within the existing churches will increase as the churches return to the traditional contents of their faith and give up self-defeating attempts to transform their traditions in accordance with the myth of "modern man."

We can't know, of course, whether these "plausible scenarios" will become realities. But the sociological prophecy is in tune with the biblical prophecy about returning for renewal.

During the gloomy days of World War II, when reflection about the past and the present seemed to obscure any clarity about the future, John A. Mackay published a tract for the times under the title *Heritage and Destiny* (1943). It was based on the biblical principle which we have alluded to, and the first chapter declared that "The Road to Tomorrow Leads Through Yesterday." Elsewhere, he spoke of "the apocalyptic power of retrospection," and in illustration of this grand-sounding affirmation, he recounted a simple story of his youth in the Scottish Highlands.

My summer vacations were usually spent by the shores of a sea loch in western Scotland. The local fishermen taught me where the best haddock banks lay, and how to find my way thither by observing certain landmarks in the hills behind the shore. . . . On an early morning, I would sit down at the oars and head my boat for the deep water. When, after a time, the roof of the Laird's house became just visible above a clump of trees, and the white foam of a mountain torrent peered over a great boulder of rock, I knew that, at the point where those two lines of vision crossed, lay the bank, and that it was time to ship my oars and drop anchor for the fishing. I had moved forward to my destination, guided by landmarks on the receding shore.

II
AN ARTICULATE FAITH

Expecting the Unexpected

The gospel is unexpected good news. That God so loved the world as to become one of us; that Jesus Christ should champion the poor, the sick, the demon-possessed, the outcast, the sinner; that the cross—a dreaded symbol of death and defeat—should be transformed into an emblem of victory and hope; that a cold corpse should be raised from the dead; that a Spirit should empower common people to preach with boldness; that a community of the concerned should thrive in Corinth and in Rome—this is melodrama more sensational than our imagining!

It was because in Christ the unexpected had happened that saints, apostles, prophets, martyrs expected the gospel to turn the world upside down. Expecting the unexpected, martyrs spilled their blood, reformers took a stand, missionaries circled the globe.

The living spark of Christian faith is extinguished when the unexpected becomes the traditionally accepted. Then God's melodrama becomes a familiar farce, a period piece in religion's versatile repertoire.

In the first quarter of the eighteenth century, Alexander Pope, daring to add to the Beatitudes, penned the blasé lines, "Blessed is he who expects nothing, for he shall never be disappointed." Contrast with this the virile dictum of William Carey, the pioneer of modern missions, who toward the close of the same century said, "Expect great things from God;

THEOLOGY TODAY, VIII (1951), 145–149.

attempt great things for God." If in the church the flame of sheer audacity for God's sake is quenched by chill conformity or the inertia of convention, judgment is nearer than we think.

When all the world knows what to expect of the church, then the church has lost its expectancy and has become conformed to the ways of the world. Symptoms of the peril of conventionality, where the unexpected potency of the gospel is no longer expected by either the world or the church, are all too common in our day.

I

In the first place, we may well be concerned by the militant campaign of an increasing number to enlist the support of the Christian church on the side of economic and political conservatism. The conflict with communism at home and abroad has made us apprehensive and suspicious of programs and platforms that defy existing social patterns and espouse the cause of the oppressed and underprivileged. For many in our own country a mortal struggle is being waged at the moment between free enterprise and the rising tide of socialism which, in turn, is taken to be a halfway house to totalitarianism and communism. And since, so this argument runs, democracy and Christianity are as indissolubly linked together as are communism and atheism, it is to be expected that the church will sponsor the one and condemn the other.

Now it needs to be said that apart from a few individuals there is no reason whatever to question the loyalty and patriotism of the American churches. But does this imply that Christian leaders must therefore become publicity agents for the *status quo?* Stanley High of the *Reader's Digest* thinks just that. In an article entitled "How Radical Are the Clergy?" a report is given of a Gallup Poll conducted among a representative selection of the clergy regarding certain questions of a political and economic sort (*Reader's Digest,* April 1951, 118–120).

The overwhelming conclusion of the poll shows that the

clergy "are on the side of the American system," which phrase apparently means for the author something considerably to the right of center. Those of the clergy who affirm their affinity with "leftward reform of the social order" are, we are told, in a distinct and inconsequential minority. Those who see in the rapid rise of communism a judgment against Christianity for its unconcern with economic justice suggest "a total misrepresentation of the convictions of most clergymen."

This survey is taken to be "reassuring." But is it? Aside from the question of the validity of such a poll (have we so soon forgotten the recent presidential election?*) and the discontinuity between the questions asked and the author's special pleading, it may be just as well regarded as an indictment against the standpat conventionality of the clergy. Where lies the spiritual leadership and the moral dynamic of those from whom nothing unexpected is expected? Have the churches become so much a part of economic and political traditions as to forfeit their freedom under the gospel?

This is not a question of party politics or dangerous sympathies with subversive tendencies but a question of the church's witness to the unexpected good news of God in Christ. It would surely be cause for alarm if the clergy were uncritically pro-communist, but what of the complacent conformity of the clergy of whom nothing radical is expected?

II

This leads to the whole question of the place and purpose of the ministry today. There are disturbing evidences that more and more the ministry is becoming professionalized. To train oneself for the ministry today means to learn the tricks and trades of a recognized and accepted profession. There are certain things to learn, certain arts to become proficient in, certain

---

*The 1948 presidential campaign between Thomas E. Dewey and Harry S. Truman. Polls throughout the campaign had given Dewey a large lead, which Truman managed to surmount.

duties to fulfill and programs to establish. Consider the popularity of books dealing with the mechanics and machinery of church administration. Students frequently come to theological school with lofty ideals and righteous zeal, only to become hardened professionals by their senior year. They go out expecting not the unexpected but the usual, the commonplace, the settled situation.

There are contributing factors in the rise of this ministerial professionalism. Students marry earlier and have families—all of which gives concern for financial and domestic security high priority. They frequently undertake "field work" on weekends partly for financial reasons, partly because this is encouraged in the interests of practical experience. But during this apprenticeship habits of study, of preaching, and of church work are fixed, and the ministry is seen as a trade which one learns and practices in conformity with accepted customs and traditional patterns.

Efforts to meet this situation on the part of the theological schools usually take the form of revising and manipulating the curriculum. Liston Pope of Yale Divinity School, in an article on "Our Stagnated Preacher-Training" (*The Pulpit*, Jan. 1951), accuses the current programs of theological education of being obsolete. "Very few creative ideas," he says, "have appeared ... in the last thirty years. ... By and large the general mood in the seminaries appears to emphasize conservation and to discourage imaginative ventures."

But the problem goes deeper than the perennial juggling of courses and hours of study. A wholly new perspective of the meaning of the Christian ministry is needed for our day. We must nurture and encourage the initial zeal of first-year students and give them every assistance to resist the temptation to become professionalized. We must redefine for them the meaning of the "pastorate" so that they look forward with eagerness and anticipation to the unexpected power of the gospel in human lives and society.

This, of course, entails risks, which have always been the cost of true discipleship. Writing in *Time and Tide*, John Betjeman, the English poet, imagines the reception given to a newly installed country parson. "If he teaches religion, if he attempts to be definite, if he admonishes and exhorts, if he really loves God and his neighbor fearlessly, he will be despised and rejected."

III

And what about theology? Do we expect the unexpected there? Or are we so bound to the clichés and dogmatisms of our particular traditions, be they conservative or liberal or neo-orthodox, that we stifle and smother the living gospel? Do we really theologize? Or do we merely talk about theology? Do we reflect upon the unexpected good news, or do we analyze trends, pitting this school against that, feeling the pulse of the times, steering a middle course between extremes, writing our little books, or big ones, for our mutual edification and review?

There are times and places which require careful and deliberate analysis of current theological trends, but our times call for something more positive and affirmative in theology. The familiar byplay of dialectic, the wearying recourse to paradox, the frustrating reduction of existential problems to a state of tension resembling a kind of suspended animation—these current trademarks of theology frequently suggest that we are dealing with puzzles and riddles rather than dynamic truth and new life. We desperately need these days to venture beyond the ideas and concepts of our theologies to the reality of our life in God's light. Liberals, conservatives, neo-orthodox—all alike need to learn anew the meaning of the new person in Jesus Christ—who not only has new ideas but is a new creature.

Touching the Untouchable

The gospel is the good news that God is in touch with us. God is not aloof or remote from us. God deliberately identifies with sick, sinful humanity. The biblical vocabulary is rich in symbolic expressions of this, the most common being the extensive references to the "hand" of God, signifying divine action, influence, power, judgment, and blessing. In Christian art one of the earliest forms used for suggesting the presence and power of God was the hand. Sometimes it was made to emerge from a cloud of mystery; sometimes it was extended in blessing; sometimes it pointed downward with the implication of lifting up. In Michelangelo's classic painting of the creation, the focal point is the outstretched finger of God as it comes into touch with Adam's languid form. The artist has captured the supreme creative moment when the vital spark is struck, the current of life established, and "man became a living soul."

I

In the New Testament this quality of electric contact, and the transference of power which follows, is frequently ascribed to Christ, who stretches out his hand in gestures of help and benediction and actually touches the blind, the sick, and the outcast. For his own contemporaries, the most striking instance of Jesus' identification by contact was doubtless the healing of the leper. After the Sermon on the Mount (in

THEOLOGY TODAY, XI (1954), 1–7.

Matthew's account), while "great crowds followed him," a leper boldly accosted Jesus with the plea to make him clean. And we read that Jesus "stretched out his hand and touched him . . . and immediately his leprosy was cleansed" (Matt. 8:1–3). If we recall with what dread and disgust the Jews regarded leprosy, and how they insisted that any contact with the disease involved defilement and pollution (cf. Lev. 13:46), then Jesus' touching of the untouchable takes on added meaning and significance not only for the leper and the spectators but also for our understanding of God's redemptive love in Christ. As Archbishop Trench put it, "Another would have defiled himself by touching the leper; but he, himself remaining undefiled, cleansed him whom he touched; for in him health overcame sickness, and purity defilement, and life death."

There is, however, another side to this divine condescension by contact. It is our wistful, sometimes frantic, attempt to get into touch with God. In Paul's Areopagus address, he spoke of those seeking for God "on the chance of finding him in their *groping* for him" (Acts 17:27, Moffatt). The word used is the same as in Jesus' invitation after the resurrection to his disciples, "See my hands and my feet, that it is I myself; *handle* me, and see" (Lk. 24:39). In the account of the woman with the incurable illness, several words are used to suggest that the crowd thronged, choked, and pressed around Jesus, yet only one dared to touch his garment (Lk. 8:42–48). The others got near enough, but only one sought the healing touch. And sometimes there were those who would have prohibited others from touching Jesus, for example, the disciples who tried to prevent the mothers from presenting their children (Matt. 19:13–15), and the Pharisee who suspected Jesus' claims because he allowed "a woman of the city who was a sinner" to touch him (Lk. 8:36–39).

Furthermore, it is to be noted that just as Jesus had raised his hand in benediction and blessing upon his disciples, they in turn continued the practice for those who had been baptized (cf. Acts 8:17; 19:6), and the "laying on of hands" became a mark of special ordination to Christian service (cf. Acts 6:6; 13:3; I Tim. 4:14; II Tim. 1:6).

Christ himself may thus be likened to the finger of God in touch with humanity, and the church—which is his body—is truly the church as it identifies itself by contact with the sick, the sinful, and the untouchable.

If we were to take seriously such a mark of the true church and apply it to our own times, what would be the result? If the biblical figures of the hand of God and the touch of Christ upon the untouchable were regarded as symbolic ways of speaking of the gospel of redemptive love in action, would we also discover that this is a distinguishing trademark of the church today?

Would we perhaps have to confess that all too often the church does not lift a finger to touch the untouchable, that this is precisely *not* the mark of the church which is most apparent today? And what about the clergy who have been called and ordained by the laying on of hands, are they distinguished in their vocation for making contact with those to whom they minister? It is the glory of the church and its ministry that contact by identification has been and is being made in all sorts of ways, but we may profitably examine some areas of contemporary life where the bold and daring touch is especially needed.

II

According to Origen, one of the criticisms which Celsus urged against the early church was the low intelligence and social standing of so many of its members. He imagines the church's invitation to be, "Let no one come to us who has been instructed, or who is wise or prudent (for such qualifications are deemed evil by us); but if there be any ignorant, or unintelligent, or uninstructed, or foolish persons, let them come with confidence." Christians thus admit, he continues, that "they desire and are able to gain over only the silly, and the mean, and the stupid, with women and children." What he objected

to, in effect, was the church's readiness to touch the untouchables of society, an objection strikingly reminiscent of the
charge brought against Jesus by the scribes and Pharisees.

It was easy enough for Origen to answer Celsus, just as Jesus
had replied to his critics—"Those who are well have no need
of a physician, but those who are sick." But do we hear such
a criticism of the church today? Is it perhaps disturbing that
no modern Celsus is accusing the church of touching the
untouchables of our day? The church has its critics, to be sure,
but they do not make *this* charge. On the contrary, we hear
that the church is not really in touch with the untouchable,
that it remains aloof from the sick and the outcast, that its
practice belies its profession. And these are exactly the kinds
of accusations which the communists repeatedly level against
the Christian religion.

The record of the church is not nearly so bad as it is made
out to be, but there is no denying the fact that today the
church is *not* associated by its critics with the untouchables of
our society. Racial segregation is the most obvious illustration.
In recent years much has been done to awaken the Christian
conscience to this increasingly touchy situation. Denominational pronouncements against racial discrimination in the
churches have become commonplace, and there is an increasing number of local churches daring to break down the middle
wall of partition. Yet it remains essentially true that the most
segregated hour of the week is eleven o'clock Sunday morning.
The churches of America, in any event, are not taking the lead
as they should in the crusade for racial equality, and they are
not giving expression to the specifically religious and Christian
reasons for nonsegregation. The reasons that are advanced
today are mostly political, economic, and sociological.

Addressing the Indians of Bombay about progress in race
relations in the United States, Benjamin E. Mays, president of
Morehouse College, Atlanta, Georgia, said: "I was not so
happy when the people of India asked me how these gains
came about. I had to tell them that most of the progress
resulted from coercive court action. . . . I wish I could have said

to them that these gains came about because the American people believe so strongly in democracy and in the Christian gospel that it was unnecessary to battle for them." The Christian motivation—which stems from God's spontaneous, uncaused redemptive love—is going by default.

But there are other untouchables in modern society who are not being touched by the church. The alcoholics, for one; the neurotics and mentally ill, for another. The church's attitude toward alcohol has been consistently idealistic, moralistic, and unrealistic. For the most part the church is associated with total abstinence, with prohibition, with temperance. Pronouncements are made against the evils of drink, the liquor trade, the perils of social drinking for family life, and the increasing traffic fatalities due to drunken driving. Is it any wonder that alcoholics turn for help, not to the churches, but to such groups as the A.A.'s?

We have learned that alcoholism is not a matter of moral degeneracy so much as it is a psychological disturbance related to the alarming increase of neurotic problems among all ages and classes of our society. In a discussion recently with a college chaplain about the kinds of questions which students brought to him, it was revealed that the most common difficulties were not problems of intellectual doubt or religious faith, but the anxieties and tensions associated with personality adjustments.

Now it may be argued that here at least the churches are aware of the problem. Certainly preachers are discussing the issues in their sermons, books by the score are being published on the general subject of religion and psychiatry, and pastoral counseling has become a recognized function of the ministry. Nevertheless, it must be said that there is a great deal of confusion as to the church's attitude on this matter. There are some who think that repeated exhortations from the pulpit on how not to worry will solve people's problems. There are others who believe that a true Christian ought not to have such difficulties at all. And there are others who think the church is not the place for such matters, and they would direct all such "cases" to the physician or psychiatrist. Thus, some would touch too lightly, and some not at all.

III

Ministers, who have been ordained by the laying on of hands, have a special responsibility to communicate the power and vitality of the gospel by contact with their congregations and communities. They must be in touch with people, all kinds of people, not in order to show how congenial and human they are, but in order to communicate the meaning and significance of the gospel. To do this ministers must be not only pastors in touch with people but also preachers in touch with the gospel as it is related to people's lives and problems. This means that ministers must be willing to touch what are often taken to be unconventional and untouchable problems of human life. "Our minister," reports a layman, "can answer more questions that nobody is asking than any minister we ever had." Nothing is more absurd, Reinhold Niebuhr has reminded us, than the answer to an unasked question, and the peculiar conceit of ministers is that they are grappling with basic issues when as a matter of fact they may not be lifting a finger to lighten the burdens of their people (cf. Lk. 11:46).

What are some of the untouched problems of life with which ministers, in their capacity as preachers and teachers, should be dealing? We usually approach a question such as this by saying that people today want to know what the meaning of life is, whether God has a plan or purpose for each individual, whether history is moving toward any goal, etc. These, to be sure, are basic questions, and the preacher must constantly throw the light of the gospel upon them; but it may be that in dealing directly with such big themes the lesser, but not unimportant, problems of life are ignored and bypassed.

We may learn something here from the secular, even atheistic, existentialists who tell us that what people are really worried and concerned about are the little daily *ad hoc* decisions and tasks which confront them. In other words, existence itself may be as much of a problem as the meaning of life. The two are, of course, related, but we may miss making contact with the former if we direct all our attention to the latter.

Consider, for example, as just one existential problem which for most preachers is an untouchable and untouched subject, namely, sex. There is a whole cluster of interrelated problems here, involving adolescence, marriage, domestic life, the unmarried person, divorce, to name only a few. But take sexual behavior itself. Surely we did not need to wait for Kinsey's statistical reports to learn that sex is a dominant, dynamic force in people's everyday lives. We should have known as much from reading the Bible! We may disagree with the scientist's methods and his implied conclusions regarding sexual behavior, but the minister will make a sad mistake to hide behind such objections and fail to touch this supposedly untouchable subject.

Even the theologians, who have discussed Kinsey to some extent, have generally taken a critical and negative approach. In an adult discussion group, when the question of marriage and divorce was raised, a young woman asked why preachers never preached on this problem. The question led to the reflection that no one present had ever heard or read a single sermon devoted exclusively to either marriage and divorce, or to the general subject of sex itself. Must we be silent because this is an untouchable subject, or because from the point of view of the gospel we have nothing in particular to say? Must we not say, on the contrary, that here as elsewhere we believe the gospel can baptize with its redemptive touch the merely biological and romantically sentimental views of sex which so dominate our contemporary culture?

IV

A criticism of what we have been saying thus far may be anticipated. Some will say that with all this talk of touching the untouchables of our society, such as the problems of race and sex, to say nothing of other matters that could be mentioned, such as the current issues of freedom, we are abandoning classic theological and evangelical emphases for something very much like an activistic social gospel. But there is a basic difference here. The liberal social gospel which has come in for so much criticism in recent years was in many respects a self-consciously anti-theological position; we have been advocating, on the other hand, a quite specific theological view of social problems.

Just as modern biblical interpreters would regard such a healing miracle as Jesus' touching of the leper as evidence not only of his compassion but also of the drawing nigh of the Kingdom with the overcoming of the forces of evil and redemptive, healing manifestation of the New Age, so too the plea for the church to identify itself by contact with the untouchables of today should be regarded as a direct evangelical and theological exhortation. If theology, as we like to think of it in the words of the motto of THEOLOGY TODAY, is "Our Life in God's Light," then it is not only a matter of creeds and doctrines and propositions but a way of thinking—a normative way of thinking—about anything and everything that relates to human existence.

In memory of the poet Goldsmith, Samuel Johnson prepared an epitaph which was inscribed on a monument in Westminster Abbey—"He touched nothing he did not adorn" *(Nullum quod tetigit non ornavit)*. That is an extravagant claim to make for anyone, perhaps especially for Goldsmith. But it is true of the touch of our Lord, and it has the force of an ultimatum for the church today.

Making Old Things New

.

The Reformation, which an increasing number of Protestant churches celebrate on "Reformation Sunday," was not something new but something old made new. The word itself should remind us that the Reformers were not concerned with the novel but with the gospel, not innovation but reformation. To them was given new insight into old truth, and that is why Luther and Calvin and the many Reformation creeds took their stand upon the Scriptures and the revelation of what God had done in Jesus Christ. To their critics, the Reformers emphatically insisted that theirs was no new doctrine, no new creed, no new church. Calvin's *Reply to Sadoleto* (1539), in answer to the charge that the Reformation was essentially divisive, puts it plainly: "Unless indeed one ought to be held a deserter who, seeing the soldiers disordered and dispersed and departed far from their ranks, raises aloft the ensign of the commander and summons them back to their posts."

It is crucial for Protestants today, as in the sixteenth century, to reject all charges of novelty and to affirm that the Reformation was the making new of something old. When Catholics argue this way, then Protestants must celebrate not only Reformation Sunday but their faith and heritage by demonstrating in word and deed that they stand for something *old* made new.

Theology Today, XI (1954), 301–306.

I

It would, however, be a virtual betrayal of the Reformation so to insist upon that which is old as to obscure the fact that the old has been made *new*. In one sense, Protestants should welcome the charge of innovation, just as the Reformers realized that new meaning and power were derived from the gospel for their own day. If nothing new or startling, nothing unexpected or exciting, happens when recourse is had to the gospel, then something is wrong somewhere. From the point of view of the medieval hierarchy or the Counter Reformation or perhaps from modern Roman Catholicism—Protestantism *does* seem to be a new thing. It would be a shameful rebuke if on Reformation Sunday we were regarded by others as doing no more than laying a wreath upon the tombs and monuments of the Reformers. If for Protestantism the old in and by and for itself becomes the center of gravity, then we have forfeited our faith in the living, dynamic, re-creative power of the gospel.

The Reformation, thus, may be appealed to as our charter for moving beyond wherever we happen to be. It is a challenge to traditionalism and to current structures of thought and action and experience. This is not in the interests of a nineteenth-century view of inevitable, automatic progress, but in line with the conviction that the gospel is the good news of a divine redemptive purpose that has a past, a present, and a future. It is a conviction based upon what God *has done,* but this, in turn, involves inexhaustible and unlimited resources of *new* life and power for today and tomorrow.

II

There is a foolish and superficial kind of optimism which, until fairly recently, has been all too common. It has been a shattering, if necessary, experience for us to realize what a mirage such an unrealistic faith can be. But there is also a biblical and evangelical optimism which takes full account of the untrustworthiness of human nature and the transitoriness of life and yet dares to think and plan for tomorrow.

Dietrich Bonhoeffer, writing from his Nazi concentration camp, says, "Some men regard it as frivolous, and some Christians think it is irreligious to hope and prepare oneself for better things to come in this life. They believe in chaos, disorder and catastrophe. That, they think, is the meaning of present events, and in sheer resignation or pious escapism they surrender all responsibility for the preservation of life and for the generations yet unborn." The narrow way, which is never the easy way, is "thinking and acting for the sake of the coming generation, but taking each day as it comes" as if it were one's last day on earth.

It is at this point that the Reformation can illumine our understanding of the doctrine of eschatology—which after all is only another way of speaking about Christian teleology. "I believe," said Luther, "that the last day is not far off, for this reason: the gospel is now making its last effort, and it is just the same as with a light which, when it is about to go out, gives forth a great flash at the end as if it intended to burn a long time yet, and then it is gone." And Calvin wrote, "With whatever kind of tribulation we may be afflicted, we should always keep this end in view—to habituate ourselves to a contempt of the present life, that we may thereby be excited to meditation on that which is to come." But neither Luther nor Calvin interpreted eschatology to mean "sheer resignation or pious escapism." Calvin, in the quotation just cited, continues by saying, "But believers should accustom themselves to such a contempt of the present life, as may not generate either hatred of life, or ingratitude towards God." The Reformers, in making old things new, injected the note of responsibility for life today and tomorrow even into their eschatology.

III

In their rediscovery of the gospel, the Reformers became aware of the contemporary relevance and the unlimited possibilities of what God had done in Christ. They were not archaeologists digging around in the dust heaps of antiquity; they were very much of their own age with an acute sense of responsibility for generations yet unborn. The Reformation was not a minor, spasmodic attempt at the reform of this and that but the revolution of a millennium of history and tradition. Thus for us who claim to be heirs of the Reformation, intoning slogans about the "continuing Reformation," "the church must always be reformed," etc., there follows the awful responsibility to make old things new. This is not only the imperative which the Reformation lays upon us, this is the evangelical responsibility of all those who take seriously the inexhaustible resources and unlimited possibilities of the gospel. Consider briefly three distinct but related verses of the New Testament which suggest this.

First, here is Paul writing to his Corinthian friends about God's gift to the world of Jesus Christ, and he is so overwhelmed by the import of this fact that he exclaims, "Thanks be to God for his inexpressible gift!" (II Cor. 9:15). That is to say, language is inadequate to do justice to this gift of God. It cannot be fully described or characterized. The gospel speaks a truth which words cannot really reproduce or the most eloquent oratory exhaust. It is not that the gospel cannot be told, but that there is always something more to say. That is why the story is taken up by music and painting and architecture so that the very stones and windows of our churches are made to speak what language cannot fully express.

Robert Browning in one of his poems searches for "one word more" that would be "fit and fair and simple and sufficient" by which he could express his love for Elizabeth Barrett. Everyone who has ever written a love letter knows what the poet means, and Paul says there is one word more to be said about God's gift in Christ. There is *always* one word more. This is not meant to discourage us or to plunge us into a semantic puzzle; Paul's exclamation is a doxology! Let us, then, give thanks that the gospel outruns our feeble efforts at definition and description, that it can never be exhausted or fenced in by our creeds and confessions, our theologies and systems, our denominations and traditions!

Secondly, here is John who in his Gospel added much to the Synoptics, and yet when he comes to the end of his account he says with a sigh of disappointment, "But there are also many other things which Jesus did; were every one of them to be written, I suppose that the world itself could not contain the books that would be written" (John 21:25). This is literary exaggeration, yet how true it is. There is more to tell about Christ and what he means for faith and life than books can contain. John's Gospel in many ways is the fullest and most complete, and yet the author apparently was conscious of its brevity, and he brought it to a close simply because he knew he could never finish it.

The gospel, in this sense, is an unfinished work. There are more than 2,000 lives of Christ in the British Museum in the English language alone! But more than this, the life of Christ has deeper and wider implications than can be summed up in a book or in a library. We have not begun to exhaust the meaning of this life for our own social, economic, political, and cultural life. He somehow is always beyond us, beyond our biographies, beyond our moral standards, beyond our attempts to catch up with him.

Thirdly, here is the author of the Epistle to the Hebrews, writing of men and women of faith, Abel, Enoch, Noah, Abraham, Sarah, Isaac, Jacob, Moses, and then as if in despair at the growing list, he says, "And what more shall I say? For time would fail me to tell of Gideon, Barak, Samson, Jephthah, of David and Samuel and the prophets" (Heb. 11:32). Time is too short to tell all that can be told about men and women of faith. It isn't that the author is too busy or interested in something else, what he means is that though he were to live and write forever he could never complete the roll call of those whom God has chosen. It is not that the chronicle cannot be drawn up, but that it is so long that it can never be completely told. And when we stop to think of it, the time is too short, for we would have to add to this list the names of Peter, Paul,

Barnabas, and perhaps the names of Irenaeus, Tertullian, Augustine, Luther, Calvin, Knox, Wesley, Carey, Livingstone, Schweitzer, and what would we do with the modern martyrs in our own time who "quenched raging fire," "put foreign armies to flight," "were tortured," "suffered mocking and scourging, and even chains and imprisonment"? And what of the unsung heroes, obscure men and women, "of whom the world was not worthy"?

What a roll call we could make! But could we? No, it could never be drawn up in final form, for God is still at work in human hearts, in different ways, in hidden ways, and the redemptive directory cannot be closed "apart from us" and our children's children. The inexhaustible power which makes old things new, which in Christ re-creates the old creature so that we become a new creation, is still at work in the world.

IV

Making old things new—this is the good news of the gospel which the Reformers recovered with surprise and joy for their own day and which we may discover for our day too. In Christ "the new has come"—the *new* commandment, the *new* name, the *new* tongues, the *new* creature, the *new* and living way, the *new* heaven, the *new* earth, the *new* Jerusalem, the *new* song, the *new* Testament—and in Christ the new continues to come.

Hard or Soft Sell?

It is no doubt a questionable procedure to compare the church's task of proclaiming its message to the philosophy and strategy of salesmanship as practiced by big business. Christianity is not a product to be advertised by hucksters interested in increasing sales, in creating needs, in meeting competition. A recurring objection to certain evangelistic campaigns is that they are too tied to the razzle-dazzle of publicity stunts and the commercialism of advertising at its worst. The church dare not make its own the standards which appliance manufacturers and brewers set for themselves.

Yet having said that, it must also be the church's responsibility to keep informed about secular discussions on such matters as sales techniques and advertising to learn what it can about human nature, about communication, and about the problems of reaching people where they are. One such recent controversy in the ranks of advertisers is a case in point.

As everyone knows, advertising at the moment is split over two techniques both of which are being plugged for all they are worth. The issue is whether *hard* or *soft sell* is the better psychology and thus brings the bigger results. "Hard sell" is typified in much TV advertising and involves repeated, loud-mouthed, bludgeoning of the public. In reaction to this tried and tested approach, there are advocates of the "soft sell," which suggests by indirection, innuendo, and even self-spoofing. This, too, has begun to appear on TV screens, and

THEOLOGY TODAY, XIII (1957), 437–442.

the obvious and stark difference between the two methods is there for anyone to see and hear. In a special comment on the problem, *Time* magazine says that "more and more advertisers are taking the position that an ounce of charm can be worth a pound of pressure." And it quotes an advertising agency executive, sympathetic to the new trend, as saying: "We are suffering from fatigue of believability."

Now the church in its evangelistic task, whether it be preaching, teaching, theology, social witness, or missions, is also confronted by the diverse claims of hard and soft sell— though we may not think in this particular vocabulary. Is it better for the church to bulldoze its public, to present its claims with hammer strokes, to shout its wares in raucous, strident tones? Or is it better to "gentle" its hearers, to suggest rather than exploit, to soft-talk rather than bamboozle? This is to put the option in favor of the latter, but suppose the church, too, is suffering from fatigue of believability, suppose its language is too hackneyed, its claims too shrill, its spiel ("gospel"— God's spiel) too stereotyped? Biblical mythology, Bultmann observes, may hinder interested hearers from ever getting to the core of the gospel. Theological clichés ("Christ is the answer to all our problems") and overextended claims ("the cult of reassurance") may fall on ears deafened by the monotony of verbal drubbing. Wherever "hard sell" hinders rather than helps, it is time to consider the merits of "soft sell"— whether it be advertising or evangelism. We suggest a three-point strategy.

I

First, in presenting the Christian faith, don't try to tell all; be selective. Lord Acton, editor of *The Cambridge Modern History,* once remarked: "Mastery is achieved by resolved limitation." That is something to think about, and it means that what is left out of our message at any particular time may be as important as what is included. A sermon should proclaim the gospel but it need not rehearse the whole range of biblical revelation; a book on doctrine should expound the Christian faith but it need not be a *summa theologica;* an evangelist appealing to non-Christians should clarify the essence of Christianity but need not detail the whole history of western Christendom.

The gospel itself is restricted. The *kerygma,* as C. H. Dodd pointed out twenty years ago, has to do with a few reiterated points—that Jesus is the fulfillment of Old Testament prophecies, that he lived and died, that he rose from the dead. When Paul wrote to the Romans, the Corinthians, the Galatians, and others, he tailored his epistles to their special needs and circumstances. He didn't try to tell everything but was highly selective. So too a widow's mite, a cup of cold water, a broken alabaster cruse may be more effective in preaching the gospel than long-winded harangues. And in the same way, St. Francis preaching to the birds, the legend of the juggler of Notre Dame, Albert Schweitzer's Lambaréné mission (whatever may be said of his formal theology)—all these in restricted fashion may speak a surer message than didactic indoctrination in all the fine points of biblical history and doctrine.

The implication of this, however, is not that we cultivate brevity for its own sake or search out disconnected episodes. Before we can be selective, we must be clear what is important and essential and what is derivative and explanatory. Mere snippets of the gospel can mislead. As in the case with the miracles of Jesus, some may only see the "wonder" and not the "sign" of divine presence and power. To be selective we must know how and what to select. This is where theology should come to our rescue, for theology should help to put the pieces together and to show the relation of the parts to the whole. It is not necessary to display the whole on every occasion, and perhaps theology's place is behind the scenes, but if we don't have to tell all, we must first know what the all is in order to be selective and effective.

II

A second rule in presenting the Christian faith would be— don't make too many claims; allow for some mystery and perplexity. This follows from the first rule. If we need not tell all, then we must necessarily be impressionistic, suggesting and implying, and perhaps intriguing and tantalizing. But for this very reason, we must beware of dubious and ambiguous claims.

In our day the "religion of relief"—whether from individual or social troubles and anxieties—is something for us to watch carefully. It is true that the Christian faith promises "peace," "rest," and "good cheer"—all, incidentally, words used by Jesus. It is also true that unless the church can offer the world something better than it already knows or has, it might as well keep silent. The gospel, we must never forget, is "good news," and it is our responsibility to proclaim the good tidings with a sense of joyful abandon and evangelical optimism. If we cannot do this, we cannot do anything worthwhile. If—theologically—we become so enmeshed in our antinomies or paradoxes that both affirmation and action are paralyzed, we are unfaithful stewards of the heritage bequeathed to us. Moreover, people today desperately want to know what Christianity has to offer, whether it adds or subtracts from life, how it proposes to solve the riddles and vexations of life, why—in a word—they should take it seriously.

Christianity must make its claims, but let us take care to relate its claims to its demands. The Christian faith not only claims to do something for us; it makes its own claims upon us. "Peace," "rest," and "good cheer" are all there for the taking, but remember it was *Jesus* who spoke these words. What peace did he know? What rest did he have? What good cheer did he express? We would quickly say in every case that it was the deepest and most satisfying. But the context of these words is rejection, antagonism, suffering, the cross.

It is imperative, therefore, that we present the claims of Christianity in context. The Christian apologist must not become a pitchman or pre-election politician, promising everything to everyone. We must make it clear—so there be no misunderstanding—that the gospel is not a patent medicine cure-all. It is the good news of a mystery—that God has become human, that a new creation in Christ is possible, that good cheer and tribulation go together.

It is conceivable that the church in our day could make its claims more obvious if it claimed more from its hearers. Instead of promising to deliver the moon or pie in the sky, more might listen if we were to woo, beguile, and whet the appetite for a life of adventure, mystery, and excitement. Can we promise to exercise the mind with life's profoundest problems, to stretch the dimensions of existence, to flex the muscles of will and imagination in a distraught and troubled world?

III

There follows a third rule in presenting Christianity to our day—don't clobber with clichés; be creative and imaginative. This is largely a matter of language, but it relates as well to the whole problem of translating traditional into contemporary forms and patterns. One reason "hard sell" is giving way to "soft sell" is simply that the former is cliché-ridden. And when a message to the public is framed in clichés, fatigue of believability inevitably sets in. Now a cliché, a stereotype, a platitude is not necessarily untrue just because it has been worn thin with too much handling. But the point is that the point is invariably dulled, the message doesn't come through, communication is thwarted. To prevent this from happening, some fresh way of presenting the message must be found. Creative imagination must be summoned and enlisted in the cause. Not in order to be tricky or devious or esoteric. Not in order to say a new thing; but to say an old thing in a new way.

Now we who speak for the Christian faith have a special problem in this matter because we are so dependent upon traditional language, whether it be biblical, theological, or experiential. The marvel is not that the church is plagued with so much stereotyped language, but that it succeeds as well as it does in communicating the ancient gospel in modern language. For, make no mistake, it is dreadfully hard work, this business of translation. That is why many preachers and theologians and missionaries never get very far with it and are content merely to reissue the obsolete coinage. Furthermore, in religion there is frequently the feeling that the old is better, hence the deliberate return on the part of some evangelists to the old phraseology, the old doctrines, the old hymns, the old altar calls, etc. And there is always strong resistance to new versions and translations of the Bible, new architectural forms, new liturgical practices, new religious educational techniques.

The question, however, is simply this: do we bring to the gospel message the best possible creative and imaginative minds and talents of our day, or are we satisfied to preach an eternal gospel in the language and molds of some previous generation or century? What are the biblical scholars, with all their linguistic and philological learning, doing to translate the sacred tongues into the language of the people today? What are the theologians, with all their existential concern, doing to revive the meaning and implication of doctrine for life? What are the evangelists, with their crowds and their emotional enthusiasm, doing to deepen and broaden the diffusion of Christianity in our day?

Much, no doubt; but is it enough, is it even as much as is possible? Religion ought not to be isolated by the verbal cliché-curtain; it should be the most interesting, colorful, exciting thing imaginable. But do we bring imagination into captivity to Christ and the church? Who today is translating doctrine as C. S. Lewis and Dorothy Sayers did some few years ago? Who is stirring the poetic imagination like T. S. Eliot and W. H. Auden? Who are the novelists like Graham Greene and Charles Williams at work in our day? And what of painting, music, drama? The names above are mentioned to show that fresh insight is possible and has been at work in our generation. But scarcely a dent has been made in our steel-like traditionalisms. May it not be said of us in our day that "the hungry sheep looked up and were not fed."

A Four-Dimension Faith

There is something depressing and stultifying about much of our contemporary mood. It is so largely inward, so little outward or upward. Our generation is post-idealist, post-romanticist, post-utopian. The norms and values of the past excite us no longer. Our horizons are more limited and our goals more immediate. We may reflect that this is therapeutic and salutary, that sentimental illusions have gone, that we are consequently more realistic, more down-to-earth, less likely to be taken in by false hopes and unattainable aspirations. But however necessary such a corrective may be, it does not apparently lift our spirits or our sights. Instead of being a means to an end, it becomes an end in itself, and we derive perverted pleasure brooding upon our moodiness.

In the novel *A Certain Smile,* by the young French writer Françoise Sagan—who, by the way, likes to drive her sports car 100 miles an hour in her bare feet, presumably not to get somewhere in a hurry but just for "kicks"—we have a stark specimen of our painful emancipation from romantic illusions. Here—where of all places one might expect it—there is no romance, no exhilaration, no wit. The contrived love affair, so French, so urbane, is completely loveless; the effect is sordid and obscene, not because the persons are so sensual but they are so impersonal. This is not just a French parable. Some of us have watched a television stunt program which brought together a young woman and a young man who have so much

Theology Today, XIV (1957), 153–158.

in common that it is, not too subtly, suggested they may marry. And how were their common traits determined? By feeding the relevant data into Univac's electronic brain!

More and more we seem to be the *uncommitted* generation. We are plagued with political neutralism, social apathy, even religious and theological expediency. The person in our day who is deeply concerned and passionately committed to a cru-sading cause is at best regarded with distant wistfulness, and at worst as a freak, a fanatic, a "square." It is in the religious and especially the theological life of our times that this mood is so perilous. Our existential protest against conventional structures, our dialectic between extremes, our contextual eth-ics—all of which have immeasurably deepened our understand-ing of the Christian faith as well as the human situation—have a way of leaving us satisfied with the second best, fearful as we are of overreaching ourselves. Thus we speak learnedly and contentedly of "proximate" goals for our faith and life, of "approximate justice" in political and social problems, of a "viable" solution which—because of the "ambivalence" of our situation—is not much but is the best we can hope for.

One suspects that much of this talk—which, to be sure, can be illuminating and helpful—is drawn more from our contem-porary mood than from the sources and resources of our faith. It is one thing to repudiate and reject the false romanticism and sky-blue idealism of an older unrealistic world view; it is another thing—and a dangerous one for Christians—to forget and neglect the farther horizons and the larger dimensions of faith and life, not as conjured up by human ingenuity, but as disclosed and revealed to us.

I

The author of the Epistle to the Ephesians writing to a group of early Christians, perplexed in many ways as we are today, was certainly neither complacent nor perfectionist when he reminded his friends of the four dimensions of their faith. His prayer is "that Christ may dwell in your hearts through faith; that you, being rooted and grounded in love, may have power to comprehend with all the saints what is the breadth and length and height and depth, and to know the love of Christ which surpasses knowledge, that you may be filled with all the fulness of God" (Eph. 3:17–19).

If Paul be the author of these words, we must remember that he is writing from prison, that here is a man who knows a thing or two about "approximate justice" (or injustice), and yet who makes the audacious intercession that the Ephesians "be filled with all the fulness of God." He is saying that the love of God in Christ has a staggering vastness and grandeur about it which dwarfs our "approximate" goals, our "viable" solutions, and lifts our eyes of faith to the farther horizons. Let us reflect briefly on these four dimensions of Christian faith as grounded in love.

First, the *breadth* of the Christian faith, or, to put it into a question, let us ask, "How much does the Christian faith take in?" Or more personally, "How much does your faith take in?" How broad is it? How wide? What are its boundaries, its frontiers? And when we put the question that way, we are at once ashamed, for we know that the Christian faith should have no boundaries, no frontiers, no barriers, no spite-fences, no middle walls of partition, no restrictions of time or space, of class or race. Yet if we are honest with ourselves, we would have to define the breadth of our faith within rather narrow confines.

We would speak perhaps of churches instead of the church, of denominations and creeds, of schools of theology, of free worship and liturgical worship, of emphasis here and emphasis there, of accents upon this and accents upon that. And if all could speak at once, we would have a confusion of tongues. And if we go further, we would begin to draw the boundary lines between religion and politics, between white and black, between labor and management, between liberal and neo-orthodox, between east and west, between continental and American, and we would find our Christian faith set and fixed within the provincial bounds of our little prejudices.

But this is clearly not the New Testament definition of the dimension of the breadth of the love of God in Christ. "God so loved *the world* . . ." "In Christ there is neither Jew nor Greek, there is neither slave nor free, there is neither male nor female . . ." The essence of God's love *(agape)* is its spontaneous, overflowing self-giving.

> There's a wideness in God's mercy
>   Like the wideness of the sea:
> There's a kindness in his justice,
>   Which is more than liberty.
>
> For the love of God is broader
>   Than the measure of man's mind;
> And the heart of the Eternal
>   Is most wonderfully kind.

II

What about the *length* of the Christian faith? To what length does our faith go? How much do we hope for? What are our endurance limits? Is our faith today marked by sustaining enthusiasm and determination born of conviction and assurance? Do we go all the way in our Christian witness? Do we go all out for communicating the gospel? Or do we go so far and no farther?

Questions such as these are sure to disturb us, for so many of us are dead tired and exhausted. We go a mile perhaps, but we just haven't the strength or the courage or the enthusiasm to go the second mile. Even among young people, there is little enthusiasm. Today it is collegiate not to be collegiate. It would be impossible to stir the younger generation today with such a slogan as "The evangelization of the world in our generation." Perhaps we are more realistic, but we are also less excited and exciting. Speaking not long ago in New Zealand, George MacLeod of the Iona Community and the newly elected Moderator of the Church of Scotland shocked his audience by saying "church members are the dullest people on earth." No doubt that is an unfair indictment, but there is enough truth in it to sting.

How unlike the New Testament description of God's love in Christ is our tired, exhausted mood! "Love knows no limit to its endurance, no end to its trust, no fading of its hope; it can outlast anything. It is, in fact, the one thing that still stands when all else has fallen" (I Cor. 13:7–8, Phillips). How do we measure up against that standard?

III

What about the dimension of *height?* How high up does our faith reach? What is the higher source of our life? Does the dimension of height give meaning to the dimensions of breadth and length? Surely we would say that faith is always reaching up, that God is acknowledged and worshiped, that it is in God that we live and move and have our being. Do we not affirm: "I believe in God the Father Almighty . . ."?

Yet, at the same time we hear a contemporary theologian speaking of "the God who is above God"—by which he means that the theologians' God, the God of many devout worshipers, is too small, too familiar, too fuzzy-wuzzy, too unlike the prophet's vision of "the Lord sitting upon a throne, high and lifted up." And because of what he saw, Isaiah confessed: "Woe is me! For I am lost; for I am a man of unclean lips . . . for my eyes have seen the King, the Lord of hosts!"

In his agnostic days, the late Professor C. E. M. Joad, the brilliant and eccentric British philosopher, used to say: "When the mind becomes old and begins to decay, it becomes matted with god-webs." But this has little to do with age. Elton True-blood tells in one of his books of an experiment with college students who were asked to regroup the Ten Commandments in what they thought was the order of importance. More than 90 per cent, he says, put the first three theocentric commandments last. We would like, if we could, to have breadth and length to our faith without too much concern for height. In this, how unlike Christ we are! In *his* summation of the Commandments, love of God precedes love of neighbor.

IV

Then, finally, here is the dimension of *depth*. Let us put it this way. How far down will our Christian faith go? Will it descend into the lowest abyss of suffering, hardship, humiliation? Will it bend to succor the brokenhearted, to extend a lifting hand to the downtrodden, to raise the sinner out of sin, to bind up the wounds of a humanity struck low? Would you welcome displaced persons into your community? Would you do something for, and not just talk about, racial integration? Would you try to help the alcoholic, the narcotic addict, the neurotic and psychotic in our society? Would you, in a word, love the unlovely?

Well, that is what the New Testament is all about. It proclaims on every page that God enters into sinful humanity. God came to us not because we were lovable or worthy or deserving, but because of a deep love for us. That love was a suffering, redemptive love which brought Christ to a cross. That is how far down God stoops. God does not stand aloof, but searches us out, becomes flesh and dwells with us, identifies with our sin and our waywardness. That is why the New Testament speaks so much of self-sacrifice and service and so little about self-realization and peace of mind. "The Son of man came not to be served but to serve." "Take up your cross and follow me." "He that shall lose his life shall find it."

These, then, in barest outline are the four dimensions of Christian faith and life. Are we depressed by their vastness and our littleness in comparison? Are they so out of sight and beyond reach as to leave us disheartened? Well, it is easy enough, and common enough, to tone them down, to foreshorten them, to make them manageable, "proximate," or "viable," as we say. But let us be sure about what we are doing. For in a real sense these four dimensions are but the outlines of the profile of Christ himself. Suppose we ask of him: how much does *he* take in? How far will *he* go? How high up does *he* reach? How far down will *he* stoop?

What Ever Happened to Dialogue?

There is an old story about a man who answered the phone and, after some conversation, said, "No, I can't have lunch with you tomorrow; I have to get my hair cut." His wife, hearing the discussion, asked him what kind of reason that was for declining an invitation. And he replied, "If you don't want to do something, one reason is as good as another." Old story maybe, but it belongs in a contemporary context that is far from funny. Conversation, dialogue, rational discourse, panel discussions, conferences, debates—all are becoming increasingly difficult and irrelevant in our day. Decisions, convictions, opinions, commitments, reasons for thinking or acting almost never emerge from a rational give-and-take but for other reasons that may be nonrational.

The current failure to communicate is not a "problem of communication" as if it could be solved by discovering better media. We have more media than we know what to do with. Our problem is that so many of us don't *want* to communicate in the first place, partly because we have nothing to say to each other, and partly because everybody seems to be mad at everybody else.

When a student complained to his teacher that the school was interfering with his civil rights by not allowing him to participate in administrative decisions, the teacher asked him what he meant by "civil rights." To which the student replied with feeling, "Definitions are irrelevant; I'm talking about

THEOLOGY TODAY, XXVI (1969), 1–4.

facts." Dialogue has become difficult because different groups speak different languages. There is no "universe of discourse," which philosophers used to assume as the premise for logical argument. Opposing factions are not on the same wavelength, or else they tune each other out. Conversation has a hard time getting started and often ends in a shouting match. Consider some random and melancholy examples.

Item: Lyndon B. Johnson, whose favorite text was "Come now, and let us reason together" (Isa. 1:18), came into the Presidency on a platform of consensus but left office amid unprecedented national dissension.

Item: At Wesleyan University, Middletown, Conn., where a special recruiting program enrolled more black students this year than ever before, the newly formed Afro-American Society set up its own residence dormitory, holds its own dances, eats together in the refectory, and some of the members won't even speak to white students. As one of them put it: "The whites seem to think I'm some sort of textbook for their liberalism, but personally I don't give a damn for educating white boys about what it's like to be black."

Item: After months of fruitless haggling, the Paris peace "talks" devoted ten weeks to a discussion of the shape of the table, finally agreeing that it should be round. When Henry Cabot Lodge was initiated into the "Grande Salle des Fêtes" of the old Majestic Hotel which is now the Paris "International Conference Center," there were no greetings, no handshakes, and no agenda.

Item: Some time before the encyclical *Humanae Vitae* and frequently since, disruption in the Roman Catholic Church has been increasing. Pope Paul VI has been methodically closing the windows and doors opened buoyantly by his predecessor, John XXIII. The hope that Vatican Council II would lead to "collegiality," with more dialogue among all levels of the hierarchy, seems forlorn at the moment.

Item: At San Francisco State College, a months-old student strike reached a stalemate. The students demanded that their complaints be accepted without negotiation, discussion, or compromise. Acting President S. I. Hayakawa is best known as an authority on semantics.

Item: The *Reader's Digest,* which is in favor of sweetness and light, and very much against the clergy's social or political involvement, recently switched by running an article which began with a paragraph based on a Gallup Poll. "Does the Christian faith have any practical relevance in dealing with the twin agonies of poverty and race in the United States today? Well, it depends upon whom you ask. The clergy overwhelmingly say yes. But through its actions if not its words the laity, all too often, says no."

Item: While students at Brandeis occupied the Communications Center Building, urging that more black students be admitted, the former President of the University, Dr. Abram Sacher, was in Africa recruiting prospective candidates.

Item: At Northwestern University's "Symposium Week," a panel of experts, speaking on the topic "Confronting Change," were shouted down by students who insisted that the format was too authoritarian.

Item: The decentralized school program in New York City, which poses an important educational innovation that deserves debate and discussion, has degenerated into a feud between the community and the United Federation of Teachers, on the one hand, and an ugly name-calling standoff between blacks and Jews, on the other hand, two minority groups that might be expected to work together.

Item: Two clippings lie side by side on my desk. One is an article from the December issue of the American Association of University Professors *Bulletin,* entitled "To Encourage Reason on the Campus: A Proposal for a New College Course in Thinking and Writing." The other is a news release on the

December conference in Princeton of a distinguished group of experts, sponsored by the International Association for Cultural Freedom and chaired by Dr. Carl Kaysen, director of Princeton's Institute for Advanced Study. The article claims that students can think and speak more clearly if they are required to write more essays. The conference, which included many authors of books and essays, never got off the ground and came to no agreement on anything.

Item: In *Commonweal's* special "Israel" number, the editorial quotes I. F. Stone as saying: "If God as some now say is dead, he no doubt died of trying to find an equitable solution to the Arab-Jewish problem."

Item: Question on a physics examination: "Show how it is possible to determine the height of a tall building with the aid of a barometer." The student's answer: "Take the barometer to the top of the building, attach a long rope to it, lower the barometer to the street, and then bring it up, measuring the length of the rope. The length of the rope is the height of the building." When asked by his professor if he really knew the conventional method, he replied that he did, but that there were many other valid and interesting answers. Another: "Take the barometer to the basement and knock on the superintendent's door . . . 'Mr. Superintendent, here I have a fine barometer. If you will tell me the height of this building, I will give you this barometer.' " The student on further questioning said he was fed up with high school and college instructors trying to teach him "how to think."

If these items belong on the docket, we all have some radical restructuring to do in our understanding of people, problems, and methods of communication. Preachers, theologians, and teachers will be increasingly confronted by the dilemma that their profession implies speaking, talking, writing while fewer and fewer are in the mood for listening or hearing. What ever happened to dialogue? It became radicalized, politicized, Balkanized, polarized.

Wash Your Language

It was in Cleveland Amory's old *Saturday Review* column, I think, that I read about a public school teacher who asked the young pupils to write down some of the classroom rules and regulations they had been talking about for some weeks. Among items such as "be on time," "keep neat and tidy," "don't talk back to the teacher," one young student remembered the teacher admonishing everyone to "wash your language." It seems an excellent revision of the traditional text, and it is especially applicable to those of us who use religious language.

When traditional language patterns change in significant ways, we can be sure that equally significant changes are taking place in culture and society. The shift, only a decade ago, from "Negro" to "black" is such a change. So is the current consciousness crusade about sexist names and pronouns that perpetuate male chauvinism. And so is the liturgical drift that has now reached flood proportions that assumes to address Deity in the second person plural ("You"—"Your"—"Yours" rather than "Thee"—"Thou"—"Thine").

Most of us are already aware of the culture shock occasioned by the linguistic insistence on "black" or "Ms." Curiously, almost no theological attention has been given to the liturgical substitution that is everywhere now accepted as standard.

THEOLOGY TODAY, XXX (1973), 211–217.

I

The forms we use to speak to each other, our names and nicknames, what we call friend or foe, how we designate others in private or in public, and ultimately how we address the Lord God Almighty—these language patterns reveal much of our attitudes, opinions, prejudices, loves and hates, as well as how much we respect others and reverence Deity.

It is not many years ago that I first heard a distant cousin describe how her father and mother always addressed each other, whether in public or in the intimacy of the home, as "Mr. Marshall" and "Mrs. Marshall." Today such an impersonal form would seem a senseless conceit to a generation for whom everyone is on a first-name basis. The royal, or editorial, "We" is seldom met with these days, and newspaper reporters are now permitted to quote the President directly without the circumlocution of writing that "the President said that . . ."

Modern English usage almost completely avoids "reverence capitals," although these were universally in vogue up until fairly recently. Old English, like German, capitalized many nouns and always the nouns, adjectives, and pronouns relating to God, the persons of the Trinity, the Saints, etc. When THEOLOGY TODAY began publication thirty years ago, we utilized "reverence capitals" for the divine pronouns and for a long list of words, such as Church, Gospel, Incarnation, Biblical, Resurrection, Creation, Redemption, etc. We soon began to simplify our style rules, for visual rather than doctrinal reasons, and we even wrote a paragraph on "Theological Orthography," which concluded with the somewhat ambiguous statement:

It may be argued that the trend away from "reverence capitals" marks a decline and an unwitting secularization of theology. But surely it may be maintained on the basis of the Incarnation itself (or is it "incarnation"?) that the divine becomes human, and that it is only through the human that we come to know the divine. (May 1951, p. 243.)

II

It is a far cry from the Old Testament Tetragrammaton (YHWH) to the Berkeley campus free-speech exhibition, but the linguistic distance tells us something about the past and something about today. The ancient Hebrews thought the name of God was too holy to be uttered, and they devised all sorts of abstract and roundabout clues, such as Ancient of Days, Lord of Hosts, and the Eternal. But most interesting of all, "Name" itself became a double for Deity, as frequently in the Psalms we read "Let them that love thy name be joyful . . ." (Ps. 5:11, etc.).

Since in ancient cultures a personal name expresses the mysterious essence of that person, the Name of God reflects the divine power and presence. So Jesus tells his disciples to pray "Hallowed be thy name" (Matt. 6:9), and his own name is "above every name" (Phil. 2:9).

It may well be that the punctilious regard for proper modes of address to God, this reverence demanding literate attention lest the sacred be profaned, accounts for the superlative character of the Old Testament writings simply as literature. If the topic under discussion is of such numinous quality as to defy expression, then exceptional creative imagination must be invoked. Perhaps this is one reason why the Scriptures have always been regarded as in some way "inspired." How else account for such a literate articulation of such an ineffable subject? It seems appropriate that the Bible concludes with a doxology rather than a definition: "Hallelujah! Salvation and glory and power belong to our God" (Rev. 19:1).

By way of obvious contrast, our age ("literate" in the sense that nearly everyone can read and write) suffers from an overload of verbalizing and a general deflation of language. Bombarded from all sides with words, names, and personal confrontations (TV talk shows, political rhetoric, consumer advertising), we have become more illiterate as we have become more loquacious. Religious utterance is a case in point. When last were we enthralled by the sheer *literate* expression of a sermon, a prayer, a modern liturgical celebration, a poem, a meditation, an article in a journal?

This deflation of language may account for the younger generation's resorting to slogans and obscenities. How else can you make anyone listen these days? Like hard rock music, the conventional figures of speech, forms of expression, and patterns of personal address must be amplified into deafening decibels to get any attention at all. The free-speech movement produced no enduring prose or poetry for its much talking, but it was a symbol of concern for *italic* expression and direct personal relationships.

The really dirty words, we were reminded during the student protest movement, are not the unprintable four-letter words but obscenities like "napalm," "incursion," "protective reaction," and now (with Watergate in mind) we can add "law and order." The polite forms of address which social etiquette prescribes for personal exchange need to be challenged when so many of us can also speak of niggers, gooks, commies, and Archie Bunker's other ethnic epithets.

The shift from "Negro" to "black" is an eloquent illustration of how names and personal identifications can emerge in our own society with something like Old Testament solemnity. Since "Negro" is a *white* appellation, it represents an identity gratuitously bestowed from the outside. Many Indians, for the same reason, now prefer to call themselves Native Americans. In any case, "black"—a mere descriptive adjective—has become intensely personalized, even sacralized. The verbal shift mirrors the emergence of a profound self-awareness. Here follow only three of innumerable cues to the new black self-identity:

> I am invisible, understand, simply because
> people refuse to see me.
>   (Ralph Ellison, *Invisible Man.*)

> For I was born, far from my native clime,
> Under the white man's menace, out of time.
>   (Claude McKay, "Outcast.")

Little Black boy
Chased down the street—
"Nigger, nigger never die
Black face an' shiney eye,
Nigger . . . nigger . . . nigger . . ."
    (Frank Horne, "Nigger: A Chant for Children.")

(From *Black Voices: An Anthology of Afro-American Literature,* edited by Abraham Chapman, 1968, pp. 193, 373, 402.)

For a whole people in the short space of a decade to achieve a new personal identity is surely astonishing and unprecedented. If some of us on the outside are not yet attuned to what has been happening in our midst, it must be because we have not been paying attention. In Eleanor Craig's wonderfully ungrammatical(?) title, inspired by a note from an emotionally disturbed pupil, *Your Not Listening.*

III

Those who are listening know very well that the women's liberation movement, often trivialized by men as "women's lib," represents a major shift of self-consciousness within our contemporary culture. Like blacks, women want to be themselves and not what others outside call them or think of them. Rather than talk about the movement itself, let me link the current sexist awareness with recent liturgical reform and refer to a specific case study.

In 1972, a coordinated committee from the Cumberland Presbyterian Church, the Presbyterian Church in the U.S. (South), and The United Presbyterian Church in the U.S.A. produced and published *The Worshipbook—Services and Hymns.* This is a manual, or "book of forms" as my minister father used to call it, of 688 pages, including orders of worship, special services, litanies, prayers, lectionaries, and a hymnal of words and music. The whole thing claims to be a contemporary revision and updating of traditional worship patterns with the addition of much new material. A major denominational publication of this sort can only hope its heavy financial investment will be met by general congregational adoption for at least the next twenty-five years.

Alas, the book is hardly fresh from the printer's before radical criticism threatens its inauguration. Liturgical classicists have been murmuring in the wings for some time, and there are still many who have not got accustomed to the "new" worship manuals and hymnals of 1955, 1946, and 1933. But the most blatant, and apparently unexpected, blast against the new book has come from a UPUSA group known as "The Interim Task Force on Women."

In an extensive and vigorous report to the UPUSA General Assembly, meeting in Omaha, May 1973, the women's committee said bluntly that the new *Worshipbook* "presents a theology that is masculinist, exclusive, and oppressive." This in spite of the directive of the previous Assembly, which agreed that all "church documents" conform with usages of "nouns, pronouns, and adjectives" that include *both* sexes.

Detailed examples drawn from *The Worshipbook* of a male-dominant sexist perspective are noted for the "Service for the Lord's Day" (". . . ruler of men . . ."; ". . . unless we love our brothers . . .") and for the "Service for Ordination and Installation," etc. Exception is taken to sex-specific references in hymns when these can easily be replaced with more sex-inclusive terms. The report concludes by recommending that *The Worshipbook* "be reprinted and issued in approved revised form within three years." The United Church of Christ, by the way, has already approved—and is the first major denomination to do so—changes in its Constitution that will eliminate all "sexist" language.

No amount of verbal juggling can justify, for *any* of our denominations, the present sex-linking language of so many of our ecclesiastical forms, documents, and publications. And it can safely be predicted that because of the new self-identity awareness of women everywhere today, a new linguistic awareness, including caution about the use of pronouns and adjectives, will become everyone's concern. It would be to the churches' credit if they were in the front of this campaign.

IV

There is another radical shift of cultural emphasis just barely hidden under the current preference for the second person plural pronoun for speaking of God. It is not too long ago when a mixing of "Thee's" and "Thou's" with "You's" and "Your's" within the same prayer was taken as a sign of liturgical innocence or religious primitivism. Now almost everywhere the second person plural has displaced the singular, in Bible translations and revisions, in liturgical formularies, and in congregational worship. The under-thirty generation probably never remember any other form.

The Presbyterian *Worshipbook,* noted above, is an impressive editorial example, where virtually everything between its covers, including revisions of ancient hymns, goes over to the "you" format. The only exception is an inside front cover form of the Lord's Prayer, though there is a "you" form inside.

In 1946, the Revised Standard Version of the Bible took the position to drop the "Thee-Thou-Thine" form "except for language addressed to God." That was a compromise that created difficulties, since address to Jesus—whether as a man or as the Christ—was put into the "you-your-yours" form. So, Peter's confession reads: "You are the Christ, the Son of the living God" (Matt. 16:16); and Paul's Damascus query asks: "Who are you, Lord?" (Acts 9:5).

Today we have no such problem since everything, human and divine, is reduced to the same pronominal plane. It seems odd that so little attention has been directed at this grammatical shift which is mostly taken for granted by everyone. There is no prospect that the purists could reverse the trend, or that it would be a good idea to try. But this seemingly minor linguistic change may obscure some highly significant theological implications. The only discussion from a theological point of view that I am aware of, and it was supplied by my colleague, Professor Bruce M. Metzger, is by C. E. B. Cranfield of the University of Durham in the recently defunct journal, the *Outlook*, of the Presbyterian Church in England (Jan.-Feb. 1972). Professor Cranfield, I think, rightly argues for a theological critique of the new forms, but he insists on retaining the old forms for the wrong reasons.

It could be said that the widespread use of the plural divine pronouns is in the interests not only of linguistic simplicity but of radical biblical theology. If, it can be asked, Jesus dared to translate the Old Testament Tetragrammaton into the familiar *Abba* form, and if his own preferred mode of divine address was "Father," can we not then move from a stilted to a more intimate and direct form for our day? If, in Luther's fine phrase, Christ brought God down to earth for us, should we not avoid all grammatical temptations to sacralize the Son of Man which might imperil or docetize his full humanity? And, as the Reformers insisted and as contemporary Catholics agree, shouldn't worship, private and public, liturgical and hymnic, be in the simple, everyday, easily understood language of the people?

It could also be added that the current familiarized divine address is simply a liturgical consequence of the intensely personalized theology of the last fifty years. Barth's Christomonism, Brunner's divine-human encounter, Bultmann's existential event of redemption in Jesus Christ, Tillich's new being in Jesus as the Christ—all could be construed as supporting "you" rather than "Thee."

Even more impressively, if paradoxically, Martin Buber's *I and Thou*, which has informed so much of modern Christian thought, could be adduced as arguing for a personal rather than an "object" referent, whether in human or divine relationships. Ironically, of course, Buber's theological point is grammatically blunted since his use of "Thou" is precisely what is unacceptable in modern English usage. But Buber's point could *not* be made by revising the title as *I and You*, as if he were simply anticipating the current best-seller, *I'm OK —You're OK.*

V

Such considerations raise the question whether the traditional dimension of transcendence can in any way be retained or renewed by means of the more familiar pronominal forms. As J. A. T. Robinson noted in one of his lesser-known books, *Liturgy Coming to Life* (1960), the decision lies between making the holy common (and therefore available) or sacralizing the commonplace (to make it holy).

Is there danger in the easygoing "you" address of homogenizing the Creator and the creation? If the "Thee" format hints at docetism, does the "you" form suggest Arianism? If the plural personal pronouns get us all together, do we then, unwittingly perhaps, domesticate God? Is there theological temptation here toward a subtle form of idolatry, or what H. R. Niebuhr used to call a "unitarianism" of the Son that virtually occludes the Creator as the Wholly (Holy) Other? (The use of "reverence capitals" here seems inescapable.)

All might agree that the familiar forms make worship more acceptable and religion more relevant. But in the personalizing process, something of the mystery and ineffable glory of the divine can be lost beyond retrieval. Rudolf Otto, in an appendix to his book *The Idea of the Holy,* speaks of the "supra-personal in the numinous," and he uses the medieval mystics as examples. The reference prompted me to look up again the so-called "negative theology" of Nicholas of Cusa (ca. 1400–1464). In his treatise *On Learned Ignorance,* he argued that the more we know of God, even with the revelation of Jesus Christ, the more we know how little we know. The revelation of the mystery does not eliminate the mystery altogether. "God alone knows himself; he is as incomprehensible to creatures as infinite light is to darkness."

It is pertinent to note that in the new Presbyterian *Worship-*

book there are dozens of prayers for everyone and everything imaginable but no prayers addressed to God as ineffable, transcendent, beyond thought or reach, and there are no entries in the Index under either "Adoration" or "Ascription." *Sic transit gloria Dei.* Or in other words, "Wash your language."

The Language of Prayer

Can prayer avoid both of the current linguistic tangles: (a) "Thee/Thou," "You/Your," and (b) sex-exclusive language? Can our prayers also: (a) retain some sort of personal address, and (b) give expression to a measure of literary grace?

What follows is an experimental response to these perplexing but crucial questions. This cycle of daily prayer, with three options for each day of the week, was prepared for the 1978 edition of *A Year with the Bible* (published by The Westminster Press).

I have been making up this little devotional lectionary for more than twenty-five years, and I am gratified that more than 300,000 copies are printed each year. The Bible readings, one for each day of the year, follow a theme, this year the Ten Commandments. The prayers are intended for personal and family use, and this section has always given me trouble and left me dissatisfied.

The wording of some of the adapted collects will be familiar; the final Saturday prayer, for example, is from Robert Louis Stevenson. A literary inspiration was John Hunter's *Devotional Services,* first published in 1890 and long out of print.

Sunday

Eternal and ever-present God, our guide by day, our guardian by night, lead us from darkness into the light of this new

THEOLOGY TODAY, XXXIV (1977), 353–356.

day. May it be a holy and a happy time, as we celebrate the divine presence through each passing hour. For Christ's sake. *Amen.*

As the sun dispels the dark, and morning follows night, we remember that Jesus rose from the dead in the early dawn. So may light shine upon every doubt and fear, every cross and care, upon our ignorance, our sin, our perplexity. Renew our minds and purify our hearts to receive the good news of the gospel of redemptive love. Through our Lord Jesus Christ. *Amen.*

O God, from whom we receive not only days for labor and nights for rest but also the peace of this special day, we pray that this time of holy quiet may be profitable to us in heavenly things, and so strengthen and refresh us that every day may be a sabbath rest of joy and praise. *Amen.*

Monday

Almighty God, who meets us at the beginning and at the end of day, give us strength and insight to live each day as if it were a free gift and a special opportunity. May no unhallowed thoughts or foolish cares disturb the hours, and may we learn wisdom, receive power, and experience the influence of things unseen. In Christ's name we pray. *Amen.*

We pray, O Spirit of the Eternal, to subdue in us all unruly passion and pride, all selfish desire and corrupt inclination. Keep alive in us all that is simple and true; all that keeps us unspotted from evil influences; all that makes us wise to improve our opportunities, strong to resist temptation, brave to live and work by our faith, and to meet calmly whatever may befall. We offer this our prayer in Jesus' name. *Amen.*

Open to us, O God, the ways by which faith, hope, and love may become more real for us. Help us to see eternal things and to hear the heavenly pleading in our hearts. Give us rest from vain desires and put us in love with serious thought. May we feel the presence of eternity in and through our devotion to Jesus Christ our Lord. *Amen.*

Tuesday

Almighty God, from whom every good prayer comes, deliver us from coldness of heart and wanderings of mind, that with steadfast thought and kindled desire we may worship in spirit and in truth. Through Jesus Christ our Lord. *Amen.*

Eternal Creator, we mortal, human creatures are ignorant how to pray, and we feel unworthy to ask for special favors. But we rejoice that the Creator of all that is in the universe around us is also the Redeemer of each and every one of us. So we approach the Almighty with fear and trembling but in hope and expectation, because of Jesus Christ. *Amen.*

God of all power and majesty, the giver of all good things, graft in our hearts the love of truth, increase in us true religion, and nourish us with the bread of life. For Christ's sake. *Amen.*

Wednesday

Almighty and Everlasting One, train us to go in the way of faith, hope, and love that we may keep the commandments of love to God and love to neighbor. Lift our affections to things above and help us to work for justice and peace, today and every day. *Amen.*

O God, the strength of those who do not trust in themselves, accept our stuttering prayers, raise us up when we stumble, and point us toward a better tomorrow, as Jesus gave new hope to the lone, the lost, and the least. In his name. *Amen.*

Almighty God, accept our humble prayers for ourselves and for all humanity everywhere. Grant that we may both perceive and know what things we ought to do, and receive grace and power to fulfill what is expected of us. In Jesus' name we pray. *Amen.*

Thursday

O God, in whom there is no darkness or error, say unto us: "Let there be light." Illumine our souls, lift our thoughts to higher things, and help us to live our faith as a service of perfect freedom. Through Jesus Christ. *Amen.*

Dear God, teach us to pray when evil and suffering overwhelm us. The mystery of life can silence our petitions, but it is better to say something than remain quiet, better to pray than to curse the darkness. Help us to say with Job: "Though he slay me, yet will I trust in him," and with Jesus on his cross: "Father, into thy hands I commend my spirit." *Amen.*

Spirit of the living God, renew our feeble faith, clarify our minds to grasp the truth, and turn us around in the direction we should go. Help us to discern the true from the false and the evil from the good so that we may walk in all humility in the paths of heavenly wisdom and peace. *Amen.*

Friday

Almighty God, nourish, we pray, the roots of our national life with righteousness, mercy, and peace. Make us a people equal to our high trust, reverent in the use of freedom, just in the exercise of power, generous in the protection of the oppressed. May wisdom and justice inform our laws, and may religion that is pure and undefiled be the stability of our people. *Amen.*

O God of peace and hope, heal the divisions that separate us from each other so that we may keep the unity of the spirit in the bond of peace. Where there are differences of opinion, help us to be one in love and devotion. Deliver us from blindness, prejudice, and false witness. We pray that the church of Jesus Christ may be a blessing and that the Kingdom of God will become a reality among us. Through Jesus Christ our Lord. *Amen.*

Almighty God, whose goodness has loved us into life, and whose mercies never fail, we pray for all who have a special place in our hearts and sympathies; those joined to us by ties of family and friendship; all children who are dear to us; all who help us to a faithful life and whose spirit turns our duties into joy. Sustain us with the assurance that underneath us all are the everlasting arms. In Jesus' name. *Amen.*

Saturday

O God, before whose face the generations rise and pass away, the strength of those who suffer, the comfort of the sick, and the destiny of those who die, we give thanks for the company of the martyrs, the cloud of witnesses that surrounds us, and for all of our own family and friends who are with us no more. Help us to make the church on earth a foretaste of the church triumphant. "Be our guard while life shall last, and our eternal home!" *Amen.*

O living Christ, whose presence is everywhere and whose love and compassion never fail, graciously regard all who are in trouble or danger and especially those known to us (whom we name in our hearts). Guide those who are wandering, defend the innocent against their accusers, restore the lost and the hopeless, comfort the sick and the dying. "Speak through the earthquake, wind, and fire, O still, small voice of calm!" *Amen.*

O God, as the day declines and the shadows of evening fall, help us confess our feelings of shame for wrongs done this day as for the good things left undone. Restore to us the joy of salvation; bind up what has been broken; rekindle the fire in our faith. Go with each of us to rest; if any awake, temper to them the dark hours of watching; and when day returns, return to us, our sun and comforter. Call us with morning faces and with morning hearts, eager to be happy, if happiness be our portion, and if the day be marked for sorrow, strong to endure. "Saviour, breathe an evening blessing!" *Amen.*

Whether the intent or the format of such prayers will prove acceptable remains to be seen. But there is no question that some sort of fresh approach to the language of prayer would be both linguistically opportune and religiously creative.

We are supposed to be in the midst of a time of inward and personal spirituality. Young people today are not embarrassed, as their elders would have been, in giving expression to their inner feelings and their personal self-analyses. Worship and liturgy these days are not so much experimental as experiential. There is a new mystical, contemplative posture to our piety, and this open, intimate mood exists alongside our theological insecurity and anxiety.

This new inner spirituality is being deplored by many for being otherworldly, introspective, vapid, and insipid. And those who think language, syntax, and literary form are still important can only wince at the kinds of prayers produced thus far by what might be an otherwise promising trend.

If prayer is the soul of religion, we need to bend every effort to find better ways to articulate what is most surely believed. As the Apostle said in another connection: "A wide door for effective work has been opened . . . and there are many adversaries" (I Cor. 16:9).

Not like They Used To

Digging through some old papers recently, I came across a dusty file labeled "Theological Verse." Once upon a time I began a collection of limericks and doggerel, mostly lampooning teachers and theologians. Like so many projects, this one was left unfinished, but I noted that there are no very recent entries in the file.

On reflection, it occurred to me that while my own student generation derived great sport from poking fun at our teachers, particularly the more solemn ones, today's students couldn't care less and would probably wonder why we wasted time on such a useless exercise. I suppose there is more equality and camaraderie today among students and their teachers, and seminarians nowadays are not likely to sit in awe before theologians.

I

In my day, professors were given all kinds of wonderful nicknames, like "Water Closet" (W. C.) Craig, "the Gnome" (Harold A. Nomer, whose daughter was of course "Miss-Nomer"), "Sandy" MacPherson, "Cap" (U.S. Army) Palmer, "King" Cole, "Se Mettre en Branle" Waldrop (getting a large object, like a locomotive, in motion), "Two-Gun" Kelso (because of the way he pointed at you), "Me-and-the-King" Slosser (for name-dropping), "Drunken" (J. Duncan) Spaeth,

THEOLOGY TODAY, XXXII (1975), 1–9.

"Root's Roots" (for Robert Root's course on language), "Grandmother" Osgood (because he sat at a table to lecture), "Old Gold" Spaulding (because in those days the cigarette advertised "not a cough in a carload," and Spaulding coughed several times during each sentence), "God-Damn" Vietzmann ("the indeterminacy principle doesn't mean a god-damn thing"), "Bo-Peep" Piper (pronounced Peep-er), "Chesty" Loetscher (a stocky man looming large), "Wee" Hodge (Caspar Wistar Hodge, contrasted with the more famous Hodges), "Das" Machen, "Jock" Mackay, "King Karl" Barth, and so on and so forth. Today students call their teachers, if anything, by their first names or initials.

We thought teaching mannerisms and convoluted dialectics were ripe sources for jokes, pranks, masquerades, and comic verse. One of my students once described a lecture by Reinhold Niebuhr by saying that he was the only speaker he ever heard who could gesture with his knees. A colleague, Norman V. Hope, used to be serenaded regularly with shouts of "Hope for Pope," and sometimes the whole campus would join in a parade, disrupting classes and bearing the luckless candidate around in an overstuffed Victorian chair, *ex cathedra* fashion. When I complained once that I could not cover Kant in an hour's lecture, a straight-faced student said to me afterwards, "I suppose for Kant you'd need two hours."

During the final weeks of my college course, a hundred or more seniors would sing on the steps of Nassau Hall and, among other things, rib various members of the faculty in twenty or more verses. Here are three examples, dating from 1931, the first of a beloved hard-of-hearing (hence "Buzzer" for his hearing aid) history professor and his famous lecture on Garibaldi, the second of a Shakespearean who took all the parts himself, spouting and sputtering (hence "slickers," or raincoats), and the third of an ROTC officer (when the unit was still horse-drawn; a most unlikely object of mirth these days):

> Here's to our pal "Buzzer" Hall
> His voice is like a clarion call.

On Garibaldi's life and death
He yells himself quite out of breath.

Here's to Duncan "Falstaff" Spaeth
Who spars with dread Ophelia's wraith.
The front row boys, when'er he snickers,
Find it best to wear their slickers.

McConnaughy's a Captain now,
A dapper leader, brave and how!
He rides just like a part of a horse.
(Which part, we will not say, of course.)

Chorus (after each verse):

Away, away with rum, by gum,
Here they come, rubby-dum-dum,
Looking as if they'd been off on a bum,
The faculty of Princeton college-oh.

These were the days of college humor magazines, Harold
Lloyd in *The Freshman,* and Joe College and Betty Co-Ed
making frolic of everything connected with academe. Nostalgic trivia, no doubt. Today we are more serious, and the state
of society, including education, is so grim that there's nothing
left to laugh at. Right? Wrong. The student humor of the '30s
and '40s grew up with and lived alongside the great depression
and World War II. Even in the Nazi concentration camps,
we're told, humor was one widely recognized means of survival.
In solemn times, perhaps *especially* in solemn times, if we can't
laugh at ourselves, at our mentors, and at each other, we are
truly a sick society and our only escape is sick jokes at others'
expense.

II

Whatever we can say about humor-in-general, it would appear that today we do not poke fun at our teachers, nor do
theologians and theological ideas present themselves as sub-

jects for comic verse. Maybe twenty-five years ago we were too
frivolous. Anyway, here are some examples, from my file on
"Theological Verse," that are representative of the kind of fun
we enjoyed the day before yesterday.

Dean W. R. Inge, the "gloomy" dean of St. Paul's, once
proposed a new line for the final stanza of Bishop Heber's
familiar hymn, this being in the early days of air travel:

> They climbed the steep ascent of heaven
>   Through peril, toil, and pain;
> O God, to us may grace be given
>   To travel by the train.

William Temple, the Archbishop of Canterbury, poked fun
at Reinhold Niebuhr after a student conference at Swanwick,
at the time when R. N. was provoking the doctrine of sin:

> At Swanwick, when Niebuhr had quit it,
> Said a young man: "At last I have hit it.
>   Since I cannot do right,
>   I must find out tonight
> The best sin to commit—and commit it."

When John Baillie returned to his native Edinburgh, he
foisted his classical Greek heritage upon the Scottish divinity
students, favoring the Hellenistic over the Hebraic perspective.
Someone scratched these lines on a desk, which I copied,
presumably to be sung to the tune of "A Bicycle Built for
Two":

> Baillie, Baillie, give us your answer true.
> Why ain't Plato found in the canon too?
>   For by your interpretation,
>   He's better than Revelation,
> His style is neater than Second Peter
> And it's true he's not a Jew.

One of my students, years ago, had this to say about Morton
Scott Enslin, the irrepressible New Testament scholar:

> If you've noticed that all I conclude
> Is in thoroughly radical mood,
>   It will be no surprise
>   When you see me excise
> The Pastorals, both Peters, and Jude.

In the late 1920's, a group of prominent theologians in Great Britain projected a series of volumes, under the editorship of W. R. Matthews and H. Wheeler Robinson, to be called "The Library of Constructive Theology." It was an attempt to be "relevant" in an age of decreasing authority for Bible and tradition. The "General Introduction" to the series spelled out the rationale for the innovative publishing effort, and the following two verses by an unidentified wag sought to explain what the series was all about:

> The Editors are certain that the church in every land
> Is confronted with a great, though largely silent, crisis and
> An equal opportunity, and, though perhaps you doubt it,
> They have a common mind on what we ought to do about it.
>   We ought to do about it. And don't you dare to flout it.
> They have a common mind on what we ought to do about it.

> "Apologetics" now have lost their hold upon the mind—
> Accepting propositions on authority defined;
> Authority itself is in a state of dissolution.
> There's certainly a questioning, if not a revolution.
>   Perhaps a revolution. But we've got the solution.
> There's certainly a questioning, if not a revolution.

My colleague, George S. Hendry, brought his classical training to Princeton, but not all the students responded to his lecture allusions, as this verse suggests:

> Dr. Hendry's a teacher unique
> But his juniors are still up the creek.
>   For with erudite thought
>   He consistently taught
> In Hebrew and Latin and Greek.

Although it would be difficult for some to imagine a more sober theologian than Karl Barth, he seems to have inspired several verses on his theology. The following is by a Lutheran missionary:

> A difficult thinker is Barth.
> His logic will tear you apart.
> With his dialectic,
> Life gets so hectic,
> You hasten for refuge to Sartre.

And this from a forgotten author in a now defunct journal which noted: "We publish it with acknowledgment to the unknown author, as a corrective against jargon, against over-solemnity in theology, and because we would be suspicious of any theology which was not strong enough to laugh at itself, or to stand a bit of misrepresentation":

> The deceitful human heart
> Has been analyzed by Barth
> With the help of neo-Pauline terminology.
> His aim is to restore
> The crisis either/or
> As the fundamental concept of theology.
>
> You will hear with apprehension
> That the dialectic tension
> Is the core of the immediate situation,
> And will understand the gravity
> Of absolute depravity
> Through an existential *Ich-du* confrontation.

Another anonymous, if not immortal, jingle tells us something, if not much, about Rudolf Bultmann:

> Hark! The herald angels sing
> "Bultmann is the latest thing."
> At least, they would if he had not
> Demythologized the lot.

Frederick R. Kling, a seminarian of twenty-five years ago, put this Gilbert and Sullivan tribute together for Paul L. Lehmann:

> I am the very model of the neo-dialectical;
> I'm always in a crisis with some tension intellectual.
> By Barthian analysis my mind is in paralysis—
> I need a metaphysic for suspension of the ethical.
> I understand explicitly what's meant by Catholicity;
> And though ecclesiastically I'm all for historicity,
> For existential rhetoric I'm classified a heretic—
> But still I am an advocate of ecumenicity.
> From all the eschatology that's humanly predictable
> My greatest comfort is that immortality is fictional;
> And since I am fanatical in matters problematical—
> I now bestow upon you all my blessing benedictional.

Another seminarian of the same generation, Robert S. Barker, heading for Japan, where he's been ever since, prepared this threnody on "Theological Thrombosis":

> O pity the pupil of Barth!
> Though he seeks to drive sin from his heart
>   And by evil he's frightened,
>   Then his fear is more heightened,
> For he knows that there's no way to start.
>
> The student of Zurich's Emil
> Knows that reason is really not real.
>   Naught but God's revelation
>   To corrupted creation
> Can conclusively consummate weal.
>
> But heed ye how Niebuhr explains
> The extent of society's pains.
>   It is human depravity;
>   And yet in some cavity
> The "imago Dei" remains.
>
> So it is that one like Haroutunian
> Is on fire to inspire a reunion

With the chaps that the church
Has left in the lurch
While becoming a banker's communion.

Oh, the madness of modern theology!
It eschews Hellenistic ontology.
In its mumbling jumble
Ancient systems must crumble
While we study abnormal psychology.

In 1938–39, Charles Clayton Morrison, the aggressive and innovative editor of *The Christian Century,* was invited to give the Lyman Beecher Lectures on preaching at Yale Divinity School. Arguing in one of his final lectures against the American revivalist experience in favor of the New Testament "church" context for evangelism, he was suddenly and vigorously interrupted by a strong voice, asking: "What about Paul?" The next day, a group of Yale students were gathered around the piano, singing a little ditty put together the night before. They asked Dr. Morrison to listen, and he joined in the fun, as follows:

Doc. Morrison came from "The Century"
To lecture to New Haven gentry;
Thundered he: "Take the Church—
It's been left in the lurch,
And the fight's become purely defensory!"

Chorus: "What about Paul?
What about Paul?
Alone on the road to Damascus."
Joined the Church,
That is all.
Good question—I'm glad that you asked us.

What we need is ecumenicity,
To return to our basic catholicity,
Purge the clergy with hyssop
Then veto the bishop,
And thus we may dwell in felicity.

Chorus: "What about Paul?" etc.

III

If there are similar kinds of nonsense verse nowadays, I'm unaware of them. The only contemporary versifier I can mention with appreciation is "St. Hereticus" who writes delightfully, but infrequently, for *Christianity and Crisis.* But for the most part, theologues today, whether in church, seminary, or divinity school don't make humor like they used to. Why not?

It is risky business to analyze what makes people laugh. That, of course, hasn't prevented some heavy-handed interpretations. Like Freud, for example (see his series of essays on "wit" in Brill's *The Basic Writings of Sigmund Freud,* 1938, pp. 633–803). Or Henri Bergson's *Laughter: An Essay on the Meaning of the Comic* (1911). But we can learn something, I think, from the two or three best discussions I know of that relate humor and theology.

I am thinking, first, of Peter Berger's intriguing suggestion that humor is one of the "signals of transcendence" (along with ordering, play, hope, and moral outrage). Instead of looking "up there" or "out there," Berger points to such intimations of the beyond as can be found within human nature itself. In this sense, "the finite has the capacity for the infinite" *(finitum capax infiniti),* and humor is not simply a trademark of the human creature ("an animal that laughs") but a theological attribute pointing to the Creator. (Peter L. Berger, *A Rumor of Angels: Modern Sociology and the Rediscovery of the Supernatural,* 1969, pp. 86–90.)

A second, and earlier, theological discussion of humor is in Reinhold Niebuhr's *Discerning the Signs of the Times: Sermons for Today and Tomorrow* (1946). It comes in a sermon, "Humour and Faith," on the text from Psalm 2:4, "He that sitteth in the heavens shall laugh: the Lord shall have them in derision." Niebuhr points out that this is the only instance in the Bible where laughter is ascribed to God, and this tends to support the critics who do not find much humor or laughter in the Bible.

Both Berger and Niebuhr agree that humor, laughter, and the comic are intimately associated with "the incongruities of our existence" (Niebuhr) and with "discrepancy, incongruity, incommensurability" (Berger). To have a sense of humor implies the ability to smile at the absurdities of the human situation, not to take oneself too seriously, and to realize the comic proportions of all human pretensions in this vast universe, not of our own devising.

Berger argues that where this humorous awareness exists, we automatically also expect that somewhere, somehow, there is a meaning and a solution and a better answer to the oddities of existence. Niebuhr distinguishes between humor (which allows us to laugh at the vicissitudes of our immediate human existence) and faith (where the ultimate riddles of life must finally be referred). Humor can cope with the local incongruities and save us from our too-solemn selves; but only faith can cope with the absolute paradoxes of existence. "That is why," Niebuhr concludes his sermon, "there is laughter in the vestibule of the temple, the echo of laughter in the temple itself, but only faith and prayer, and no laughter, in the holy of holies."

A third discussion of the relation of humor and theology can be found in a collection of essays edited by M. Conrad Hyers of Beloit College, *Holy Laughter: Essays on Religion in the Comic Perspective* (1969). Most of the chapters are reprints, two of them from THEOLOGY TODAY, but there are illuminating original contributions by Hyers himself and by his well-known colleague at Beloit, Chad Walsh.

Hyers laments the reluctance of theologians to make a place for the comic element in their sober discussions. In a follow-up article in *The Christian Century* (Dec. 11, 1974), "The Nativity as Divine Comedy," he finds the Magnificat of Mary a wonderful expression of "scattering the proud" and "putting down" the mighty. This, he notes, is a classic symbolic device in the ancient repertoire of clowns and fools. "That sense of marvelous absurdity and incredulous, wide-eyed wonder that attaches itself to great surprises, sudden amazements and comic twists, seems to get lost in the prosaic thickness of theological pedantry."

Chad Walsh in a retrospective concluding chapter twits his fellow contributors, including Hyers but neglecting himself, for writing about the comic in a very noncomical prose style. Like Freud and Bergson, already mentioned, Walsh detects among writers on religious humor "a solemnity of tone and style that seems more suited to earning a degree in philosophy or being nominated to a bishopric than to inviting men to celebration and laughter." Both Hyers and Walsh disagree with Niebuhr's caveat against laughter in the holy of holies. Hyers thinks Niebuhr's distinction between humor and faith is too simplistic; Walsh thinks Niebuhr's view of the comic excludes what he calls the "baroque," and that "the believer who does not laugh within the holy of holies is deficient not merely in humor but in his awareness of that glorious absurdity that we label the sacred."

But Niebuhr's main point seems well taken, and even Hyers admits that "humor by itself is not enough" and is "powerless to solve the deepest problems of human existence." Some things are just not funny and should not be treated comically, such as disease, death, and crucifixion, just to mention three. The widely acclaimed TV production *VD Blues*, with Dick Cavett as host, was an original, and in visual ways a brilliant, educational experience. It had its very funny moments. But syphilis is definitely not funny, and jokes about it must inevitably take on a sick quality. In one of the *Dick Van Dyke* shows, a deceased vaudeville comic requested in his will that his friends conduct a memorial service appropriate for his humorous career. Dick obliges. But the service is "funny as a crutch," as we used to say. There is lilting joy and youthful exuberance in both *Jesus Christ Superstar* and *Godspell*. But these contemporary Passion plays end with the crucifixion, and the concluding scenes abruptly change key and tempo and seem aptly somber, reflective, and quiet. Niebuhr is surely right about the ultimate solemnities of faith and life. "For everything there is a season . . . a time to weep and a time to laugh" (Eccl. 3:4).

IV

Whatever we may say about the serious discussion of humor and faith, there appears in our day an observable lack of theological nonsense verse, doggerel, and sheer fun—about those things and persons that need "putting down." If we return to our original venture, that twenty-five or so years ago we were more inclined than we are today to laugh at our teachers, our theologians, and our religious pretensions—what accounts for the contemporary loss of a sense of humor?

There may be many reasons, if indeed the assertion is true. But let me note just one reason. It could be that seminarians, clergy, and church people today don't find much to laugh at simply because there is so little substance to our theology. As Churchill once said of Clement Atlee, "he was a modest man with much to be modest about," so too we don't poke fun at our theologians, because they are so few and so mediocre that they can't be readily identified. Such a state of theological affairs is surely depressing. But empty-headedness, intellectual vacuity, and fuzziness about real issues have always been ripe resources for jokes and japes.

Theological fun, anyone?

III
A FAITHFUL MINISTRY

Counting the Cost

It is part of the good news of the gospel that God's redemptive love in Jesus Christ can be had for the taking. Like a gift freely offered, all we have to do is to reach out and take it. It is as simple as Jesus' invitation, "Follow me," or Paul's exhortation, "Believe in the Lord Jesus, and you will be saved." All preaching, evangelism, and missionary activity derive from this basic conviction that the gospel has a way of making its own appeal and of eliciting its own response. The task of the preacher, the evangelist, the missionary is simply to proclaim the gospel, and in doing so to "preach for a verdict," to urge people to make a "decision" and to "accept Christ as their personal Savior."

It is all just as simple as that, and we should never forget it. Yet perversely enough, it is not simple at all! To proclaim the gospel or to respond to it may be the most difficult and staggering thing imaginable. That is why so many well-meaning "decisions for Christ" never seem to come off. And that is why Jesus never oversimplified the demands of discipleship. Read the Gospels, and it is clear that while he sought disciples wherever he went, he wanted no one to follow him under the false pretenses that it would be easy or simple. Decision is one thing; discipleship is another. And the cost of discipleship comes high. Before one enters upon it, it is well to count the cost, just as a farmer would estimate whether a new silo for his barn could be built before actually going

THEOLOGY TODAY, XII (1956), 424–429.

ahead with the decision (cf. Luke 14:28–33). This, too, is part of the gospel, and we had better not forget this side of the matter either.

It is possible to make converts too easily, to rejoice prematurely in the number of "decisions for Christ" which our preaching produces, to lead people under false pretenses to the life of discipleship. We must be on our guard against such possibilities, not in order to dampen our zeal but precisely in order to proclaim the gospel aright. And this is especially important in a time like ours when there is much talk both about the return to religion, in some places, and the falling away of church people, on the other hand. It is true that we are to say the same thing in both situations—"Here is the gospel; it's all yours!" But there is something more to be said, particularly in an age when anxiety and meaninglessness predispose people either toward or away from the claims of Christianity. To those on the threshold of decision and discipleship, we must speak our Lord's word of caution— "count the cost." To those withdrawing more and more, we must rigorously and honestly proclaim the superlative demands and requirements of Christian faith over against the disillusioning possibility of being strung along under false pretenses. How would this affect our invitation to accept Jesus Christ as Lord and Savior?

I

First of all, we must make it clear that to accept Jesus Christ as Lord and Savior involves an extravagant theological claim. Too often this phrase is allowed to become a pious cliché, the trademark of self-styled evangelists and so-called Bible-believing Christians. They are right in regarding the phrase as the heart of the matter, but they mislead when they suggest that it is plain as a pikestaff and as simple as ABC.

We are told that the first Christian creed or confession of faith was "Jesus is Lord" (cf. Rom. 10:9; I Cor. 12:3; Phil. 2:11). For Jewish and Gentile converts this summed up the meaning and content of their faith. Soon the phrase became a baptismal formula, and in course of time it was developed and extended to include all the affirmations that we now associate with the Apostles' Creed. That is to say, a whole theology is at stake here and not merely an emotional response or feeling. To say that Jesus is Lord is to say that he is one with God; to say that Jesus is the Christ is to say that a particular historical person is the personification of God's redemptive purpose. This is what the Christian faith is all about, and it is a stupendous claim. It means that the Eternal has entered time, that the Infinite has been confined by the finite, that God has come to us personally in a particular person, in a particular place, at a particular time. This is the incarnation, central and determinative, and at the same time it constitutes the scandal and offense of the gospel which makes the Christian claim seem so absurd and impossible.

This is, of course, the good news of the Christian religion—that God is not aloof but personally involved in the human situation. For this reason, theologically speaking, Christology is the center and norm of all doctrine, and it is instructive to note that even in the most radical reinterpretations of Christian faith in our day the Christocentric emphasis is retained. Paul Tillich's concern for the "new being" is related to Jesus as the Christ; Rudolf Bultmann's concern to "demythologize" stops short of "the event of redemption" in Jesus Christ.

But to say that Jesus is Lord is to utter a paradox, to affirm that mystery and miracle are inextricably interwoven with fact and faith. It is not self-evident that Jesus is Lord. It was not so during his days on earth, and it is not so today. The Gospels make it plain that his closest disciples were confused and unsure about his claim to be the Messiah. This means that to accept Jesus as Lord and Savior is to reflect deeply upon basic theological issues, and we do the cause of Christ no service by reducing, toning down, or oversimplifying its theological demands.

II

We must go a step farther. To accept Jesus Christ as Lord and Savior involves not only an extravagant theological claim, it commits one to an exorbitant standard of living. If decision for Christ is the initial down payment, discipleship with Christ is the total cost. And this comes high; it cannot be had cheaply or at reduced prices. As the hymn has it, this "demands my soul, my life, my all."

The high cost of discipleship is repeatedly emphasized in the Gospels. Jesus never slurred over the requirements and demands of following him. To follow Christ is to follow one who had no place to lay his head, who required undivided allegiance even to the forsaking of parents and family, who promised persecution, ridicule, and at the end a cross. To walk in the steps of the Master is to stagger under a cross on the way to Calvary. No wonder Jesus did not encourage those well-meaning disciples who were not ready to face all the prerequisites of discipleship!

The high cost of Christian living has never gone down, though we have frequently tried to soften its full cost and have even intimated that it can be had at reasonable rates. There is a widespread heresy today that to be a Christian means that all one's problems and questions will be answered, that peace and power will be won, that trouble and anxiety will vanish. There are rewards to be sure in being a Christian, but they are the by-products of rigorous and demanding discipleship. Christian faith and life not only answer questions but, even more, they raise new questions. Peace and power are to be found, but the daily cross is always there too. Troubles and anxieties may be lifted but Christians—if they really follow their Lord and Savior—are concerned as Jesus was in his self-identification with sinful humanity.

Let us make no mistake about it, and let us not lead others to the Christian life under false pretenses—to accept Jesus Christ as Lord and Savior is to enter upon a new kind of existence and not merely to enhance the best that we already know. That is why the New Testament talks so much about the "new creation," of dying and rising with Christ, of being born again. And the classic theological vocabulary contains words that emphasize this, such as justification, sanctification, repentance, conversion, regeneration, etc. But there is no doubt that in much of our preaching, evangelism, and theologizing today we undercut the demands of discipleship by offering a reduced Christianity which we think will be more attractive and enticing. Modern advertising methods have so accustomed us to expect something for nothing or next to nothing that we have unwittingly applied the same approach to the Christian faith. That is why the increase in church membership and the revival of interest in religion on the college campus are fraught with peril as well as with good. All such evidences of interest are welcome and can be used constructively, but we must not sell Christianity short. There's a big price tag on Christian discipleship, and those who get it cheaply may soon become disillusioned when they discover they have an inferior substitute for the real thing.

III

"Decisions for Christ"—as the history of evangelism shows —are fairly easy to get whether by fair means or foul. They are a dime a dozen. But real discipleship, day by day Christian living, is harder to come by, and that is why it is so rare in our midst. The Christian life, as anyone who has really tried to live it knows, is a difficult, seemingly impossible undertaking. It is much easier *not* to be a Christian in our world today, and the church in all honesty and humility ought to be bold enough to proclaim its invitation in such a way that everyone can see how much it costs and therefore how much it is worth.

It may be said that to stress this side is to lay a stumbling block in the way of the seeker. But Christianity is itself a kind of stumbling block, and no good can result from smoothing it out so that it seems plain and easy and simple. Furthermore, the proclamation of the sheer difficulty of Christian discipleship may actually be better advertising than we think. The big causes that are enlisting the loyalties of people today do not offer easy or simple solutions to life's most pressing problems. Young people especially are not attracted these days to phony-sounding panaceas or utopian promises. They know that struggle, conflict, danger, and adventure are part of the stuff of life, and that discipleship in any field comes high and demands everything. It is surely conceivable that they would be more interested in a Christianity that required something than in one that can be had dirt cheap.

In the early days of the American frontier, a request for itinerant preachers was circulated in this form: "We offer you: No Salary; No Recompense; No Holidays; No Pension. But: Much Hard Work; a Poor Dwelling; Few Consolations; Many Disappointments; Frequent Sickness; a Violent or Lonely Death; an Unknown Grave." No doubt that scared many away! But it brought results. How about reissuing that challenge when we urge people today to accept Jesus Christ as Lord and Savior?

In but Not of the World

To be in but not of the world is one way to define the mission of the church and the vocation of the Christian. The phrase suggests the delicate balance required if worldliness, on the one side, and otherworldliness, on the other, are to be avoided. It sums up Paul's exhortation: "Do not be conformed to this world but be transformed . . ." (Rom. 12:2).

A Christianity that is not *in* the world has forgotten what the incarnation is all about; a Christianity that is *of* the world has forgotten that "our commonwealth is in heaven" (Phil. 3:20). All too often one or the other *is* forgotten, and it would not be too difficult to write the history of the church or the history of theology by simply noting how delicate has been the balance between worldliness and otherworldliness through the centuries, and how one and then the other seemed to prevail. And strong temptations to tip the balance (perhaps we should call it "tension" rather than balance) are with us today as in the past.

I

Taking a quick look around and venturing a generalization, there is plenty of evidence that *otherworldliness* is a strong temptation today for many churches and individual Christians. This seems somehow quite out of character in our unromantic age, in a world which discredits panaceas and utopias, when

THEOLOGY TODAY, XV (1958), 293–298.

neither the old dream dreams nor the young see visions. Or is it precisely because our world is so disillusioned and disheartened that Christianity's claim to offer something "out of this world" is so appealing and captivating? "If the foundations are destroyed, what can the righteous do?" (Ps. 11:3). Well, they can "take refuge," like the Psalmist, "in the Lord" whose "throne is in heaven." They can find asylum in their faith; they can go to church; they can hope in the Lord—eschatologically and apocalyptically—that sometime in the future "on the wicked he will rain coals of fire and brimstone."

This is one way to be in but not of the world, and there are persuasive reasons, historical, biblical, and theological, for abandoning the world. It takes a time of crisis, such as ours, to demonstrate dramatically not only the futility of our feeble efforts to save the world from itself but the significance of Christian eschatology which beckons us to raise our eyes from the dust to look at the far horizons. These are apocalyptic times, and yesterday's "liberalism" seems effete, and the "social gospel" bankrupt.

We should not be surprised, therefore, that the Jehovah's Witnesses with their prediction of Armageddon just around the corner is one of the fastest-growing religious groups in the world today. We should not find it odd that Billy Graham attracts huge crowds with his old-time religion, or that there is a renaissance of fundamentalism in our day, or that there is a revival of interest in worship and personal piety in our churches, or that many on the edges of organized religion at least profess their faith in faith. All these movements may remind us, if only negatively and in a corrective sense, of Christianity's stance outside of *this* world, that "here we have no lasting city, but we seek the city which is to come" (Heb. 13:14).

But it must also be said that to be in but not of the world in this fashion often means that we are not really *in* the world at all. Instead of bringing the gospel *to* the world in its confusion and perplexity, we try to keep the gospel *from* the world by keeping it to ourselves. "To keep oneself unstained from the world," we often retreat to the seclusion of our church or our theology, but we forget that the apostle who urged this advice preceded it with the curious definition—"Religion that is pure and undefiled before God and the Father is this: to visit orphans and widows in their affliction" (James 1:27). The gospel to orphans and widows, the most detached, lonely, unaccepted of all people, cannot be preached or declared by defining the world as "out of bounds," "off limits," or by quarantining the church and Christian piety *from* the world.

Too much of our religious and church life is strictly "out of this world" not in a proper eschatological sense but in an unrelated sense. So much of our Sunday worship, our pastoral prayers, our hymns and anthems, our pulpit homilies, our sacramental ceremonies, our vested choirs and divided chancels, our processing and recessing—so much of this and more is simply unrelated to reality. It is otherworldly not in a good but in a bad sense. And were it not so soporific and hypnotic, it would not be tolerated by people who otherwise are very much *in* the world. The prankish, irreverent pastor in Peter de Vries's novel *The Mackerel Plaza*, praying about a local flood, intoned: "May a merciful Providence deliver us from this act of God" —knowing full well that his congregation hearing two pious phrases strung together would not question the theological discrepancy. We may improve on this utterance and pray: "May a merciful Providence deliver us from this kind of otherworldly religion."

II

The evidence is not all on one side, however, and there is plenty of religious *worldliness* in our midst today. The fact that this statement immediately strikes us as ambiguous is an indication of how strong the otherworldly tendency is among us. To be *in* the world may mean *either* that we are so much concerned and enmeshed with the things of this world that the church and the Christian life become indistinguishable from the world, *or* that we proclaim the gospel in word and deed to

the world in a redemptive and healing way by self-identification
and participation in the world's woes and ills. The first possibility is the stronger temptation, and it too is a peril that threatens
the Christian witness today.

It was the glory of "liberalism" that it sensed the inconclu-
siveness of church membership or theological orthodoxy as a
test of true religion. It was the incontestable insight of the
"social gospel" that it took seriously "the world" which God
loves and seeks to redeem. Both were worldly rather than
otherworldly. But putting the accent on being *in* the world,
they often obscured the other side of the equation—not to be
of the world. The "liberal" credo regarding "the Fatherhood
of God" and "the brotherhood of man" (or the infinite value
of human personality, as Harnack originally defined it) was
wide open to the temptation to stress the latter and ignore the
former of its two articles of faith, and thus to become indistinguishable from other, secular programs for democratic reform.
The "social gospel" was so patronizingly concerned with society that it frequently forgot that it was the gospel which inspired and initiated its crusade.

Is it any wonder that, especially in American Protestantism,
there emerged an "activism" that was very much *in* the world
simply because the world had penetrated deeply into the
church, its theology, and its piety? One result of this has been
what Richard Niebuhr has called our "utilitarian faith," the
belief that piety pays off in prosperity, that faith in faith is
therapeutic, that religion is a good thing. So we witness the
phenomenal growth of the cult of religious reassurance, that
present-day "Coué-ism" which affirms: "Every day in every
way through religion, prayer, and piety I am getting better and
better."

III

We have hinted at another way to think about being in the
world, namely, by proclaiming the gospel in word and deed to
the world in a redemptive and healing way. This is not just a

theoretical or alternative possibility but a direct implication of
the incarnation. It is in Christ that we see what it means to
be in but not of the world. "Though he was in the form of God
. . . he humbled himself" (Phil. 2:6, 8). In his identification
with sinful, sick humanity, Jesus was charged by the respectable religious leaders of his day for being the friend of sinners,
a breaker of the sabbath, a glutton and a winebibber. But
nowhere is there any evidence that he demeaned himself or was
degraded by his contact with tax collectors, paralytics, harlots,
Samaritans, or demoniacs. His association was always one of
mercy and forgiveness, of sympathy and acceptance, of redemption and restoration.

As over against an escapist type of otherworldliness, this
would mean that we must not be tempted to relinquish the
world to its own self-destruction. We must not be content to
judge the world, to condemn it, to deny it, or to stand aloof
and remain apart from it. And over against a worldliness that
reduces Christianity to a secular philosophy or moralism, this
would mean that we must not be tempted to equate the gospel
with mere humanitarianism, or sky-blue idealism, or conde-
scending social service.

When Jesus said, "No servant can serve two masters. . . . You
cannot serve God and mammon" (Luke 16:13), his words can
be, and have been, taken to underwrite the Christian's withdrawal and detachment from the world. But this phrase, "you
cannot serve God and mammon," is preceded in Luke's Gospel
by the parable of the unjust steward, that clever rascal whom
Jesus applauded not for his dishonesty but for his ingenuity.
And the moral of the parable contains the astonishing statement, coupled with the equally astonishing advice, that "the
sons of this world are wiser in their own generation than the
sons of light. . . . Make friends for yourselves by means of
unrighteous mammon . . ." (Luke 16:1–9).

The world of Christians and of Christian churches is not a
separate, spiritual realm safely inoculated against the diseases
of another, earthly world. We may pretend that this is so, in
which case the world ignores us, either because we remove

ourselves so far from it, or because it senses that we too are deeply involved in the world we condemn. The mission of the church and the life of the Christian cannot be fulfilled on a line which is parallel to the world but which never intersects or penetrates that sphere.

But beyond that, to be *in* the world, to make *friends* of the unrighteous mammon, means that we not only expose and condemn the evils and ailments of the world, but, what is more difficult and distasteful for most of us, that we seek to appreciate and welcome every evidence and contribution for good which the world offers. The astonishing thing about Jesus' parable is that he tells us we can *learn something* from the clever, if unscrupulous, steward. The world is not only the arena in which the struggle for life is staged, it is not merely the realm of perdition and judgment, it is where we are, and both we and it stand in need of forgiveness and redemption. "For God sent the Son into the world, not to condemn the world, but that the world might be saved through him" (John 3:17).

Education in General
and Theological Education

Anyone who undertakes to survey a segment of education today soon discovers that everything is related to everything else. Starting at one level leads inevitably to another. The problems of higher education are of course not those of secondary education. Theological schools differ from community colleges. Graduate-professional training is not the same as adult continuing education. But having noted such obvious diversities, there is more that unites than divides.

Until recently it has been the educational fashion for each separate division to operate its own enterprise without paying much attention to other levels of education. I don't know any theological educators, for example, who trouble to acquaint themselves with what's happening in the high schools today. Even educational groups with the same kinds of problems seldom get together. I have never heard of a conference for medical, law, education, and theological students, all of whom belong to the graduate-professional designation. Educationally and professionally we tend to insulate ourselves, living within very narrow parochial confines. In the same locality, there is likely to be very little communication among elementary, secondary, college, or graduate teachers and students.

But today there is a growing sense of common cause throughout all the ranks of education. We are all in this thing together, and most of us know that the times are changing. We are all involved with teachers, students, classrooms, textbooks,

THEOLOGY TODAY, XXVII (1970), 434–452.

libraries, exams, essays, grades, and degrees. But the mere mention of these commonplaces exposes our current frustrations and anxieties. And since we have so much in common, we should know about each other to help each other and to learn from one another. An illustration from another field may suggest the changed situation in education.

The current interest in ecology and the environment has disclosed the principle of the interdependency of all of nature. Environmentalists point out that all of us and our world are dependent upon a chain-of-being in which every part is related to every other part. To concentrate on one aspect to the neglect of others is to be not only parochial but foolhardy. We live in an implicative system of elaborate and intimate design. What affects one area affects all areas. Educationally, this suggests that any particular category, theological education for example, should be viewed within the total educational complex. At least this approach promises something different and possibly something fresh.

I

To look at theological education as one small piece of turf within the total educational landscape requires a wide-angle perspective. Instead of beginning with the special problems of graduate-professional education in the area of theology, ministry, the church, and other forms of Christian service, we must allow all these matters to remain unexplored until we get our bearings within general education at various levels. To see theological education as a piece of all education may seem uncongenial since we are not used to operating this way. But if we try to make the adjustment, as I have tried to do in an intensive way for the past three years, it is just possible that we may catch a new vision of our own educational responsibility. In desperation it might be argued that there is no other alternative anyway. Concentrated attention in the past on theological education as a special category has produced so little for such a long time.

While I was making up my mind about this, the following statement caught my eye, and I use it as supporting evidence. The comment refers to a consultation on professional education held at the Episcopal Theological School, Cambridge, Mass., in 1967 to which speakers from various professions were invited.

There have, it is true, been various studies of American theological education in the past quarter century, but the recommendations resulting from them have been rather obvious and anything but radical. There have been no significant breakthroughs comparable to those resulting from the Flexner report in medical education or the case method at the Harvard Law School under Langdell. Thus, it seemed *necessary to look outside theological education for new ideas.* [1]

For a starter, let me select three observations regarding general education which suggest implications for theological education: (a) the sheer massive size of the educational enterprise, (b) the academic "upward mobility" syndrome, and (c) the creeping selectivity of the whole educational system. All three are obvious and all are portents of possible disaster. Theological educators seem not to be aware of what's happening elsewhere in education, and so it is important to dwell on what is more apparent when looking at the whole scene. The ominous perils to which these three factors point are even less a part of the normal purview of theological education. The drift toward disaster, which many general educators sense and fear, seems actually to be a vigorously pursued goal for many of us in theological education.

(a) Wherever you look these days, *education is very big business and getting bigger.* Theological education is such a tiny drop in the ever-expanding pool and beset with so many problems of mere survival that it is easy to forget how flourishing are other forms of education. In round figures for 1969–70, we are talking about 61 million students, teachers, and administrators. We are financially involved for nearly 65 billion dollars. The U.S. Office of Education publishes, among other things, a monthly three-column, 300-page journal called *Research in Education* which lists hundreds of current research projects on education all across the country. There are twenty regional Educational Resources Information Center clearinghouses (ERIC) which feed reports into the Washington office. The National Education Association (NEA) operates 34 departments and publishes a *Handbook* of 400 pages that simply lists local and state associations of all kinds.

Several of the larger foundations (Carnegie, Ford, Guggenheim, Danforth, Kettering) and hundreds of smaller ones are deeply involved in educational research. Many industrial corporations (Exxon, Westinghouse, Kodak, IBM, Xerox, Scott Paper) sponsor educational projects. The Committee for Economic Development (CED) representing 200 businesses has produced several basic educational documents. Manufacturers of school equipment have their own organizations, and they exhibit their wares at the various association meetings; sometimes as many as 500 such exhibitors are present at one time in one place. Every campus I visited was in the process of putting up at least one new building. Instant schools and brand-new campuses are springing up all over the country.

The sheer massive size of the educational enterprise represents one of its greatest potential dangers. Bigness and growth are typically American virtues. But we are coming to see that while economic survival may depend on groupings and clusters, the whole purpose of education may be lost if our schools mass-produce students and dehumanize them in the process. Today students are peculiarly sensitive to this possibility. The sorting out of the priorities in our expanding educational development confronts all of us with a decisive question about the chief purpose of what we're doing. A special urgency marks those of us in the smaller institutions who easily become envious of the larger institutions. Only a few years ago the multi-university concept looked like the wave of the future. Today it is almost everywhere held up for ridicule. The bigger the institution, so students argue, the more oppressive and depersonalized it becomes. And the more the system requires extra administrators and bureaucrats, the less open it will be to renewal and reform.

(b) Not only are the various levels of education intertwined, but *the momentum of the whole enterprise propels everything in it onward and upward.* This is not merely a matter of onward with the population growth, of more schools, more teachers, more students. The total drift is *academically upward* in the sense of raising standards and tightening requirements. For the past several decades, we have witnessed an evolutionary climb from the lower to the higher rungs of the educational ladder. The expectation of all educators is to move upward, and it is taken for granted in higher education especially that everyone is involved in academic gamesmanship.

College presidents try to entice more Ph.D.'s for the faculty from the more prestigious graduate schools. Previously isolated land-grant colleges hope to become full-fledged universities. Universities develop their graduate schools. And all along the line, everyone wants to upgrade the curriculum and screen the applicants for proper motivation and academic aptitude.

In this process from lower to higher, it is assumed that meritocratic values correspond with "quality" education. Upward mobility, it is hoped, gets translated into "excellence." Foundation and government funds for research support this upward climb. Learned societies and accrediting associations enhance the mystique of academic prestige. Not every institution can become another Harvard, but every present level can be superseded by a higher. Perhaps, as Harold Taylor has suggested, the ultimate achievement would be a graduate school of such rigor that only a few highly gifted students could be admitted and from which none at all would be graduated.

Academic upward mobility accelerates in the university-graduate school echelon. The more rigorous the graduate school, the more prestigious its reputation. There are today probably not a hundred really first-class university-graduate schools in the country. These presumably act as pacesetters and models for everyone else farther down the line.

Theological education almost everywhere now emulates this

upward academic pattern. This has not always been the case. Except for a very few well-established seminaries and divinity schools, many theological institutions have only recently climbed up from the level of ecclesiastical trade school. But theological education today, even of the denominational variety, derives its academic norms from university-graduate education. The accrediting influence of the Association of Theological Schools, the rapid development of departments of religion in colleges and universities, and the pressure to defer to university-based standards have all contributed to theological uniformity.

There are two perils in this upward mobility game. For one thing, students are increasingly restive under a system that uses cognitive, rational, intellectual, cerebral criteria as the only measures for ability, quality, excellence, and maturity. The life of the mind is fine, but there is more to life than mental gymnastics if this means, as in graduate school, the locked-in structure of comprehensive exams, documented dissertation, and oral defense.

And secondly, graduate-professional education, if it is to be faithful to its dual responsibility, must give as much attention to professional training as to academic scholarship. If theological education continues to make the academic the norm for the professional, then the logical future for seminaries is for them to become departments of religion in colleges and universities. In any case, the question of priorities is forced upon us. In some ways, this is the most crucial decision for theological education in the very near future.[2]

(c) The inevitable corollary of academic upward mobility is *increasing selectivity based on predetermined standardized tests.* If ability, excellence, and quality education are linked directly with high cognitive performance, then the best education and the best schools must practice restrictive admission policies. Only so, it is argued, can the incompetent be excluded in order for the high achievers to progress at their own pace. For the past thirty or forty years this has been the driving aspiration of all institutions of higher education, including theological seminaries. Some can enjoy more selectivity than others, but scarcely any upward-bound institution advertises that it will admit anyone regardless of academic qualifications.

But this is exactly what the current debate on "open admissions" is all about. If academic achievement, based mainly on reading, writing, and verbal skills, is the major test for admission to higher education, then clearly this principle negates any pretensions to equality or democratic education for everyone.

Strict constructionists view with panic any assault on the hard-won principle of selectivity. So do those who have only recently and with great difficulty climbed up a rung or two on the educational ladder. But the issue has now been joined by many outspoken educators, by most students, and by all blacks. Let three quotations point up the problem and the peril of academic selectivity.

The most common educational justification for ability tracking is the assumption that the student will develop better educationally if he is grouped with students of similar ability. . . . The available evidence indicates that it does not work: the intellectual development of the bright student is apparently not impeded if he attends a relatively unselective college, nor is the development of the less able student adversely affected if he attends a highly selective college.[3]

To reward superior natural endowment is, in effect, to substitute an aristocracy of genes and talent for the older aristocracy of family and title. To reward the socially advantaged is to render the already fortunate more fortunate still. Clearly, neither of these principles is acceptable in a school system that professes to be democratic.[4]

It is abundantly clear that seminary admissions committees which continue to operate in their usual way thwart all efforts to increase the number of Black students. . . . This process is designed to be highly selective and to produce the best possible student body in conformity to the standards of AATS and the socio-cultural-economic norms of the white Protestant majority.[5]

Once again, the sorting of priorities becomes an educational imperative. We are *not* talking about relaxing academic schol-

arship; we *are* talking about "full equality of educational opportunity." However the open admissions debate proceeds, and it
promises to heat up, graduate-professional schools must reappraise their goals *so that academic standards serve rather than
dominate* the whole educational program.[6]

II

Even a cursory survey of general education today leaves the
overpowering impression of a halting, stumbling, failing system. From all sides and from all levels we are hearing substantive criticism that the educational system is not working as it
should. In a relatively short period, many of the myths that
sustained the whole enterprise have been disputed or rejected.

Just when we were beginning to pride ourselves on a developing system of standard requirements and goals, all moving
majestically from lower to higher, we are being confronted by
direct attacks against everything regarded as so essential just
yesterday.

Teachers and faculties have been organized for professional
recognition and status, salary security and tenure. Students
move from level to level by way of standardized tests, grades,
and exams. Research, scholarship, and specialization at the
upper reaches presumably have set academic norms for the
whole educational hierarchy. Isn't the educational system getting bigger and better, more efficient and utilitarian, more
essential for entering into the good life of modern society?
More high schoolers each year go on to college. More college
students go on to graduate school. We must be doing something right.

All of a sudden, so recent has the change come over us,
practically all such assumptions are challenged at every level of
education.

Dissatisfaction with American education is everywhere evident.
. . . Since the late fifties, the federal government has granted billions
of dollars to finance curriculum reforms, innovations of all kinds in

thousands of schools, and a large program designed specifically to improve the instruction of the disadvantaged. Yet the outcome of much of this endeavor and expenditure has been, to put it mildly, disappointing.[7]

If what I've done all year is what an education is, then taking a diploma from high school is hypocrisy. It's ridiculous. What I've learned all year is what I've done on my own outside of school—what I've read, what I've learned from others. You just can't sit there all day; it's so boring. Parents don't realize it. I know parents say you have to learn to accept things that are boring, that everything can't be exciting, but, dammit, it's four years of my life![8]

Because adults take the schools so much for granted, they fail to appreciate what grim, joyless places most American schools are, how oppressive and petty are the rules by which they are governed, how intellectually sterile and aesthetically barren the atmosphere, what an appalling lack of civility obtains on the part of teachers and principals, what contempt they unconsciously display for children as children.[9]

Comments such as these which fault the system for being boring, uninteresting, or a waste of time are commonplace today among students and educators at all levels. A more direct criticism has to do with the lack of relevance in much that passes for education. One needn't go outside theological education for evidence. The conventional pattern of religion and theology courses in colleges and seminaries strikes many students today as completely irrelevant.

Courses on the literature and formation of the books of the Bible, philosophy of religion and language, the development of Jewish and Christian thought down the centuries, the history of comparative religions, analysis of great thinkers—these kinds of courses form the backbone of most instruction in the field.

What students today most want from the study of religion they hardly ever get. The personal-mystical enthusiasm which many find meaningful comes too close to subjectivism for their teachers. Trained in the intellectualism of the typical graduate school, most teachers of religious subjects try to avoid anything as intangible as inner faith experiences. They want to demonstrate that religion can be studied as objectively as any other discipline. Their subject, they keep saying, is a humanistic field of scholarly inquiry.

Many theological students, and an increasing number of pastors, know that theology and the churches are being criticized not because they have no resources to draw on, or no meaningful ideas to contribute, but because they engender so much sham, hollow piety, sentimentalism, conventional moralism, and social irrelevance.[10]

Of a much more crucial nature than charges against education as boring or irrelevant are the current convictions of many educators and students, though not many in theology, that *the whole educational enterprise represents an oppressive self-serving social system.* The big problem with the school system, so this attack argues, is not merely with the inadequacies of teaching and curriculum, bad as they may be. The problem lies with education's cellular structures which support the onward and upward momentum of the whole thing.

Much of the recent student rebellion is directly related to this growing resentment against a repressive system that allows very little critical reaction. Such a mood faults the whole educational enterprise from top to bottom as oppressive since it undergirds the meritocratic society it is set up to serve. It is oppressive because it favors the elite and depresses the disadvantaged. Not only so, but in many ways even the favored elite, who might be expected to approve their privileges, are the very ones who proclaim the loudest that the system demeans them as much as anyone else.

The focal point of this issue is the black-white dichotomy in American society. The racist tendencies in our midst, so accurately predicted by the National Advisory Commission on Civil Disorders, the "Kerner Report" of 1968, are apparently forestalling significant educational integration. But at a deeper level, we are beginning to see that adult expectations for an integrated public elementary school are hopelessly unrealistic so long as the whole society itself is divided.

From the side of education, especially from the students themselves, the system perpetuates the evils we all deplore but refuse to face. This kind of interrelation of education and the social-political realities of the times helps to account for the ultramilitant claim that nothing useful can be accomplished anywhere until everything in society is overturned.[11]

Curiously, theological students for the most part have not thus far adapted this critical stance toward their own situation. Some, but not many, note that seminaries and divinity schools tend to support the church status quo. Where churches and denominations financially support theological education, the possibilities of prophetic renewal issuing from within the seminary must certainly be lessened.

If general education perpetuates the social conventions, could it not be argued that seminaries contribute to the rigidities and unrealities of institutionalized religion? There is some evidence that this issue will be articulated more forcefully soon.

III

If there is fault to find with education, and if the system appears to be breaking down, we assume that the first place to look for trouble must be teaching and the teacher. Students, we imagine, go to school to learn. "School" means faculty, teaching, curriculum, courses, textbooks, assignments, instruction, exams, essays, and grades. If students are dissatisfied with the school system, or if they are not learning what is being taught, then presumably the trouble spot can be located in teaching and the teacher (assuming that students are not just plain lazy, uninterested, or delinquent).

Primal attention to teaching runs like a theme song through much of the educational literature and discussion of recent years. The tune runs like this: teaching has been neglected, more attention needs to be given to methods of teaching, in higher education teaching rates below research and publishing, good teachers are scarce, all teachers are impoverished and unappreciated, lectures are not as good as seminars, electronic aids may or may not be useful, the purpose of teaching is to transmit content, teachers should be experts in their fields, if graduate students know their subjects they can teach them, teachers pursue an objective search for truth.

The neglect of teaching methodology, especially in higher education, is astonishing. Teaching is apparently a skill, art, craft, profession for which there is no special training outside the mastering of one's discipline. In graduate schools, where most teachers for higher education are trained, it is rare to find any instruction whatever in teaching methods or learning theory. It is a safe bet that very few theological professors have ever studied teaching-learning theory, or have ever read any educational literature, or have attended any educational conferences, or have ever been videotaped in class, or have ever had their teaching evaluated in any way at all.

There is no question that education would be better in many ways if more attention were directed to teaching and to methods for improving teacher effectiveness. But we should be clear about the purpose of teaching within the whole process of education. Are we trying to find new and better ways for continuing the traditional authoritarian method of telling, training, inculcating, and indoctrination? Are we thinking of teaching as transmitting? Is learning receiving? Must education be teacher-subject oriented? Is teaching telling? Is learning listening?

If teaching is primarily the passing on of the western intellectual and cultural tradition, and if the test of effectiveness is measured by some sort of student examination or paper, then the fact is that almost any method will suffice. Some teachers and some students will prefer one method to another, but repeated surveys show little measurable differences in methods used or in content mastered.

We have reported the results of a reanalysis of the data from 91 comparative studies of college teaching technologies conducted between 1924 and 1965. These data demonstrate clearly and unequivocally that there is no measurable difference among truly distinctive methods of college instruction when evaluated by student performance on final examinations.[12]

Emphasis on teaching and the teacher, important as this may be, tends to obscure the other side of the educational formula, namely, learning and the student. We assume that because faculty and administrators traditionally determine curriculum whatever is decided about teaching will automatically benefit the student.

IV

My own research on general education began with teaching as the primary focus. But I have come to see that *the real problem in education today is not teaching and the teacher but learning and the student.* The big question is not how to teach but who the student is and how the student learns. Where do students come from? Where do they want to go? What are their abilities? How do they think of themselves? How do they relate to others? What do they think of the world around them? What do they read? How do they study? What do they want to know? What music do they like? What are their hobbies? What creative arts or crafts interest them? How do they express themselves? How do they evaluate their own education thus far?

The crucial issue in education is the student, not the teacher, not the curriculum, not the requirements, not the subject matter, not the test scores, not the transcript, not any number of other matters, important as they may be, which usually get prior attention by faculty and administrators. The learning process is a much more complicated affair than teachers have acknowledged. Students today want to find out for themselves. They want to be allowed to make their own mistakes. They know that learning depends on being personally involved. That does not preclude the role of the teacher, but it changes the teacher's function from a lecturer to a guide, from an authority to a participant. Learning is something students do for themselves, with or without help. It is no longer possible anyway to teach everything about a subject. But it is possible to indicate what a subject is all about and how the student can discover what is worth knowing.

There is no doubt in my mind that we have come to the end of a long and energetic era of education in which teaching and content have dominated the whole process. The next stage will completely rearrange every campus in the country, and in the resulting dislocation, and possibly confusion, at least one clear perspective will emerge: *a new educational concern for the student and the learning situation.* This will mean taking seriously the student-as-person.

The importance of the inward personal factor in education, from the student's point of view, can be gauged by the way students tend to evaluate teacher performance. Almost invariably, whenever such evaluations are operative, students rate teachers on the positive side when they exhibit traits of friendship and caring. In the 1970 *Yale Course Critique,* for example, freshmen are advised to take courses on the basis not of subject matter but with regard to the teacher's accessibility and willingness to listen to students' suggestions about improving the course.[13]

The personal factor in the teaching-learning linkage ought to be of particular concern for theological education. Christian faith, professedly at least, is more on the side of persons than principles, institutions, or organizations. The gospel, as personified in Jesus, is good news for people, especially for the poor and the oppressed. It is somewhat ambiguous, however, whether seminaries and divinity schools (or for that matter, departments of religion in colleges and universities) exhibit special regard for personal values. Is it universally agreed that churches, Sunday schools, or church-related colleges make a special contribution, *because of their faith commitment,* in the area of caring about people, especially the poor and the oppressed?

Love, honesty, openness, compassion, friendship, regard for

the poor, the stranger, the sick, the victimized, the worker, the artist, the musician, all kinds and conditions of men, women, children, animals, and nature itself—these are the values and virtues the student generation extols, and they are very close to the biblical characteristics of religious faith and life.

If education, whether general or theological, were to redirect its whole program so that it would be student-oriented rather than content-oriented, a new day in our schools would dawn. Some would hope never to see that day! The situation would be, perhaps, analogous to General Motors determining its policy for the benefit of the consuming public and not merely for the sake of the board of directors and the stockholders. Let's face it: this for many would be a frightening prospect.

The personal dimension in education would threaten, as some fear, to turn the whole educational enterprise *inward.* Might this emphasis transform theological education into therapy sessions and sensitivity training? To focus on the student would seem to many a perverse, even a backward step. Certainly it is a controversial issue.

But there is another side to the student, and that is definitely and aggressively *outward.* If students want education to pay more attention to them as persons, they also demand that education become directly involved in the life and politics of the community. The cloistered campus is already a relic of the past. Students now require that the campus be dragged, kicking and struggling if need be, into the community and that the community be invited to participate in the campus.

The whole community ought to be the school, and the classroom a home base for the teachers and kids, a place where they can talk and rest and learn together, but not the sole place of learning. The classroom ought to be a communal center, a comfortable environment in which plans can be made and experiences assessed. However, one can open up the classroom as much by moving out of it as by changing the life within it.[14]

Education in the future will require a greater public involvement, a greater partnership between the home and school, between the community and the school. The school cannot be indifferent to the social conditions of the area it serves.[15]

Just as the overintellectualism of college and university education is being questioned today, so too the secluded research lab and uninvolved campus are being translated into direct social action. Teachers, professors, educators, trustees, and administrators are being challenged by students to put their feet in step with their ideals. Mouthing platitudes about liberal humanism will not do; indeed that is today branded as hypocrisy and regarded by students as dishonest, irrelevant, even obscene. Religion and its institutions are just as much at fault here as colleges and universities. The church stands for so much that is humanizing and ennobling, but too often the message gets blurred with pious rhetoric.

V

To look at theological education from the wider angle of general education is to be startled into awareness of rapid and total change. But change brings pain, and for every innovation there is corresponding resistance. Education today, whether general or specialized, is engaged in a colossal tug-of-war. The old assumptions of academic scholarship are being confronted by the new demands of personal involvement.

Unless theological education is content to continue its uncritical imitation of an academic tradition now under fire on the college and university front, then certain decisions about tomorrow must be made today. The most important of these, in my opinion, relates to a redefinition of the "professional" side of the graduate-professional label. What does it mean today to train young men and women for church leadership and Christian service?

Our answer to this question should force us to reappraise the goals and aims of theological education *with special attention to what we think the church should be in today's world.*

By raising the "professional" question, I do not suggest

furthering the unfruitful distinction between scholarly and practical subjects. I am thinking rather of the kind of question asked so frequently these days in general education. Until today, the big question has always been content-oriented: "What *is* education?" But now high school, college, university, and graduate students are asking a different kind of question: "What is education *for?*" When translated into the area of theological education, this becomes a "professional" question.

If the church is primarily the custodian of the sacred tradition, then theological education will be of a certain type. If the church is regarded as an agent for social and cultural change, then theological education will be quite different. This is a "professional" decision of utmost urgency which seminaries and divinity schools have mostly avoided. It is not primarily a question of academic prestige, of raising standards, of accreditation, of clusters, of university connections, of curriculum revision, of teaching methods, of new forms of ministry. It is a question about the purposes which theological education should seek to serve.

NOTES

1. Owen C. Thomas, Professor of Theology, Episcopal Theological School, quoted in the Foreword to *Theological Education as Professional Education* (Dayton, Ohio: American Association of Theological Schools, 1969), p. ix. (Italics added.)

2. On academic gamesmanship, see: Christopher Jencks and David Riesman, "The Triumph of Academic Man," in *Campus 1980*, ed. by Alvin C. Eurich (Delacorte, 1968), pp. 105, 109, 112; Harold Taylor, *Students Without Teachers* (McGraw-Hill, 1969), p. 16; E. Alden Dunham, *Colleges of the Forgotten Americans* (McGraw-Hill, 1969), pp. 7, 23; *An Assessment of Quality in Graduate Education* (Washington: American Council on Education, 1966), Foreword by Logan Wilson; Kenneth Underwood (ed.), *The Church, the University, and Social Policy* (Wesleyan University Press, 1969).

3. Alexander W. Astin, "Responses to 'Spiro T. Agnew on College

Admissions,' " *College Board Review,* Summer 1970, No. 76, p. 4.

4. Melvin M. Tumin, "Some Basic School Ideas That Need Rethinking," *Princeton University Magazine,* Fall 1969, No. 42, p. 29.

5. "The Black Religious Experience and Theological Education for the Seventies," ed. by C. Shelby Rooks, *Theological Education,* Vol. VI, No. 3, Supplement (Spring 1970), p. S-13.

6. Robert Stevens, "Aging Mistress: The Law School in America," *Change,* Jan.-Feb. 1970, pp. 32–41; Alan Wolfe, "The Myth of the Free Scholar," *The Center Magazine,* Vol. II, No. 4 (July 1969), pp. 72–77; Nevitt Sanford, *Where Colleges Fail* (Jossey-Bass, 1967), p. 34.

7. *To Improve Learning,* Report to the President and the Congress, Commission on Instructional Technology (U.S. Government Printing Office, 1970), p. 11.

8. Leslie Gregg, high school senior, *Princeton Town Topics,* May 21, 1970, p. 27.

9. Charles E. Silberman, "How the Public Schools Kill Dreams and Mutilate Minds," *Atlantic Monthly,* June 1970, p. 83.

10. Henry B. Clark, "Tradition, Impotence and the Seminary," *Reflection* (Yale Divinity School), Vol. 65, No. 2 (Jan. 1968), p. 7; *Theological Education,* Vol. VI, No. 2 (Winter 1970), pp. 89, 146; Douglas W. Johnson, *A Study of New Forms of Ministry* (National Council of Churches, 1968), pp. 1–14; Connolly C. Gamble, Jr., *Continuing Education and the Church's Ministry: A Bibliographical Survey* (Richmond, Va.: Union Theological Seminary, 1967), pp. 116f.

11. The literature on the school as an oppressive system is substantial. The following items are typical: John Holt, *The Underachieving School* (Pitman, 1969); Jonathan Kozol, *Death at an Early Age* (Houghton Mifflin, 1967); Herbert R. Kohl, *The Open Classroom* (Random House, 1969); Ronald and Beatrice Gross (eds.), *Radical School Reform* (Simon & Schuster, 1969); Diane Divoky, *How Old Will You Be in 1984?* (Avon, 1969); John Birmingham (ed.), *Our Time Is Now* (Praeger, 1970); Marc Libarle and Tom Seligson (eds.), *The High School Revolutionaries* (Random House, 1970); Alvin C. Eurich (ed.), *High School 1980* (Pitman, 1970); Richard Shaull, "The Challenge to the Seminary," *Christianity and Crisis,* April 14, 1969.

12. Robert Dubin and Thomas C. Taveggia, *The Teaching-Learning Paradox* (University of Oregon Press, 1968), p. 35.

13. *Yale Course Critique,* published by the *Yale Daily News,* 1970; "Advice to Freshmen," p. v. A typical positive evaluation: "The strength of the course rested in Mr. . . .'s interest in his students and his receptivity to their suggestions."

14. Herbert R. Kohl, *The Open Classroom* (Random House, 1969), p. 75.

15. *Living and Learning,* Report of the Provincial Committee on Aims and Objectives of Education in the Schools of Ontario, the "Hall-Dennis Report" (Toronto: Ontario Department of Education, 1968), p. 14.

Classroom as Community

When seminarians complain nowadays, as they have been doing for years and years, about the lack of campus community, they are not referring to the fragmentation and tribalism of modern life. Most students have learned to live with the breakup of traditional structures. They are thinking rather of the routines of seminary existence which have a way of becoming unbearably dull, robbing life of expected curiosity, excitement, and joy.

I

It's not fun and games students are looking for, but common gestures of personal worth, honesty, respect, and mutual regard. And where they sense the greatest lack of these simple virtues is in their dealings and relations with their professors and in their daily classroom situations. It's not an all-campus commune they grope after or even a highly cerebral society of scholars all busy and happy in their research. They yearn for less classroom formality and more openness about what to study and why, they have a desire for more personal recognition as individuals and less academic ranking, a need to see professors and administrators as human beings with all their oddities and quirks, a reaching out after mutual understanding in an

THEOLOGY TODAY, XXIX (1972), 394–401.

atmosphere of acceptance and nonjudgmental trust.

All they are saying is to give common humaneness a chance. They want their teachers to relate to them not only as scholars but as humans. They think their instructors could try a little tenderness, maybe a little profanity on occasions, maybe a confession of failure, or an outburst of pure pleasure about something. Teachers, I think—and I include myself at the top of the list—have been so busy teaching their subjects that they have little time for their students. This is especially the case with the researchers on the faculty. As the old joke has it, with one professor saying to a colleague as they enter the library, "A campus would be a great place to live if it weren't for the students."

Much of the current controversial literature on new educational forms has to do with the emerging interrelation between teacher and student. In addition, the sensitivity movement, the youth subculture, the political and antiwar protests, the black identity movement, women's liberation, the reduction of the legal voting age, the commune movement, the establishment of free schools—all these and many other factors converge on a new compelling awareness of what the teaching-learning experience can and ought to be.[1]

II

One evidence of student concern for more personal communication with professors can be found in the growing body of material relating to student evaluations of teachers and courses of study. Almost invariably, two major criteria are mentioned by students: first, that their professors be prepared, competent, and interested in their fields, and second, that they show some interest in students as persons, spending some time in or out of class talking with them, counseling with them, listening to them, eating with them, and taking the trouble to learn their names.

Typical of this student evaluation of teachers, though per-

haps more blunt and brutal than most, are the following random samples from the directory given to Yale University in-
coming freshmen:

"Mr. . . . did not seem very concerned with the course" . . . "One
gets the impression that Mr. . . . has been teaching the course for
twenty years with little, if any, change in his style or content"
. . . "He was most unsympathetic to student suggestions" . . . "The
strength of the course rested in Mr. . . .'s interest in his students and
his receptivity to their suggestions" . . . "Mrs. . . . brought tremendous enthusiasm and knowledge to her lectures" . . . "Says he encourages discussion, but his style and the level of most of his remarks seem
to leave the class silent" . . . "Most people felt somewhat guilty taking
a course that was so much fun" . . . "Mr. . . . is a personable instructor
who is genuinely involved with his students' work and sensitive to
their individuality" . . . "Mr. . . . is a scholar first and appears to accept
the task of teaching only grudgingly . . . he holds no regular office
hours, and reaching him by phone can fatigue your dialing digit"
. . . "Mr. . . . is easily approachable and encourages students to have
lunch with him."[2]

A somewhat different but corroborative approach to the
importance of a more personally involved relation between
teacher and student can be found in some special studies made
recently on the so-called "helping professions." For more than
ten years the University of Florida at Gainesville has been
exploring "the principles governing the nature and effective
practice of helping relationships," including control groups of
teachers, counselors, nurses, and Episcopal priests (but keeping
in mind also doctors, social workers, human relations experts,
social action workers, school psychologists, public health directors, psychiatrists, rehabilitation counselors, play therapists,
sensitivity facilitators, etc.).

Effective helping personnel "tend to be people-oriented
. . . are characterized by a generally positive view of their
subjects . . . tend to see persons they work with in essentially
positive ways as dependable, friendly, and worthy people
. . . appear to see themselves as one with mankind . . . [and as
having] an essentially positive view of self." Helping profession-

als who take an "objective" view of their roles, no matter what their training or competence, are apparently not as effective in actually helping people as those who take a more "subjective" or person-directed view of their work.[3]

III

In my own fumbling way, I have been trying to arrange my seminary classes in recent years in accordance with some of these student concerns. I take their quest for a more humane educational environment seriously, and since the initiative should come from the instructional side, I feel some obligation to respond positively. There is little likelihood, I think, of creating a complete campus community in this day and age, but the classroom seems an obvious format with which to experiment.[4]

Hoping my experience may be of interest to others, I shall describe and evaluate two different kinds of courses given last year that tried to make a community of sorts out of the classroom. The first course was an elective of about 35 students on "Symbolism and Theology." Some of the standard conventions were followed, such as a syllabus and outline, a bibliography, suggested topics for term papers or projects, a list of questions and issues on the topic, and a few initial lectures to get things started.

Students had certain options: letter-grade or pass-fail, a paper or a project of some sort; teams of two or more were encouraged to work together, suggestions about future class meetings were solicited, and several unscheduled slots were left open in the calendar for class presentations. The students were a mix. Most were white, Protestant (of a dozen denominations), and male, but there were eight women, seven Roman Catholics, a black graduate student, a student from Switzerland, an Air Force chaplain on leave. About half the class lived *off* campus. Several, as I already knew (and later on discovered), were loners, used to staying to themselves and uneasy about making friends with anyone. The Catholics at first seemed unsure of themselves and suspicious of the rest of us.

My hidden agenda for the course, which soon became transparent, was to see if such a mixture of students could really get to know each other and their instructor in an open and friendly way, and whether this community approach would have any effect on the teaching-learning situation itself. The community goal, with some minor reservations, was a big success; the academic achievement, on balance, probably was more than in standardized classes.

We tried various kinds of common projects. I arranged during the first week for a picnic down by the lake at the lunch hour. It was optional but nearly everyone attended. We had a sacramental meal of bread and wine, and also cheese, cider, and apples. Everyone just stood around and ate, but I prodded them to learn the names of some classmates whom they didn't already know, and it was a chance to talk informally about the symbolism of names and naming. And since we were by the lake, we talked about water symbolism, putting together baptism and the "new name." The whole thing was not so didactic as the retelling sounds, and everyone agreed that we should try the picnic idea again.

We did. A second time at Thanksgiving on a cold, windy day, in a public park, with a bubbling cauldron of soup, and a chance to talk, while strolling to keep warm, about the symbolism of eating and thanksgiving (eucharist), civil religion, and the onslaught of winter, all very unorganized. And again at Christmastide, inside this time beside an open fire with a huge Wassail bowl and Pfeffernüsse. My prepared talk on the symbols of gold, frankincense, and myrrh got drowned out with spontaneous carol-singing. Since the picnics were my idea and optional, I paid for the provender out of my own pocket. By this time, nearly everyone knew everyone else by first names, and the Catholic students were almost ecstatic at being drawn into the group.

Keeping only a jump ahead of the class as to schedule and calendar, we arranged for some short films, a music program in the chapel, a slide presentation on death and dying, a pre-schemed confusion of conflicting notices for a class from which I absented myself (to see how students would react to "chaos"), a demonstration of sign language for the deaf, a panel discussion of James Dittes's "little-adult" construct, and a stage dramatization of the Apocalypse which in the last scene had lots of people, including the instructor, dancing in the aisles. Students were encouraged to bring symbolic objects to class for "show and tell," and reams of Xeroxed releases of all kinds were duplicated and distributed for everyone.

The releases which I prepared for the class were intended to provide theological "content" and bibliographic suggestions, and were offered as an alternative to lecturing. This device, while not altogether successful, freed us to use the classroom sessions for anything that struck us as important.

Whether the classroom esprit helped the learning process, it is not easy to say. But at least three things can be said: (1) the actual work done was certainly no less than in more formalized classes and for several students it was much more; (2) whatever was or was not accomplished, we had a good time together for a period of more than ten weeks—a somewhat novel if difficult-to-evaluate classroom experience; and (3) who knows, really, whether mastery of content is more important, educationally, than communal enterprises in which students express themselves as persons in a context of mutual acceptance?

IV

The second course was a team-taught omnibus on "The Life of Jesus" which enlisted the cooperation of a New Testament colleague, J. Christiaan Beker, and capitalized on the current Jesus movement. The point of the course, as announced in advance, was to correlate biblical-doctrinal views of Jesus with popular expressions found in films, biographies, music, and other art forms.

The registrar warned us of a large enrollment, but when the first class met there were nearly 150 students signed up. Such a big group required some readjustments in our plans. We set up fifteen small seminars to meet once a week with a syllabus of readings and with preceptors drawn from teaching fellows and senior class members. We arranged for some introductory lectures, prepared an extensive bibliography, and published our calendar of topics and presentations, with some open slots for student projects.

In addition to the discussion seminars, which were not uniformly a great success, we had a two-hour space each week for some feature-length films (*The Robe, King of Kings,* the Hungarian *St. Matthew's Passion,* Pasolini's *Gospel, Green Pastures,* Buñuel's *Nazarin*). We invited a colleague, Edler G. Hawkins, who directs the Black Studies program, to talk after *Green Pastures* on the "Black Jesus," and we had a Chinese-born professor in the Far Eastern Studies department at Princeton University, James T. C. Liu, lecture on "Jesus—East and West." A local team of "Jesus People" gave their witness before the whole class. We had a rock music festival of deafening decibels, a "Jesus wants me for a sunbeam" display of Sunday school materials, several student-made films and slide shows, and a concluding "Messiah" stage extravaganza, involving about 50 students and open to the whole campus, based on a tongue-in-cheek interpretation of Jesus by way of popular songs of the 1930's ("Someday I'll Find You," "My Heart Belongs to Daddy," "Stouthearted Men," "Love for Sale," etc.).

At the end of semester my team colleague said to me, "I really don't know how we pulled this off; when we first got into it, I felt sure the whole thing would fall apart." Some things never did get together. The readings and the films remained unrelated; some wanted more lectures, some less; reading and research got scant attention; our attempt to relate biblical-doctrinal scholarship and popular piety was mostly ignored by the students.

But curiously enough, even with such a large and unwieldy class, a sense of community quickly emerged and continued to the end. It was nothing like the community of the Symbolism class. Part of the mystique, I'm sure, came from the theme and the current youth-culture excitement about Jesus. Like a contagion, some students got involved when they saw that others were involved.

For the teacher, this kind of classroom format is just about ten times more exhausting than traditional lectures or discussion-type seminars. It is absolutely essential to work from an overload of preparation, with lots of substitute plans available. The instructor must stay ahead of the crowd but be able to back up and join the human race, to be free and spontaneous in remarks and comments yet with thoughtful insight and background content. Most important of all, teachers must show that they can accept and respect differing and even repugnant opinions coming from all kinds of students, not because of lack of convictions, or because pluralism means flattening out all truth, but because students are persons, and no teacher has the right to violate anyone's integrity and dignity.

I *don't* think that community classrooms appeal to everyone; I *don't* think sensitivity groups are the answer for modern education; I *don't* think theology can be translated into therapy; I *don't* think festivity is a substitute for intellectual reflection; I *don't* think films and happenings contain more content than books or scholarly articles; I *don't* think every student wants to be exposed to others and shouldn't be forced to do so against his or her will.

As one student said to me after the Symbolism course, when I told her we had missed her at several of the sessions, "Well, you know, some of us aren't that excited by the enthusiasm of an in-group." I think I know what she meant, for I was that kind of student myself. But for those who do want some show of common humanity, and their number increases every year, the classroom offers a built-in format just waiting for imaginative reform.

V

I conclude with three quotations which say what I want to say about the problems of contemporary education. The implications for theological education, though indirect, are in my judgment inescapable.

First, an extravagant, preposterous, radical statement about educational myths that still claim the allegiance of many teachers:

The teaching business has generated dozens of superstitions. Among the more intriguing of these are the beliefs that people learn most efficiently when they are taught in an orderly, sequential, and systematic manner; that one's knowledge of anything can be "objectively" measured; and even that the act of "teaching" significantly facilitates what is known as "learning." By far the most amusing of all our superstitions is the belief, expressed in a variety of ways, that the study of literature and other "humanistic" studies will result in one's becoming a more decent, liberal, tolerant, and civilized human being. (*The Soft Revolution,* by Neil Postman and Charles Weingartner, Dell Publishing Co., 1971, p. 38.)

Second, a statement from a sociologist about his, and my, goals for education, adopted from the Pennsylvania State Quality Education Project:

Quality education should help every student to acquire: (1) the greatest possible understanding of himself or herself and an appreciation of his or her worthiness as a member of society; (2) understanding and appreciation of persons belonging to different social, cultural, and ethnic groups; (3) a positive attitude toward school and toward the learning process. ("Some Basic School Ideas that Need Re-thinking," by Melvin M. Tumin, *Princeton University Magazine,* Fall 1969, No. 76, p. 34.)

Third, an excerpt from an interview by an editor with an educational researcher:

Frank McLaughlin: "Is there any one thing that you would like to see happen or that you predict might happen to help schools become humane institutions?"

Arthur Combs: "I think your question runs directly contrary to what I'm convinced is the final solution. We keep looking for something, some gimmick that will make the difference, and I'm convinced that you're not going to change American education until you change the teachers. The change must occur in the hearts, understanding, thinking, beliefs, the values of the people who are running the business. We found in our research that there's no such thing as a good method or right method of teaching." ("Conversation: Two Humanists," *Media and Methods*, Dec. 1971, p. 29.)

NOTES

1. The literature on the current student mood as it pertains to education is extensive, and I have tried to assess some of it in previous articles, e.g., "Education in General and Theological Education" and "The Student as Person," *Theology Today*, Jan. 1971, pp. 434ff., and Jan. 1972, pp. 395ff.; cf. also "The Seminarian and Self-Directed Study," *Princeton Seminary Bulletin*, March 1971, pp. 69ff., and "Technology and Tradition," in *The New Teachers*, edited by Don M. Flournoy (Jossey-Bass, 1972), pp. 50ff.

2. *Yale Course Critique 1970*, published by the *Yale Daily News*. In "Advice to Freshmen," the *Critique* says to "select courses by considering the teaching ability of the professor rather than the specific content of the course." See also Gertrude M. Lewis, *The Evaluation of Teaching* (National Education Association, 1966); Kenneth E. Eble, *The Recognition and Evaluation of Teaching* (Salt Lake City; Project to Improve College Teaching, 1970); Milton Hildebrand, Robert C. Wilson, Evelyn R. Dienst, *Evaluating University Teaching* (Berkeley: University of California, 1971). (The last two items contain extensive bibliographies.)

3. Arthur W. Combs *et al.*, *Florida Studies in the Helping Professions*, University of Florida Monographs, Social Sciences No. 37. (University of Florida Press, 1970), pp. 72–74. "The future pastor should become increasingly familiar with himself, with the structure of his own perceptual world. . . . The effective pastor is the one who perceives in a certain way rather than the one who possesses a corpus of professional knowledge, psychiatric or theological" (pp. 46f.). See also *The Helping Relationship Sourcebook*, ed. by D. L. Avila, A. W. Combs, and W. W. Purkey (Allyn and Bacon, 1971), 412 pp.

4. My own seminary has a somewhat spotted record on building a campus community. Although geographically unified, the campus was split asunder in 1929 over the fundamentalist controversy, and

the scars and wounds lasted for a generation. In 1952 when the Campus Center building was dedicated, an impressively inscribed tablet was installed in the entrance foyer, carrying some majestic words from the mind of the then-president, John A. Mackay. "This building erected by the sacrificial gifts of many alumni and friends of Princeton Theological Seminary is dedicated to the creation on this campus of a Christian community, whose members, drawn from diverse lands and churches, shall serve in all the world the one church which is Christ's body." The brave vision, alas, can hardly be said to have been realized. Students in recent years voted to remove a similar statement from the annual student *Handbook*, not because they rejected the vision but because they objected to its pretensions. Now, in the 1972–73 edition of the *Handbook*, the statement on "Princeton Seminary as a Christian Community" has been restored.

Where Are the People?

People-related professions, such as teaching, the ministry, and politics, assume the importance of keeping in touch with their constituency. Teachers, preachers, and politicians must know *who* their people are and *where* they are. There's an old saying that to teach John and Mary arithmetic, you must not only know arithmetic, you must know John and Mary. The ministry, as with all helping professions, depends on personal relationships. Politicians know all too well that to get elected, and reelected, they must go to the people—which means they must know who and where the people are.

In a presidential election year, when politicians are so much in the news trying to be everything to everyone, those of us in teaching and ministry may learn something about communicating with our own constituency. No doubt one reason why the political situation seems so confusing is simply that it is no longer easy to categorize the people as Republicans or Democrats, liberals or conservatives, rural or urban, north or south or east or west. We are a fragmented, variegated people, jealous of our individual and group independence, suspicious of government for the people, weary of political rhetoric, and unpersuaded by high-sounding platforms.

It may be that political candidates get elected not because of their stand on "the issues" but because they know where more people are than those who get defeated. A cynical comment, no doubt, but no politician can get elected who ignores

Theology Today, XXXIII (1976), 219–223.

the public, talks past them, or offers answers to questions no one is asking.

A familiar way of signing off a friendly letter or concluding a conversation is to say: "Keep in touch" or "We'll be in touch." To keep in touch with our clientele, our audience, our congregation, whoever they are out there somewhere—this is surely imperative for those whose reason for existence depends on knowing where the people are.

I

Those of us in theology, religious studies, ministry, and church come under special obligation to be in touch with our people. We think of ourselves as in some sense "servants," "witnesses," "apostles" of the truth. Presumably, we speak *"from* faith *to* faith" (Rom. 1:17). But alas, all too often we are "unprofitable servants" either by pandering to the public, a sin we readily attribute to politicians, advertisers, and hucksters, or by being out of touch with our people, in which case we may have much to say but no one listens.

Not to know where the people are, to ignore them and pretend they don't exist, or to talk around them while talking mostly to ourselves—this is a subtler form of professional malpractice that deserves some attention. Two significant examples may be noted.

(1) There is a growing awareness at the present time that much of the business of biblical scholarship is simply unrelated to where the people are. The complicated apparatus of historical critical methodology apparently makes little impact on church people or those who might be expected to be interested in the Bible. And many biblical scholars themselves seem not to care, since they mostly study and write for other scholars and for the learned societies. Seminarians dutifully learn all about the various critical schools, because that's what their professors are themselves involved in, but those who go into the parish ministry confess that very little of this training gets translated into preaching. There is no discernible wave of expository

preaching today and no evidence that enlightened scholarship has illuminated the text so that the Word of God speaks clearly and unambiguously to our times.

The problem is not with preaching, but with teaching. The biblical professors in seminaries and religion departments have become trapped in the critical maze of their own discipline. They talk to and for themselves but for almost no one else. Fascinating as the game may be to the expert, the specialist, and the researcher, it often looks to those on the outside as "the Rube Goldberg school of scholarship," to use Roland M. Frye's caustic figure of speech.

But it isn't only outsiders who are raising questions about the irrelevancy of biblical studies. Several prominent and reputable names within the field can be cited. Walter Wink in his perceptive little tract, *The Bible in Human Transformation* (Fortress Press, 1973), speaks of "a chorus of voices raised in the name of God and humanity against a form of scholarship gone to seed." Biblical studies, he suggests, are meant "so to interpret the Scriptures that the past becomes alive and illumines our present with new possibilities for personal and social transformation." But if this is so, then we must say that "historical biblical criticism is bankrupt," and that, in fact, the net result of much study and research is to reduce the Bible to "a dead letter." Included in Wink's reasons for this state of affairs is the separation of biblical studies in seminaries and religion departments from "a vital community" of seekers and believers. It is not at all obvious that biblical studies are "from faith," nor are they addressed "to faith."

Two others in this "chorus of voices" are James M. Robinson of Claremont, writing on "The Future of New Testament Theology," in *Religious Studies Review* (Jan. 1976), and Paul S. Minear of Yale in his brief but provocative essay, "Ecumenical Theology—Profession or Vocation?" (THEOLOGY TODAY, April 1976). There are others, and the outcry is of such crucial importance that we hope to return to it again in a future issue. [See "Symposium on Biblical Criticism," THEOLOGY TODAY, XXXIII, 1977, 354–367.]

(2) Our second example of religious studies losing touch with where the people are is a somewhat unexpected one. It is embodied in a rigorous critique of "liberation theology" by Jürgen Moltmann, the well-known Tübingen theologian. Moltmann's point is made in response to reading Míguez-Bonino's book *Doing Theology in a Revolutionary Situation* (Fortress, 1975), and is printed as "An Open Letter to José Míguez-Bonino" in *Christianity and Crisis* (March 29, 1976). Primarily directed at Latin American and third world liberation movements, the critique at many points applies to other sorts of liberation theologies.

It is ironic, as Moltmann sees it, that while liberationists think they are speaking and acting on behalf of "the people," they are in fact often as isolated as the biblical scholars from a "vital community." There is no question that all societies could use some socioeconomic reformation, even revolution. But we must never forget that the "subject" of such liberationist concern is "the oppressed, exploited people themselves." Now what happens when the liberators are out of touch with those who need liberation?

The intellectuals and the students are certainly not the subject. They can at most throw the revolutionary sparks into the dried-up and parched woods. But if the people are not "burning" and do not rise up, the most beautiful sparks are of no use. The sparks then become sectarian candles around which elite circles gather ceremoniously in order to confirm themselves.

Working people who punch time clocks are not likely to take kindly to students and professors who are free to cut classes, protest, demonstrate, and riot *in* public *for* the public. Sometimes, in Moltmann's quaint analogy, the locomotive tears loose from the coaches in its urge to move forward. "It seems more important," he observes, "to maintain a connection with the people than to travel alone into the paradise of the future. It is more important to live and work in and with the people than to relish the classless society in correct theories."

A similar kind of critique can be found in Julius Lester's

review of the anthology *The Black Experience in Religion,* edited by C. Eric Lincoln (Doubleday, 1974). Lester teaches Afro-American Studies at the University of Massachusetts at Amherst, and his review appeared in *Christianity and Crisis* (March 31, 1975). "Black theological thought," says Lester, "is little more than political polemics in religious language."

The issue is not racial justice, liberation, or the need for black identity and integrity—all indisputable goals. The problem is that many black theologians are out of touch with their own constituency. They are talking mostly among themselves, just like the biblical scholars and the third world liberationists.

Despite the ardent wishes of black theologians, blackness is not a spiritual value but a psycho-political attitude which has arisen in reaction to white racism. To embrace it is to affirm one's relationship to white society and, unconsciously, admit that one's life is wholly defined by that society. Ultimately, it is to deny that blacks have souls of their own. To reduce the message of the Gospels (which is not social revolution) to black nationalism (and that is all black theology is) is irresponsible.

As Lester sees it, the black "vital community" of religious experience (cf. the spiritual—"If anybody asks you who I am/ Tell 'em I'm a child of God") is being ignored and bypassed by many black theologians. The irony, once more, is plain but painful. Biblical scholars entrusted with communicating the living Word of God, talking mostly among themselves; liberators unable to muster a quorum; black theologians forgetful of the religious experience of their own people. And all three believe they know who and where the people are and what is good for them.

II

Where the people *are* is, of course, not where they *ought to be.* Richard M. Nixon was quite happy to accept the mandate of the people, just as they were, without confronting or challenging them in any way. In marked contrast, the biblical prophetic tradition implies that the true prophet not only stays in touch with the people but, in God's name, reminds them of their past and provokes them toward their appointed destiny.

We need many more radical biblical scholars who will translate the Scriptures for the people of today, as Augustine, Luther, and Barth did for their day. We need all the liberationist theologians we can find who will stay in touch with the people where they are and, like Moses, lead them out of bondage, through the wilderness, and toward the promised land.

Staying in touch with the people where they are is not the criterion of gospel truth. As always, we must find that in Jesus, the personification of God's will for humanity. But those of us who are teachers and preachers of the Word made flesh may profitably study that intriguing passage in John's Gospel which anticipates the cross and reflects the evangelist's concern to italicize the incarnation:

> While he was in Jerusalem at Passover time, during the festivities, many believed in him as they saw the signs that he gave. But Jesus, on his side, did not trust himself to them—for he knew them all. He did not need anyone to tell him what people were like: he understood human nature. (John 2:23–25, Phillips)

It is not enough just to know where the people are or even, as in politics, to go after and receive their support, acclaim, or mandate. Those in Christian ministry who serve the people must know what people are like because, through Christ, we also understand human nature.

The Pastor and the Prophet

In the Editorial for the October 1976 issue, "Where Are the People?" it was noted that "people-related professions . . . assume the importance of keeping in touch with their constituency." This applies, we said, especially to teachers, preachers, and politicians. But we also observed that "where the people *are* is . . . not where they *ought to be.*" Further reflection on this theme suggests a somewhat different analysis for those of us in "people-related professions."

I

In a less complex age, such as the one I grew up in as a seminarian, we generally understood ministry-in-the-church to include the combined roles of pastor, preacher, priest, and prophet. In more recent years, we have added the extra responsibilities of administrator, counselor, and enabler. But in the process something has changed, and a ministry priority system emphasizes one or two roles while obscuring others.

Take the "preacher," for example. Is preaching a first-priority trademark of contemporary ministry? Well, preaching is still a requirement in most Sunday worship services, and ministers agree they spend much of their weekly time preparing next week's homily, and they would spend more, if they could. But are there any great, outstanding, or significant preachers in American churches today? If we discount the mass media evan-

THEOLOGY TODAY, XXXIII (1977), 325–328.

gelists, Billy Graham, Oral Roberts, Robert H. Schuller, and a few others, can anyone compile a list of a half dozen provocative preachers? Contrast this odd silence of the pulpit with the '30s and '40s when great preachers were everywhere all around the country. Just to mention some: Oscar F. Blackwelder, George A. Buttrick, Harry Emerson Fosdick, James G. Gilkey, Teunis E. Gouwens, Charles E. Jefferson, Edgar DeWitt Jones, E. Stanley Jones, Harris E. Kirk, Halford E. Luccock, J. V. Moldenhawer, Joseph Fort Newton, George C. Pidgeon, Paul E. Scherer, Joseph R. Sizoo, Ralph W. Sockman, John Timothy Stone, Ernest F. Tittle, George W. Truett. At least as many more could be added, but isn't it a glorious and incomparable list?

Some of these were better preachers than pastors, but all would have agreed that ministry can be prophetic only when the Word of God is vigorously and uncompromisingly proclaimed. In the authentic biblical tradition, the prophet exposes the people's sin of religious infidelity, their myopia regarding the political situation, their confusion of rite and ritual with true faith, their insensitivity to the oppression of the poor, and their need for radical repentance and conversion. Prophetic preaching has always stressed this agenda.

If there are few outstanding preachers today, where else can we look for the prophets? A few years ago, we could have invoked the names of Kierkegaard, Barth, John R. Mott, Martin Buber, William Temple, Reinhold Niebuhr, Pope John XXIII, and many others. Who qualifies today as a prophetic voice in contemporary American religious life?

These are loaded questions, but apparently today "ministry" means mostly pastoring, that is, congregational caretaking. That may well be a very useful and necessary vocation in the contemporary church situation. But it does not usually give much prominence to either provocative preaching or prophetic challenge. The pastoral proclivity for getting diverse people to work together tends to overshadow the prophetic itch to disturb, irritate, or disrupt the even tenor of congregational complacency. To which it may be replied: to be a pastor nowadays is hard enough; who needs a prophet's mantle when a clerical robe is all we can handle?

II

The pastor-prophet typology is not just a ministerial-clerical problem; it applies equally well to the political and cultural situation in contemporary America. "Pastors" are everywhere (in politics, education, business management, scientific research, media programming, and consumer advertising); "prophets" are in short supply everywhere. The distinction is most obvious in the political sphere where candidates for office claim to debate the issues while the populace can't see much difference and more and more every year deliberately absent themselves from voting at all. In recent years, political parties, platforms, campaigns, and oratory all have made the pretension of prophetic challenge. But in our day and age, for whatever reasons, political strategists know that it is much more realistic to be "pastoral" than "prophetic." Prophets don't usually get elected to anything.

It may be that we live in a time, politically and ecclesiastically, when prophets are unwelcome, ineffective, absurd. In a perceptive article that starts off with the women's movement and ends up with the political situation, Garry Wills, Adjunct Professor of Humanities at Johns Hopkins University, asserts that "prophets are a scandal in democracies."

They are not representative. They cannot be controlled or called off by their "constituents," because no constituency sent them. They create their audience, and compel it. They do not follow or submit to it. They make a claim because it is right, not because it is wanted. . . . No wonder the prophet is feared. He cannot be bought off, or made to deal. There is no real way to stop him but to kill him. ("Feminists and Other Useful Fanatics," *Harper's,* June 1976, pp. 40, 42.)

If we recall the few prophetic voices of recent years, such as Margaret Sanger, Wendell Willkie, Norman Thomas, Walter

Lippmann, Adlai Stevenson, Rachel Carson, John F. Kennedy, Martin Luther King, Jr., Ralph Nader, we realize that "prophets" are usually rejected by the people and often demeaned, vilified, and destroyed.

On the other hand, "pastors" easily become leaders in almost every sector of society, and the more representative they are, the more they can cope with compromise, the more they contain their constituencies, the more they assume that "all is OK," then the more they are needed and welcomed in our midst. And of course they serve a very useful social function. They protect us, as Garry Wills puts it, against "the oddballs, the crazies, freaks, and street people." And they encourage us, rightly or wrongly, to put our trust in majority rule, representative government, and the will of the people.

III

There is still another area where the pastor-prophet tension applies, and that is theology itself. James I. McCord's blunt declaration that "theology is now a shambles" seems as obvious today as when it was first made some years ago. With the death of Rudolf Bultmann, the last in the line of theological latter-day prophets, there are few voices worth listening to in the religious field and fewer creative ideas that command attention. If ministers and politicians seem reluctant these days to adopt the prophet's mantle, theologians are not notably eager to do so. And yet, withal, seminaries and divinity schools flourish, religious books pour from the press, graduate students continue to write dissertations, scholars' guilds debate the issues, and there is probably as much organized theological activity around and about as ever.

But the evidence suggests that theology in our midst is mostly of a "pastoral" caliber. That is not to downgrade it but to describe it. To be "pastoral" in theology means to get things together into a working coalition so that persons and ideas can live together with mutual respect, support, and composure. Rough edges, undocumented theories, disruptive critiques, calls for repentance and conversion—all must be viewed with suspicion and carefully analyzed.

The result is that theology in academe today is mostly comparative and derivative, neatly structured according to approved procedures, solemn and cautious, prosaic and dull. The evidence? Look at the course descriptions in the catalogues of our theological seminaries, scan the annual programs of such learned societies as the American Academy of Religion and the Society of Biblical Literature, read the titles of graduate dissertations, sit behind the desk of an editor of a religious journal and see the manuscripts submitted for consideration.

IV

The problem is not that there is something wrong about the "pastoral" office, whether in ministry, politics, or theology. But when the pastoral occludes the prophetic altogether, then we are in trouble. For if we have no prophets, who will prick our complacency? Who will remind us of our heritage and destiny? Who will goad, prod, and disturb our easy consciences?

As Gregory Baum reminds us in his book *Religion and Alienation* (1975),

The prophets of Israel addressed the people as if they were involved in collective sin and suffered from communal blindness; the prophetic message was meant to raise their common consciousness, to make them aware of what they refused to look at, and to open them to the summons of the divine Word.

In his new book, *To Heal and to Reveal,* Paul S. Minear takes a close look at "the prophetic vocation according to Luke." He notes that the third evangelist was particularly eager to connect Jesus with Moses as *prophet* (not as lawgiver, much less as caretaker or enabler). What united the two, Jesus and Moses, was the whole prophetic tradition from Abel to Zechariah (Lk. 11:51) in which "rejection, suffering, and martyr-

dom" was the common experience. Little wonder that "virtually no one in our own day, whether inside or outside our own
parishes, actually responds to our work as if we were prophetic
revealers of God's mysteries."

Apostles
to the People

An epic chapter in modern Christian history is waiting to be assembled from the biographies of a dozen extraordinary pioneers of fifty to seventy-five years ago. From the turn of the century, 1900, to about 1925 and a little later, a steady succession of unusual emissaries provided spectacular Christian witness to untold numbers of people in many parts of the world.

We are not talking about that enormous cloud of witnesses, men and women, young and old, of every country and denomination, who girdled the globe about the same time as representatives of the great foreign missionary movement sponsored by so many churches. Their names, and their faithfulness and endurance, are written in the book of life. That, too, is a chapter that needs rewriting for our day.

We are thinking, rather, of a special group of about a dozen who were distinguished not only for their mass evangelism but more especially for what might be called their benevolent philanthropy. Here is a partial roll call:

James Emman Kwegyir Aggrey (1875–1927)
General Evangeline Booth (1865–1939)
G. Sherwood Eddy (1871–1963)
Sir Wilfred Grenfell (1865–1940)
Sam Higginbottom (1874–1958)
Sheldon Jackson (1834–1909)
E. Stanley Jones (1884–1973)

THEOLOGY TODAY, XXXV (1978), 33–41.

Toyohiko Kagawa (1888–1960)
Frank Laubach (1884–1970)
John R. Mott (1865–1955)
Sadhu Sundar Singh (1889–1933)
Robert E. Speer (1867–1947)

I

The message of these expansive evangelists was simple and direct. Christian faith, they all agreed, whatever its personal rewards in terms of religious assurance, also promised education, health, and social progress to all sorts of deprived and oppressed peoples. In our less romantic age, we may smile at this simplistic creed, sugar-coated with token benefits, thinly hiding a political and economic policy of western imperialism. Well, that may be part of the story, and the debunking of the foreign missionary enterprise has gone on apace in recent years. But it would be futile to impugn the motives of these apostles to the people. Their record of astonishing achievements is available for all to examine.

Though active just the day before yesterday, these extraordinary humanitarians are almost forgotten in our day. Often self-appointed and fiercely independent, these ambassadors to the poor, the oppressed, and the derelicts of society were untiring in their lifelong witness that Christian faith uplifts, enlightens, heals, and empowers all who accept the message of Good News. Well known in their own times, they should not be forgotten in our time, for they still stand as models of excellence especially in an age such as ours that belittles selfless service, mass evangelism, and ambitious programs of social betterment for marginal people.

What distinguishes this particular group from other mass evangelists of yesterday or today is the social and humanitarian conviction they held that Christian faith could make a real difference for multitudes of people in their quality of life. So they organized schools and colleges, they taught the illiterate to read and write, they provided health and medical facilities, they fed the undernourished, they combated epidemic disease, they introduced new farming and agricultural techniques, they gave outcasts a caring community, and—most of all—they held out hope to the hopeless.

In many instances they were the only ones devising such programs. No one else was doing it, not government, not university education, not the freethinkers or agnostics, not the humanists or artists, not the scientists or political theorists. The humanitarian movement of 1900–1925 was inspired by specific Christian principles, naïve and guileless perhaps, but conceived and carried out on a grand scale.

Today our mass evangelists, Billy Graham, Oral Roberts, Rev. Ike, Sun Myung Moon, are mostly interested in preaching their brand of the faith, soliciting decisions and contributions from the churched and the unchurched. They are primarily concerned with personal religious experience, not social or humanitarian programs for the poor and the indigent of society. Some are interested in education and faith healing, and all would doubtless say they offered their hearers a chance for a better life.

But the evangelists of the first quarter of the twentieth century, the ones we're talking about, seemed to reverse the expected sequence. They didn't usually ask people to accept Jesus Christ so they could receive promised educational or medical dividends. They appeared to be genuinely interested in helping people who needed help. It is true they also preached the gospel, made converts, and based their social programs squarely on their Christian faith. But unlike Billy Graham, for example, who says he is so busy winning souls for Christ that he has no time or inclination for social witness, these earlier mass missionaries were humanitarians first and evangelists second. Or, they probably would have preferred to say, their understanding of evangelism included social witness whether anyone was converted or not.

II

The dozen names we have listed were not especially distinguished as theologians, though they were often engaged in controversy. They began no new religions, sects, or denominations; they wrote no new creeds; they did write books, lots of them, that were read far and wide, but their ideas and their doctrines were all more or less familiar and conventional. They weren't interested in theological methodology or biblical hermeneutics; they thought the Christian faith was intellectually respectable, that the Bible was an obviously inspired piece of ancient literature, and that those who troubled to take Jesus and his teachings seriously were in for the thrill of their lives.

Perhaps we are straining to make something special of this select list. But in retrospect, they seem today more like visionaries than missionaries. They dreamed their dreams on a worldwide screen, they often overrode ecclesiastical and administrative bureaucracy, creating their own ways of doing things, working with great groups of people and even whole populations, and they were in their own times individualists, independents, and what we could call today "loners."

Some were striking in appearance (Booth, Mott, Singh) and gifted intellectually (Eddy, Laubach, Speer). But not all were so obviously endowed (Kagawa was half-blind; Grenfell was known to his intimates as "Non-Sequitur" because he could scarcely string two coherent sentences together; Speer's voice was harsh and rasping). But as a group, these heralds were charismatic exemplars of faith in and hope for humanity.

The special breed has not, of course, died out completely. In our own recent times, the successors of these turn-of-century Christian humanitarians can be spotted immediately in Albert Schweitzer, Dorothy Day, Martin Luther King, Jr., Pope John XXIII, Mother Teresa, and perhaps a few others. These, too, are remembered as charismatic persons, highly independent, unafraid of criticism and controversy, dreaming grandiose schemes for human betterment, sublimating what personal faith and religion they may have had to these wider programs of mass education, health, and welfare.

III

Assuming that many today scarcely know the names, much less the achievements, of those on our list, suppose we venture a few profiles in Christian humanitarianism. Maybe we can learn something.

AGGREY OF AFRICA

A small, wiry African, born in Anamabu, Ghana (formerly the Gold Coast), Aggrey attended a Methodist mission school and then went on to Livingstone(!) College, Salisbury, North Carolina, sponsored by the African Methodist Episcopal Zion Church. He received his A.B. degree (with honors) in 1902 and later began doctoral studies at Columbia University (he passed his comprehensive exams but never finished his dissertation). He was unusually well versed in the Greek and Latin classics, and he sprinkled his sermons and speeches with numerous tales from ancient times.

Aggrey spent his relatively short life (52 years) traveling back and forth between America and Africa. Twice he served on the Phelps-Stokes Commission to study education in Africa (1920, 1924), and he combined his talents for oratory, preaching, and teaching in what he regarded as his Christian service on behalf of better race relations between white and black. Africa in Aggrey's time was dreaming of something better than white domination and exploitation, and he thought of himself as providentially poised to act as mediator.

There is a pathos about Aggrey's life and career that can only remind us today of Martin Luther King, Jr. Both were keenly intellectual, both were deeply committed Christians, both believed in nonviolence, both gave their lives to further better understanding and cooperation between races, both were dreamers, and both were cut down too soon. Eloquent spokesmen for their own peoples, they were also widely criticized by militant blacks and apprehensive whites.

Aggrey's death came just when he was appointed to the administrative staff of Achimota College (Accra) which he helped to establish, and just when he returned to Columbia to complete his thesis. Yet with all the frustrations of being misunderstood, Aggrey's name was widely revered throughout his native land, which he called "Africa—my Africa." His picture hung in thousands of schools, and his wit and humor endeared him to multitudes of village folk.

Three Aggrey epigrams to remember: "You can catch more flies with molasses than you can with vinegar." "You can play a tune of sorts on the white keys, and you can play a tune of sorts on the black keys, but for harmony you must use both the black and the white." "I am anxious that Africa should be civilized, not westernized, and that the civilization should be Christian. . . . Only the best is good enough for Africa."

"LITTLE EVA"

In 1865, William Booth moved from Nottingham to London where, with Catherine his remarkable wife, he established the Salvation Army. In the same year, on Christmas day, Evangeline Booth was born, the "Little Eva" (the name was borrowed from *Uncle Tom's Cabin*) who became an Army "Commander" and then the "General." Also in 1865, Abraham Lincoln was assassinated by John Wilkes Booth, who with his father and his brother was one of the famous Shakespearean actors of the day. Apparently, if you find a Booth, you will be in touch with dramatic action. There were good and bad Booths, but for our purpose let us select Evangeline.

Nurtured within the Army family circle of her striking and dominant father, her gentle but determined mother, and a half dozen brothers and sisters, Little Eva soon learned the ways of street-corner evangelism. With her guitar or concertina, she sang the gospel songs, handed out copies of the *War Cry*, was one of the first women to ride a bicycle to work, and, dressed in shoddy, she appealed to and identified with the down-and-outer.

But the most effective era of her career, from 1896 to 1934, took place in Canada, Alaska, and especially in New York. This is exactly the time span for others on our select list of extraordinary humanitarian Christians.

Evangeline Booth was both an evangelist and an administrator—two vocations not often successfully combined. She could counsel with individuals and speak to enormous crowds. Her father was conspicuous everywhere he went by his patriarchal and prophetic appearance, with his long, pointed beard. Evangeline's own dramatic presence was enhanced by her red hair, the way she wore the uniform, and her vibrant voice (coached, we learn, by the brilliant film star, Nazimova).

A treasure from her London days, which she transported all over the world on her evangelistic missions, was the original crude wooden table at which William Booth had made his first Christian commitment. It bore a plate, reading: "God shall have all there is of William Booth." It always made a poignant and convincing altar call.

As an administrator, Evangeline Booth pulled the United States Salvation Army staff together and initiated extensive developments in all the traditional welfare programs. The New York office soon became the central headquarters for the Army throughout the world. Statistically, the Army record is almost incredible—established in more than 70 countries, working in 170 languages, with 17,000 evangelistic centers, and over 3,000 hospitals, schools, camps, and welfare institutions of all kinds. No other religious or social organization anywhere in the world can touch its consistent record of helping the helpless without concern for creed, class, color, recompense, or reward.

During World War I, Evangeline organized the Army's much-appreciated presence among the Allied troops, and toward the end of her long career she was instrumental in persuading France to abandon the infamous Devil's Island penal colony, and it was under Salvation Army auspices that the thousands of hapless inmates of the "dry guillotine" were repatriated.

During all this time, the Salvation Army was often ridiculed, vilified, and made fun of—even by church people and denominational leaders. For many, not familiar with the serious work of the Army, their only information was derived from Damon Runyon's *Guys and Dolls* and George Bernard Shaw's acidic *Major Barbara.*

Near the end of her active leadership, Evangeline Booth insisted that the administration of the Army be democratized. In this she withstood her older brother in London, General Bramwell Booth, but she had the considerable assistance of Gladstone in London and Rockefeller in New York. Her views prevailed; Bramwell fell ill and died; Little Eva, in 1934, was appointed "General" by the newly established High Council. Five years later she was "promoted to Glory."

Evangeline Booth could draw a crowd wherever she spoke. Once in a packed Madison Square Garden, a Vice-President of the United States said that the greatest man of the day was a woman! When asked why she didn't write her autobiography, she replied, "I won't write about myself, and that decides it." As her father before her had said, "I do things—I'm too busy to write about them."

IV

What we have tried to do for Aggrey and the Booths, thumbnail sketches at best, could be extended to include the others on our list of a dozen Christian humanitarians. But we must be content here with only a few identifying marks.

Sherwood Eddy of the "Y" and the Student Volunteer Movement circled the globe more than once, reported on revolutions in Russia and the Far East, announced himself as an "absolute pacifist," and toward the end of his long and eventful life was convinced, through psychic research, of personal immortality, so his last of thirty-six books was entitled *You Will Survive After Death* (1950).

Grenfell of Labrador, medical missionary and explorer, worked for more than forty years to bring some measure of comfort, health, and social order to the Eskimo and Indian peoples of a bleak and desolate land. He established hospitals, schools, child welfare centers, seamen's institutes, hospital ships, nursing stations, clothing distribution centers, cooperative lumber mills, a supply schooner. Knighted in 1927, he was an immensely popular exemplar of Christian humanitarianism.

Sam Higginbottom was an agricultural missionary or, less grandly, a farmer. He introduced revolutionary techniques into a country, India, that desperately needed more productive methods. As originator and moving spirit of the Allahabad Agricultural Institute, Sam and his wife, Ethel Cody (who wrote appreciatively of Indian women), became legendary figures and paragons of practical Christianity.

Sheldon Jackson comes somewhat before our quarter-century, but he can stand for all the others as a pathfinder, for that is what he was. Variously dubbed as "the St. Paul of America," "the wild horseman of the Rockies," "the missionary with the flying coattails," "the bishop of all beyond," Jackson traveled more than a million miles in the American northwest and in Alaska. He established more than a hundred frontier churches, schools, and health centers. Among other things, he introduced the reindeer into Alaska by importing them from Russia, Norway, and Lapland. Short of stature and frail in health, he infuriated his denominational superiors by doing things his way. All agreed that he was Christ's fool in Seward's folly.

E. Stanley Jones was a missionary entrepreneur. From Gandhi and Rabindranath Tagore, he adapted the Ashram formula for Christian purposes and created in several north India centers what we would call Christian communes. His Round Table Conference extended the format to include non-Christians, and his later interest in the "Federated" church plan was another attempt at innovative dialogue. Jones's book *The Christ of the Indian Road* (1925) was especially popular among high-caste and educated Indians, to whom his ministry was mostly directed. Suspicious of institutional and western-ized forms of Christianity, he insisted that Jesus was the guru, not the missionary, and that Indian Christians should carry over their native culture into their new faith and life. Later, Jones expanded his outreach to include social programs for the poor, such as mobile dispensary trucks, and he argued that Christianity was the only "answer" to communism. Elected a Methodist bishop during a return trip to America, he quickly resigned so he could continue his evangelistic work in India and elsewhere. A pacifist and an advocate of home rule for India, Jones was often criticized by British government officials and American missionaries, but his influence on behalf of a native and indigenous Indian Christianity was incalculable.

Toyohiko Kagawa became a Christian at the age of fifteen when he prayed: "O God, make me like Jesus." In the years that followed, his prayers were answered, as he went about doing good, preaching to the poor, living for ten years with the slum derelicts in Kobe, Japan, and later establishing labor coop-eratives, farmer unions, nurseries, and social welfare centers of all kinds. When a newspaper ran a competition for the ten greatest names in Japanese history, Kagawa was at the top, and the only Christian mentioned. Yet in Japan he was not always honored, because he tended to bypass the institutional churches. When in English he spoke of "denominations," his listeners thought he said "damnations." He replied: "They are very much the same thing." He was, he said, not a Christian because he was interested in society's problems; he was, rather, a convinced socialist because he was a Christian.

Frank Laubach began his remarkable missionary career in the Philippine Islands, but within his lifetime he visited practi-cally every country in the world, including Afghanistan (off-limits for Christians). His ruling passion was to teach the illiter-ate to read and write. "Each one teach one" became his trademark, and over the years he prepared more than two hundred literacy primers in as many languages. Of his many books, some on specifically religious subjects, two early titles are indicative of his astonishing contribution—*The Silent Bil-*

lion Speak (1913) and *Teaching the World to Read* (1917).

John R. Mott was a perennial Christian optimist. His eloquent speeches, to very large audiences everywhere, always included the refrain that never before in history has there been greater opportunity for the Christian cause. An elegant, handsome person with bristling brows, he could sway whole masses of people, especially among the younger generation, to evangelize the world in this generation. A born leader, he chose to remain a layman, and his special appeal was directed toward the Student Volunteer Movement and the World Student Christian Federation. The recipient of the Nobel Peace Prize in 1946, he was at the very center of the ecumenical movement and guided the variegated missionary forces into the first World Missionary Conference (Edinburgh 1910), which later issued, through the first Oxford Faith and Order Conference into the World Council of Churches, of which he was an honorary President.

Sadhu Sundar Singh was born of a well-to-do family in the Punjab and reared in the Sikh religion. He had, like Paul, a sudden conversion and became an ardent Christian. He studied at various missionary schools but did not take to institutional Christianity. He began on his own to preach the gospel throughout India, and later on he traveled to many countries. Those who were deeply influenced by his witness were C. F. Andrews, Canon B. H. Streeter, Nathan Söderblom, and F. Heiler. Singh was a strikingly handsome person. He was an ascetic, a mystic, a prophet to his people. In 1929, in poor health, he set forth to visit Tibet, alone and on foot. He was never heard of again. The Sadhu (holy man) experienced trances, lived outdoors in extremes of weather, enjoyed affinity with wild animals, and lived what today would be called a life of "radical discipline." Several of his books were translated into forty or more languages and sold in the hundreds of thousands throughout the world.

Robert E. Speer served for nearly fifty years as an ecclesiastical Secretary of State. He headed the Presbyterian Board of Foreign Missions, and through his writing, recruiting, public

speaking, and administrative leadership he exalted the wider
mission of the church throughout the world. He visited every
continent and became familiar with both the missionary and
native Christian churches. Against the wishes of many at home
and abroad, he urged that native churches become autonomous
and independent of foreign control. Increasingly, he saw the
missionary possibilities of the ecumenical movement, and he
constantly worked for greater cooperative programs. Drawn
into the controversy over the uniqueness of Christianity and
other religions, following the *Layman's Missionary Report* of
1931 which suggested a more receptive attitude toward the
"non-Christian" religions, he insisted on "the finality of Jesus
Christ." A layman who was at home in the pulpit, Speer was
a ramrod figure of a man who gave dignity, vision, and imagination to the office of church administrator.

V

To recall this fairly recent history is to stir nostalgic feelings
and, perhaps, to engender remorse that things today in the
worldwide mission of the church are so different, so unexciting,
and so unimaginative.

The opportunities for mass evangelism at home or elsewhere are not what they once were, and we should of
course live in our own time rather than in some supposedly
golden age of the past. Yet some lessons can be learned,
and some carryover influences from our dozen Christian
humanitarians could be as creative and effective for our day
as for theirs. Such as?

Well, for one thing, a humane concern for the poor and
needy—stemming from Christian faith but not tied too closely
to conversions or decision cards. A global vision could raise our
sights from current parochial and nationalist perspectives.
Imaginative planning and action based on individual conviction and initiative would certainly be fitting for a generation
of young people who talk so much about doing your own thing
and being your own person.

Most of all, we can learn from this recent past that personal Christian experience, instead of being an end in itself, can become the motivation for daring commitment to human need. After all, we ought to know from one who spoke with authority that this is the essence of the matter—to love God and neighbor.

The Sacred, the Holy, and the Soul

These three common words in the biblical vocabulary and throughout the classic Christian tradition are, curiously, quite uncommon in contemporary religious language. Well, there are reasons. We have been instructed in recent years to blur the distinction between sacred and secular; the holy implies transcendence (not a popular concept today); the soul has been obscured by, presumably, more identifiable psychological components of the self. Are we any better off than our forebears who innocently raised their voices to sing "O Sacred Head, Now Wounded," "Holy, Holy, Holy," "Jesus, Lover of My Soul"?

Once upon a time, these three little words were universally understood as meaningful pointers to important religious realities. The words have dropped out of current use, but it could be that the referents they suggested remain as significant as ever—under a different vocabulary. The possibility merits some attention.

I

The *sacred* sets aside some place, time, person, or action and, as it were, "baptizes" it with special significance. It may be, in itself, very earthy, secular, or profane (such as water, bread, wine, a name, a mountain top, a birthday, a death, a hero, a teacher, a wedding, a family ritual).

THEOLOGY TODAY, XXXV (1978), 135–138.

The sacred achieves its halo because it enshrines and perpetuates creative and recreative power. We remember the
exodus because then God's people were liberated from bondage; we still read about Job because he trusted in God even at
the brink of total despair; we celebrate the nativity at Bethle-
hem every year because there a new beginning began; and
Pontius Pilate's name is spoken whenever the Apostles' Creed
is recited because under his reign Jesus Christ was crucified.

These sacred markers stand in the midst of secularities and
are themselves instrinsically neutral. Wine, for example, can
symbolize the precious, saving blood of Christ, but it can also
stand for gross, disgusting drunkenness. The sacralizing of the
secular is not an arbitrary rating system, separating élite quality
from mundane entities; it ensures that the separated realities
will continue to engender the initial creative, redemptive ener-
gies. To go back to original sacralities is to be re-born, re-
created, and re-generated. To "do this in remembrance" is to
"proclaim the Lord's death until he comes."

Are there any sacred things today? For many, especially
within the younger generation, the answer would include: (a)
nature and the environment, (b) personal and interpersonal
relations, (c) the proper nurture and function of the human
body. Not very religious, perhaps, but in many ways serving the
same purposes in our day as traditional sacred designations. In
any case, it is not true, as we so often hear, that "nothing is
sacred anymore."

II

The *holy* adds a dimension of mystery and awe. If the sacred
sets aside the secular for special purposes, the holy reminds us
that some things are ineffable and inexplicable. They remain
outside the sphere of understanding; they evoke a sense of
reverence; they are, as Rudolf Otto noted, "tremendous" and
"fascinating." The holy can easily slip into magic and supersti-
tion, but at its highest it becomes one of the essential divine
attributes.

> Thus says the high and lofty one
> Who inhabits eternity, whose name is Holy:
> "I dwell in the high and holy place,
> And also with him who is of a contrite and
>   humble spirit." (Isa. 57:15.)

In biblical thought, since God is holy, the faithful are also expected to be holy, and so "holy" is one of the marks of the church, and faith, hope, and love are nourished by the Holy Spirit—who, like the wind, can be felt but not seen.

There is something uncanny about the holy, simply because we do not invent or command it; we experience it, receive it, and marvel at its awe-full presence wherever it becomes manifest.

It is one of the oddities of our time that in the midst of so much secular, technological, skeptical, and hedonistic culture, there also exists a persistent fascination with the inscrutable and incomprehensible—in other words, with the mysteriously holy. We need only mention the current vogue in things occult, psychic phenomena, TM, Yoga, eastern mystical practices, Atlantic booms, and UFO's.

Those who listen to late-night talk shows are well aware that a favorite topic of discussion revolves around the dimension of the nonrational and the arcane. I have myself experienced in recent years a peculiar run of coincidences, what Jung called "synchronicity." At certain unpredictable times, unusual names of persons or places recur in groups of twos or threes, and then the associations stop as suddenly as they began. I attach no religious significance to these sporadic experiences, any more than I'm willing to denominate many other psychic phenomena as "holy." But if the word is uncommon in our vocabulary today, the element of mystery is certainly very much with us.

III

The biblical scholars have been telling us for years that the Hebrew-Christian view of personality is psychosomatic rather than dualistic. The self can therefore be defined properly as an animated body or an incarnated soul but not as body *and* soul. The latter, so we've been taught, is Greco-Roman psychology, and its effects have been mostly disastrous. So the body is the prison-house of the soul (Plato); sin has something to do with sex (Augustine); when we die our immortal souls float free, waiting for the resurrection of our bodies (Westminster Confession of Faith).

But it simply must be that the radical distinction between the Hebrew-Christian and Greco-Roman views can be drawn too tightly. Either that or we must admit that most of the whole of the Christian tradition has not yet learned its first elementary psychology lesson. For one thing, the biblical psychological vocabulary is exceedingly complex, as any concordance or dictionary will demonstrate. And for another, those of us who cherish the classic humanist tradition cannot imagine that the Greco-Roman perspective on personality was all that skewed. I happen to believe in "the resurrection and the life everlasting" according to the Christian gospel, but I am still moved, spiritually and intellectually, by the death of Socrates and his confidence that every human being possessed an immortal soul.

The plain fact is that in the Christian tradition the "soul" has everywhere been acknowledged as the best and most inclusive term to designate the God-given life principle that distinguishes the human creature from the rest of creation. The English word "soul" doubtless obscures the rich biblical vocabulary in which even physical organs (heart, liver, bowels, etc.) can function as emotional and psychic faculties.

I have been reading recently ("dipping into" would be more accurate) the two-volume set, *The Penguin Dictionary of Quotations* and *The Penguin Dictionary of Modern Quotations*. In the first volume (which goes up to 1900 and was first printed in 1960 and frequently thereafter), there are nearly 150 indexed references to "soul." Most of these are from English literature, though many come from Christian piety, hymns, poems, etc. In the second volume—of "modern" quotations (published in 1971)—there are only 19 "soul" references. In the classic tradition, "soul" nearly always carries a religious as well as a psychological connotation, and very often it implies some sort of immortality. In the modern references, these suggestions tend to disappear. Today, apparently, the word is only a relic of what it once meant.

But, as in the case of the "sacred" and the "holy," we are now being exposed to a secular variety of the classic understanding. I refer to the little book with the astonishingly big circulation, *Life After Life*, by Raymond A. Moody, Jr., M.D. (Mockingbird Books, 1975; Bantam Books, 1976). Here we have, not from the side of religion or English literature, but from medical research, impressive evidence that there may be something after all in the Greco-Roman view of the immortality of the soul.

Dr. Moody's evidence is based on the recorded experiences of several hundred people who were pronounced clinically "dead" but who later somehow managed to survive. The doctor was at first reluctant to use his data as a basis for affirming the soul's immortality (psychic existence apart from the physical body). But now he tends to think the evidence is compelling, and he gets even more positive response from Dr. Elisabeth Kübler-Ross. As with the "sacred" and the "holy," perhaps the "soul" isn't as dead as we thought.

IV

These scattered reflections are prompted by the current, widespread fascination with inner spirituality and mystical meditation which is probably *the* most lively aspect of American religion in our midst today. The departments of religion in colleges and universities, the theological seminaries and divinity schools, religious and theological journals, and the clergy in our mainline churches pay little serious attention to this popular trend.

It is true, of course, that many of the secular examples of the "sacred," the "holy," and the "soul" verge on the bizarre, the shallow, and the ephemeral. But surely those of us who believe in the rejuvenating power of the gospel are missing an evangelistic opportunity if we ignore these contemporary stirrings of the human spirit. That does not mean we should be uncritical; but we might just discern that many current fads can revitalize for us not only the old biblical vocabulary but the power and presence of divine reality.

As the Apostle to the Gentiles put it: "I am under obligation both to Greeks and to barbarians, both to the wise and to the foolish . . . I am not ashamed of the gospel: it is the power of God for salvation to every one who has faith . . ." (Rom. 1:14–16).

IV
TO LIFT THE HUMAN SPIRIT

Time Out

We appear to be living in a time of reassessment. Amid the confusing movements of the day, many feel the need for a respite, a recess, a referee's "time out," to do a little reflecting and restructuring. This mood follows inevitably on the disruptive and exhausting conflicts of the past decade, especially the divisive consequences of Vietnam and the political paroxysm of Watergate. There is a French phrase that applies, *reculer pour mieux sauter,* or as a pole-vaulter might translate it, "drawing back in order to leap forward."

The agonies and frustrations of the political situation change every day with every new disclosure. But the mood of "time out," of taking a good second look, seems inescapable in so many areas of contemporary thought and life, including the churches and theology.

I

Unwelcome as it may be, this modern mood of retreating in order to advance is reflected in some areas by way of debunking and demythologizing. We are taking a good second look at some recently instituted reforms that only yesterday promised so much. For example, in a single issue of *Change* magazine, which has itself advanced the innovative ideas of many progressive educators, three books are reviewed that question previously accepted educational assumptions. These books may be summarized as follows:

(a) There is no evidence that school reform can be expected to bring about significant social changes outside the schools. (Christopher Jencks *et al.*, *Inequality: A Reassessment of the Effect of Family and Schooling in America*, Basic Books, 1973.)

(b) Complete equal educational opportunity . . . will not eliminate the advantages (or disadvantages) of different socioeconomic backgrounds. (Murray Milner, Jr., *The Illusion of Equality*, Jossey-Bass, 1973.)

(c) Equal education can be dissipated by tracking minority and poor students into dead-end vocational programs or creating a system of superior and inferior schools. (Doris B. Holleb, *Colleges and the Urban Poor*, D.C. Heath, 1973.) (The three books are reviewed in *Change*, Feb. 1973, pp. 56–59.)

Reappraisal of educational theory parallels the shift that has taken place on most campuses. Those who hoped the student generation would lead the way into a new tomorrow of social justice and humane consciousness-raising now see students busy with their books and concerned about careers. Some who previously applauded youth's politicizing of education now wonder how we could have expected so much from so few, remembering what a small fraction of students bothered to vote in the last election.

Leo Rosten, writing in *World* magazine (Feb. 13, 1973, p. 8), desacralizes youth's halo in a bitter indictment. He characterizes the old New Left as:

demonstrating its love of free speech by denying it to others, its devotion to peace by using violence, its love of Love by preaching hate against everyone from professors to Presidents, its dedication to democracy by abusing it like Nazis, its thirst for education by wrecking classrooms and burning buildings, its sensitive soul by hurling obscenities, its superior thinking by silly slogans drawn from mushy ideologies, its non-conformity by playing sheep to unstable shepherds or demented demagogues.

Even the women's liberation movement, so recently launched with such vigor and conviction, has come under critical attack from spokeswomen within. Betty Friedan, that doughty matriarch whose *Feminine Mystique* in 1963 may be said to mark the beginnings of the current crusade, has turned against some of the sisters. In "Up from the Kitchen Floor" (*The New York Times Magazine,* March 4, 1973, and in her reply to *Letters,* March 25), she takes to task those who usurp the women's movement as a man-hating opportunity for lesbian takeover. (Two books attacking the movement on other grounds: Midge Decter, *The New Chastity,* Coward, McCann & Geoghegan, 1972, and Esther Vilar, *The Manipulated Man,* Farrar, Straus & Giroux, 1972).

And, to name only one other current debunking, John Maddox has taken on the environmentalist Jeremiahs in his book, *The Doomsday Syndrome* (McGraw-Hill, 1972). Tilting against those who fear the future because there will be too many of us, notably Paul R. Ehrlich and the authors of the Club of Rome's *The Limits to Growth,* Maddox thinks population explosions, for example, will be regulated by factors such as education and better health care for children.

When childhood mortality is high, the average woman's ideal family is a large one. Who will be surprised at that? But the consequence, paradoxical though it may seem, is that one of the most powerful ways of keeping the birth rate low may be a vigorous attempt to keep children alive. Education also plays an important part in helping restraint. In Latin America and Taiwan, as throughout the developing world, people with several years experience at school or university tend to produce smaller families. . . . For better or worse, social advancement and educational ambition have been powerful influences in stabilizing the population of advanced societies. Why should the developing countries not be similarly sensitive? (P. 63.)

II

For some time now the churches, the seminaries, and theological studies have been living in a "time out" limbo. Many bold programs of only a few years ago have already stopped short of their goals. There is little enthusiasm for the World Council of Churches or for COCU. The socially oriented theology of secular liberals has produced meager results. And the mood of nervous exhaustion casts gloomy shadows in many places.

During the dark days of World War II, some British church leaders asked Karl Barth what he would say to the churches if he were in London. Barth addressed a short open letter to the British church leaders which was broadcast over the BBC. He said, in part:

> Why are you not saying what you ought to say, and saying it with power and eloquence? Why don't you force us to pay attention to you and listen to you? We should like to see you less timid, more consistent, bolder. We often have the impression that you are afraid—of what really? And you spread so little light and joy around you. When you make yourselves heard, it is usually with cares and complaints, lamentations, and accusations.

Today, as in times past, there may be much to be gloomy about. Deeply committed religious people apparently tend also to be deeply prejudiced, particularly as anti-Semitic, according to the Glock and Stark report. Clergy often complain that their social action sermons fall on deaf lay ears, but the evidence indicates that very few preach such sermons and for the most part no clear position is taken. Those who work for change within church structures usually get little support and often leave in despair. Billy Graham publicly eschews the role of Old Testament prophet and interprets his ministry as calling the uncommitted to Christ.

It is in this context, and much more of the same that could be documented, that we must read Dean M. Kelley's probing study on the growth of conservative churches. As I have already noted, "Dean Kelley's book serves the constructive, if painful, purpose of reminding those who are *not* in the conservative camp that they are remote from the very resources they seek to marshal for their social and ecumenical crusades." If the leaders, in church, seminary, or theology, are to lead, they must get in touch with the people—wherever they are, whoever they are, whatever they believe. Here again, many of us will need to back up and take time out if we want to move ahead.

A current illustration of this need for reassessment, and a reassuring one in many ways, is the new book by Andrew M. Greeley, *Unsecular Man: The Persistence of Religion* (Schocken Books, 1972). Greeley's vantage point is the sociology of religion, and he insists that in spite of the eloquent doomsayers, religion in America is alive and well. The theological and biblical content of what passes for popular religion may not be very sophisticated, but there is plenty of religion around, and it is found in some unlikely places. Places like the college and university campuses, for example, which the liberal theologians and secular seers have been *mis*reading for a long time.

Greeley's thesis, that religion is as prevalent as ever, rests upon two "empirical" observations: "(1) The available statistical data simply *do not* indicate a declining religiousness in the United States. (2) The resurgence of bizarre forms of the sacred on the secular university campus has now persisted long enough that it cannot simply be written off as a passing fashion." (P. 7.)

Secular man, to the extent that he exists, may say that he no longer needs to experience the sacred, that he can maintain contact with himself, his community, and his world by purely rationalistic and scientific means. It is, then, not so surprising that witchcraft should be flourishing, that Buffy Sainte-Marie sings, "God is alive, Magic is afoot," or that Donovan's stories about the origins of the gods and the lost continent of Atlantis should be so popular with young people. The sacred seems to be playing the same function in the life of the new mystics that it traditionally has. It provides meaning and contact with the really real. (Pp. 159f.) (A fascinating collection of essays in further development of this theme has been edited by Andrew M. Greeley and Gregory Baum under the title *The Persistence of Religion,* Herder & Herder, 1973.)

A perhaps unintended illustration of Greeley's point, that religious academics are out of touch with their own students, can be found in the March 1973 issue of *Reflection,* the opinion journal of the Yale Divinity School. In the lead article, theology professor George Lindbeck argues cogently for "The

Place of Scholarship in a University Seminary." But in the following article, written by three seminarians, very different issues are raised. "What can be done," they ask, "to foster a ministerial education at YDS which: (1) ensures that all students know the basics of Christian faith, as well as the more technical pursuits; (2) unifies the technical and practical studies; and (3) emphasizes that Christian ministry is grounded in Christian faith?"

III

One of the promising constructive developments to emerge out of the current religious confusion, and not unrelated to the campus religious scene, is the revival of interest in the discipline of the devotional life. Not only is there a renewed concern for what used to be called "spiritual exercises," but the long uncritical assumption that all things religious should be done in *corporate* context is being challenged.

For the first time in a long teaching career, one of my seminary students asked if he could write a term paper on Christian solitude as distinct from Christian communal experience. He had just bought a few acres in Nova Scotia and meant to spend his vacations in relative isolation and quiet meditation. It is tempting to put down such a gesture as withdrawn, privatistic, even irresponsible. But it fits in with so much of the current mystical search, and of course it has respectable justification in Scripture and church history.

James Denney of Glasgow used to say that the test of doctrine was whether it could be preached. George S. Hendry, my colleague at Princeton Seminary, thinks that the test of a theological system is what it has to say about prayer. He notes that, with the exception of Barth, most contemporary theologians avoid the subject. (See his article "The Life Line of Theology," *The Princeton Seminary Bulletin,* Dec. 1972, pp. 22ff.) I think he is right, and I have often reflected that, with the exception of Bonhoeffer, most modern theologians have very little to say to the seminarian seeking guidance for individual religious devotion. Theologians, it must be said, are not very good models of the spiritual life.

But on our doorstep, as it were, and in the secular press and in every bookstore in the country, the phenomenon of Carlos Castaneda and his books of spiritual wisdom is well known and eagerly accepted. In the same issue of *The Christian Century* (March 28) that ran an article on the relation of Castaneda to Buddhism, there was also an article by Huston Smith of M.I.T. on the discipline of "the Jesus prayer." As Smith puts it: "What people today seem to want is not morals and belief, not even new morals and a new belief. They want a practical discipline that will transform them."

In her usually provocative way, Monica Furlong, the British journalist and author, picks up the theme of private meditation in her book, *Contemplating Now* (The Westminster Press, 1971). The contemplative person, she notes, likes solitude and seeks it. But the question arises how the contemplative can find what others enjoy by participating in a group. "Where will he find all that he needs to form the pattern of life, i.e., good and bad, male and female, saint and sinner, the hermit and the village idiot. Answer, and this is the simple mystery of contemplation, inside himself" (p. 16).

But, it will be asked, isn't all such mystical, private, contemplative solitude essentially *a*-moral, *non*-ethical, and socially *un*-aware? To that question perhaps an answer of Aldous Huxley, written twenty years ago, is sufficient:

Half at least of all morality is negative and consists in keeping out of mischief. . . . The sum of evil, Pascal remarked, would be much diminished if men could only learn to sit quietly in their rooms. . . . Contemplatives are not likely to become gamblers, or procurers, or drunkards; they do not as a rule preach intolerance, or make war; do not find it necessary to rob, swindle, or grind the faces of the poor. (From *The Doors of Perception*, 1954, pp. 36f.)

Such inward privatism must surely go against the grain of our corporate, communal, ecumenical, and societal presuppositions. For the past fifty years, at least, theology and church life have been set in corporate contexts. Theology, we assume, must be *church* dogmatics; worship and the sacraments, we take for granted, must be within the structure of the *fellowship.* Maybe all to the good, but is there no place for the individual-as-individual, no opportunity for one to be alone with the One, no "time out" Christian life style for those who—for whatever reasons—seek solitude rather than participation in groups?

It is not at all clear that the recent "corporate" emphasis in church and theology owes more to the Bible and Jesus or to sociological, psychological, and cultural factors. In any case, both church and theology in future will need to step back away from these uncritically assumed premises and take a good second look at the possibility for solitude as authentic Christian witness.

Ecosystems and Systematics

The reason for the writing of this essay may well be more important than the essay itself. The invitation to contribute to a Festschrift, honoring the name and work of a longtime friend and former colleague, is of course reason enough. But there is another reason. As the biblical people say, the "provenance" of the document is an important clue to its contents and tells us something about the author and how his mind works. Instead of leaving all this subjective rationale properly hidden from public view, as modesty might prescribe, I propose to display it at the outset and make something out of it.

Several years ago during a misspent sabbatical, I drew up an outline, and actually wrote out several chapters, of a book that never got published because it never got finished. I was then immersed in comparative symbolism, and I was eager to see whether the current multivalent approach to archetypal symbols could be constructively applied to the interpretation of doctrinal theology. I dreamed of "The Many Levels of Faith" as a descriptive, if not catchy, title, and I half completed a chapter on "The Harmony of the Spheres" which involved some research into the chain-of-being motif.

As I say, the project never saw the light of day, and so I am dusting off that unfinished symphony as a pretext for this present assignment. But it is not just dredged up from the

This essay appeared in THEOLOGY TODAY, XXIX (1972), 104–119, as part of a special issue designed as a Festschrift for Paul Lehmann.

bottom of a barrel (otherwise, I would not tell anyone about
it). The reason I'm making something out of this is to allege
that the conclusion which I drew from my research a few years
ago no longer satisfies me, and in fact I now think the same
data can support a quite opposite point of view.

Whether this switch is earth-shaking for anyone besides
myself, I can't tell without trying it out. It would be simpler
to settle the matter immediately by revealing the first and
second conclusions and let the reader decide. But that would
spoil all the fun, and I'm inclined to think that some quirky
perversity of approach might just appeal to the one whom we
want to honor with this issue.[1] So some of the background on
"The Harmony of the Spheres" will act as preface to the first
conclusion, and this will be followed by the occasion for the
switch to the second conclusion and its implications for the
task of theologizing.

I

Traditional apologetic theology has usually presented the
truth-claims of Christian faith within a context of meaning
structures. Whatever the mysteries of revelation, the paradoxes
of thought, or the limitations of language, the primary presupposition of theology is that the gospel provides a clue to the
riddle of the universe. Bible, creed, and liturgy have always
been taken as embodying the divine purpose in various kinds
of meaningful patterns.

In addition to the implied unity of purpose disclosed in the
divine revelation itself, theology has also gratefully exploited
the presumed grandeur and uniformity of the cosmos. In this
sense, "the cosmological argument" pertains not only to a
proof for the existence of God but functions as supporting
evidence for the meaningfulness of Christian faith.

The meaning of the revelation and the harmony of the
cosmos, when taken together, has always provided convincing
presumption of design and purpose, the interpretation of
which has been theology's major responsibility. In this way,

both Bible and cosmology could be invoked to authenticate Christian truth-claims.

Cosmologies, of course, antedate the Bible and are found among all peoples everywhere. In its fourth volume (1914), Hastings' *Encyclopaedia of Religion and Ethics*—which still endures as an exhaustive resource on such matters—devotes more than 50 double-columned pages to an extensive article on "Cosmogony and Cosmology." It includes discussions of American Indian, Babylonian, Buddhist, Celtic, Chinese, Egyptian, Greek, Indian, Iranian, Japanese, Jewish, Mexican and South American, Mohammedan, Polynesian, Roman, Teutonic, Vedic, as well as Hebrew and Christian views. Certain common features underlie these otherwise diffuse views, such as the implication of time and seasons, arrangement and sequence of the created order, relation of nature to human nature, and the design of the world as teaching religious or moral lessons.[2]

But it is more instructive, for our purposes, to examine in some detail the cosmological contours of two specific world views, and we will single out the Gothic image of thirteenth-century France and the Elizabethan chain-of-being of sixteenth-century England.

II

In his classic volume on Gothic art, Émile Mâle has convincingly demonstrated from original sources the unifying harmony of medieval culture.[3] Concentrating his examination on the High Middle Ages, when Gothic architecture was at its most advanced form in thirteenth-century France, Mâle has amassed abundant evidence of the interlocking spheres of faith, truth, and life which constituted the basic assumptions behind the medieval world view.

If we may speak of "the Gothic image" as a whole, we note that it is composed of a prior sense of order, symmetry, proportion, and arrangement. All things work together to form the whole, and the cathedral itself teaches like an encyclopedia.

The realms of nature, of learning, of ethics, of history, as well as of the Bible, are all neatly and completely interwoven. Nothing is omitted or excluded from sacred consideration. Every level of truth and reality corresponds to every other level. What is true of the animal kingdom finds its parallel in the kingdom of heaven.

Divisions and subdivisions in the scale of virtues and vices are paradigmatically related to the hierarchy of angels and demons. The biblical revelation is endlessly adumbrated as associations are made with extra-biblical sources. Bits and pieces are put in their proper place, for even the most minor scrap of created matter, of isolated wisdom, of the lesser beasts, makes its appointed contribution toward the total harmony. As the cathedral building itself suggests, all God's universe is harmonious, and everything joins together in aspiration to sing doxologies to the creator.

The history of the world from the time of creation, the dogmas of the creed, the lives of the saints, the structure of the virtues, the range of the natural sciences, the organization of the liturgy, the canons of artistic craftsmanship, the dispensations of the divine revelation—all were incorporated into the Gothic image and were continuously reproduced according to fixed standards of interpretation.

For example, and here we simply single out and rearrange for our purposes a few of Mâle's innumerable illustrations, a vertical nimbus behind a human head is everywhere understood as an expression of sanctity. But a nimbus including a cross is the sign of divinity reserved for the persons of the Trinity. The aureole or radiant nimbus, suggesting eternal bliss, belongs to the Trinity, the Virgin, and the souls of the blessed. The three persons of the Trinity, the angels, and the apostles are always depicted with bare feet. A tree or plant in sculpture, painting, glass, or tapestry implies that the scene is on earth; concentric lines mean the sky or heaven; wavy lines mean the sea or water. Peter always wears curly hair and a short beard; Paul is always bald with a long beard.

Such conventions were everywhere observed so that departure from them or attempts on the artist's part at freedom of expression would have been the equivalent of heresy. The rules of design were almost mathematical in their precision. The cathedral itself is positioned with its head toward the east where the sun rises in the sky at the equinox; the north region of the building points to the Old Testament, the south to the New, and the west is the scene of the last judgment.

Peter stands to the right of his Master, and in crucifixion scenes Mary is to the right and John to the left. The twelve patriarchs are related to the twelve prophets, twelve tribes, and twelve disciples. The four major prophets correspond to the four evangelists, and the twenty-four elders of the Apocalypse bring to mind the twelve prophets and twelve disciples.

Twelve is, of course, a mysteriously wonderful number, for it is the product of three by four, the respective numbers for the divine Trinity and the basic material elements (earth, fire, air, water). So we have a combination of heaven and earth, spiritual and material, God and the world, divine and human. So, too, seven is the addition of three and four, and thus earth (the body, matter) is made to give glory to things spiritual (heavenly, divine). Therefore human life runs through seven stages; there are seven virtues and seven sins, seven petitions in the Lord's Prayer, seven sacraments, seven planets, seven ages of history, seven days of creation, seven hours of worship, seven tones in the Gregorian mode, and so on and on. Eight, which is one beyond seven, gives the baptismal font its octagonal shape, for eight is the number of the new life which begins after the traditional stages are transcended, as in music the octave begins another series all over again.

Contrived as this network may appear to us today, the whole world of heaven and earth was put together into a book to be read for Christian and moral lessons as well as for information on life and nature. Every creature, every part of creation, everything, contains a divine thought available to the ignorant as to the wise. The sun and the moon, the changes of the seasons, the grain of the field, the grape and the vine, the birds and beasts, the metals and stones, the infant and the elder—all have many levels of meaning, and all are easily and readily interrelated within the harmony of creation.[4]

III

The Elizabethan chain-of-being provides us with still another harmony structure of intricate and elaborate design.[5] Sixteenth-century England echoed the successive levels of the medieval Gothic image but with a distinctive accent and with a native instinct for orderly arrangement.

The connecting links in the chain of creation, from top to bottom, owed their importance to their place within the whole pattern of meaning. Endlessly reticulated in Elizabethan literature, with prompting from the wings in the drama of the period, the chain-of-being constituted an accepted world web of hierarchical relations.

Two brief samples of the chain may be cited. First, from Sir John Fortescue (1531–1607), Chancellor of the Exchequer, statesman and jurist, who wrote of the chain in a Latin work on law:

In this order, hot things are in harmony with cold, dry with moist, heavy with light, great with little, high with low. In this order, angel is set over angel, rank upon rank in the kingdom of heaven; man is set over man, beast over beast, bird over bird, and fish over fish, on the earth in the air and in the sea: so that there is no worm that crawls upon the ground, no bird that flies on high, no fish that swims in the depths, which the chain of this order does not bind in most harmonious concord. . . . God created as many different kinds of things as he did creatures, so that there is no creature which does not differ in some respect from all other creatures and by which it is in some respect superior or inferior to all the rest. So that from the highest angel down to the lowest of his kind there is absolutely not found an angel that has not a superior and inferior; nor from man down to the meanest worm is there any creature which is not in some respect superior to one creature and inferior to another. So there is nothing which the bond of order does not embrace.[6]

The second description is from the *Natural Theology* of Raymond de Sebonde (Sabunde; d. 1437), the Spanish-born theologian whose work was in wide circulation in sixteenth-century England. The gist of the argument is given by Tillyard:

First there is mere existence, the inanimate class: the elements, liquids, and metals. But . . . water is nobler than earth, the ruby than the topaz, gold than brass. . . . Next there is existence and life, the vegetative class, where again the oak is nobler than the bramble. Next there is existence, life, and feeling, the sensitive class . . . the creatures having touch but not hearing, memory, or movement. Such are shellfish and parasites on the base of trees. Then there are animals having touch, memory, and movement but not hearing, for instance, ants. And finally there are the higher animals, horses and dogs, etc., that have all these faculties. The three classes lead up to man, who has not only existence, life, and feeling, but understanding; he sums up in himself the total faculties of earthly phenomena. . . . There are vast numbers of angels and they are as precisely ordered along the chain-of-being as the elements or the metals. . . . The chain is also a ladder. The elements are alimental. There is a progression in the way the elements nourish plants, the fruits of plants beasts, and the flesh of beasts men. And this is all one with the tendency of man upwards towards God.[7]

One of the interesting aspects of this chain is the way the top of one level is linked with the bottom of the next higher, and this connection can be either vertical or horizontal, natural, moral, or within the context of divine revelation. In each class there stands a primate: the lion among beasts, the whale among fishes, the eagle among birds, the king among men, the sun among the planets, fire among the elements, the oak among the trees, the rose among flowers, the apple among fruits, the diamond among gems, gold among metals, justice among virtues, the head among the limbs, reason among the faculties, man among the creatures, and God above all.[8]

The organization of all creation into a symphony of sight and sound, proportion and reciprocity, was regarded in the Gothic image or the Elizabethan chain-of-being as a necessary corol-

lary to the existence of God and faith in the divine providence
and purpose. All such harmonies include at least four common
characteristics. (1) They are *theocentric* in a normative and
cumulative sense; (2) they are *didactic* as devices for instruction in science and wisdom; (3) they are *implicative* insofar as
one can move from one level of reality to another; and (4) they
are *reconciliatory* in bringing together apparent opposites, such
as faith and reason, sacred and profane, heaven and earth,
spirit and matter, soul and body, God and humanity.

IV

The cosmological structures which I examined in some detail some years ago, such as the Gothic image and the Elizabethan chain-of-being, struck me at the time as representing a net
of interconnections that was no longer viable. Fascinating and
intriguing, certainly; but hardly relevant or germane for today.

The harmony of the spheres, which once we hymned in
praise, has turned cacophonous and dissonant. The grand alliance between earth and heaven, the majestic architecture of
the Gothic image, the homogeneity of a multifaceted perspective, all have fallen on days in which such presuppositions are
both meaningless and inconceivable. It is not that there is no
meaning anymore anywhere, or that cynicism has taken the
place of faith, or that *finis* has usurped the possibility of *telos*.
The plain fact is that contemporary culture has no confidence
in the traditional views of cosmic harmony as *evidence for faith*
or as *apologetic support* for Christian truth-claims.

The gospel for today can scarcely be good news about the
revelation of a mysterious world order in which, among other
possibilities, an ox (who has seen one lately?) can stand for a
huge beast, a sacrificial animal, the Jewish nation, an Evangelist, a Christian virtue, and Jesus Christ himself. The gospel,
so Bultmann has instructed us after demythologizing the biblical cosmology, is good news about new creation. However that
is proclaimed or structured, it does not depend upon any particular view of the world, even the traditional biblical view.[9]

The evangelistic and apologetic problem for today is not how to revive older harmony patterns to induce ourselves to believe in an overarching Gothic wholeness. That option, like the Gothic cathedral itself, is stone dead. The issue rather is twofold: first, how to disengage ourselves from the obsolete systems as gracefully as possible; and second, how to present the uncomplicated nucleus of the gospel to a fractured contemporary humanity without worrying too much about getting everything all together neatly and completely.

This was the drift of my thinking and the way my mind was changing ten years ago. As a professor of systematic theology, I was perhaps vocationally uptight about abandoning structures of all kinds in favor of free forms and pluralism everywhere. Yet it seemed clear that the eager search for tidy meaning-structures that inspired so many sermons, biblical studies, and theological discussions in years past could not be commended today. We have learned in the name of science, psychology, and the arts to claim less and to relax our grip on the whole universe.

This means that everything is up for grabs, that any view is permissible, that truth, reality, gospel, theology, church are all laid out in bits and pieces, that authentic meaning can be found in any one or more of the integers but not necessarily, or only, in all together in unison. Any particular link, therefore, can be as significant as the chain itself. Tennyson's sentimental reflection about the "flower in the crannied wall" still makes sense today not because it holds the secret of "all in all" (including God and the world), but because it has its own validity and ought to be gratefully appreciated as such without being artificially immortalized within some grandiose divine-human schema.

Many different lines of investigation appeared to converge toward this point of view. Books like Barrett's *Irrational Man* seemed to me to point in this direction. So did the theater of the absurd, abstract expressionist painting, and the new wave of films. I even tried my hand at a little book which sought to retain the deeper significance of symbolism while casting loose

from the larger cosmological meaning-structures. I felt somewhat vindicated when Harvey Cox advised, some years later,
that "we should oppose the romantic restoration of the sprites
of the forest."[10]

That then was the *first* conclusion, and while I still hold to
some aspects of that point of view, the reasons have changed.
The first conclusion, I thought, emerged out of research data
for various chains-of-being, and since the very idea of a chain
has become obsolete, I imagined the inferences once drawn
were now untenable.

It never occurred to me that a *new* chain-of-being was about
to be discovered and that it would almost immediately capture
everyone's attention. It is, of course, ecology.

V

Ecology is not a new word. Biologists and botanists have
used it for a long time as indicating the interrelation of organisms and plants with their environments. And of course conser-
vationists and nature lovers have been telling us for decades
that we are recklessly expending the world's natural resources.
What is new is the melodramatic realization, just recently
come over us, that ecology represents an implicative system in
which nature and humanity are mutually interdependent for
survival.

Water and air pollution, the pillage of mineral resources, the
increasing list of extinct or endangered species of birds and
animals, the far-reaching effect of pesticides, the wanton
dumping of industrial chemicals on land and sea, the overwhelming accumulation of waste, garbage, and junk, and especially the spiraling of the population explosion—all add up to
instant awareness of apocalyptic crisis.

What started me rethinking the first conclusion based on
the Gothic image and the Elizabethan chain-of-being was an
article in *Natural History* magazine, with the intriguing title,
"Ecology: The New Great Chain of Being."[11] The editorial
preface to the article quoted the passage from Fortescue which

was already familiar to me and which has been cited above under the Elizabethan chain. And the first paragraph of the article noted a contemporary chain effect of simple but frightening implications.

It seems that the World Health Organization some years ago in Borneo used DDT to eliminate the mosquito. In the process, certain predatory wasps were also killed, and since the wasps kept the caterpillar population in control, the roofs of the houses began to collapse because they were eaten by the caterpillars. DDT was also used indoors to kill flies, which in turn were eaten by the gecko lizard, and they in turn by the cats. So the cats died from ingesting too much DDT, and then the rats began to multiply, and with them came the threat of plague. In order to restore some balance in this disrupted ecosystem, new cats were parachuted into the region.

In the biosphere, where human beings and a million other species live, the energy cycle is regular and stable. Plants are nourished from the soil and transform the sun's rays into food. Herbivores eat the plants. Carnivores feed on herbivores and are eaten by scavengers. With decomposition, the nutrients return to the soil, and the process is renewed. That is, unless an intruder such as a chemical or human pollutant disturbs the cycle. As in the case with DDT, it is the scavenger birds, the eagles, ospreys, and hawks, which die out first because the concentration of the chemical builds up as it moves from stomach to stomach, and from level to level. DDT incidentally has been detected in the penguins of the Antarctic, thousands of miles from any possible contaminating source.

One of the baffling aspects of the ecological chain is the possible damage already done but as yet unrecognized. It is only recently that industrial discharging of mercury into rivers and lakes has been spotted in fish. Mercury poisoning can cause brain damage, and it is especially toxic in the unborn fetus of pregnant women. Massive mercury pollution has been found in Lake Erie, San Francisco Bay, the Delaware River, Lake Champlain, the Tennessee River, and in many other areas.

Surprisingly, it has now been found in the livers of the Alaskan fur seals. These wonderful creatures roam miles from land in the open Pacific Ocean.

Mercury, used in pulp mills and paper processing, is absorbed from the water by plankton which is eaten by fish and in turn eaten by the seals. Ironically, the livers of the seals are being used to make an iron supplement "blood booster" for humans. "You can just figure from this," said a biologist, "that there isn't any place in the whole world that isn't contaminated."[12]

The ailing environment has become a current crisis, as everyone now knows, because of our exploitation, destruction, and pollution of the very resources on which our survival and well-being depend. We can hardly be excused for pleading ignorance of the law of ecosystems, and our only salvation requires that we learn to live within the limits of the biospheric chain-of-being. This represents a *new world view* as comprehensive and inescapable as the Gothic image or the Elizabethan chain-of-being, and it is not a matter of contrived imagination and inflated metaphor but an empirical matter of fact. It imposes on us, whether we like it or not, a new systematic ordering and harmonious structuring which we can resist only by willing our own and the world's extinction.

The first conclusion, to which reference has been made, must therefore give way to a *second* conclusion. Chains-of-being are not so obsolete after all. The harmony of the spheres is not only a romantic reminder of a simpler and more credulous age, it is the only option before us. If previously everything appeared to be fragmented in bits and pieces with authentic existence found, if at all, here and there but not everywhere, now we must reconsider our pluralistic, discrete, and individuated inferences in the light of new evidence.

Ecology speaks of the interdependency of organisms and things within the whole system. Entities in isolation do not exist. What seems to solve one problem may create another worse problem in another area. What affects one segment affects the whole system. Ecologists cannot afford the luxury of specialization; they must be generalists. So a new commitment and compulsion to systematics is upon us.

VI

The ecological emergency of our day has reopened the cosmological argument. This may appear to claim too much for an environmental situation of great ambiguity. To imply that ecology is the matrix of a new systematics, as the Gothic image and the Elizabethan chain were in their time, may seem an extravagant conceit. But if ecological predictions of the immediate future are justified, and here numerology reappears with statistical vengeance, we may have no choice about the contextual situation in which future deliberations *in any area* are to be pursued. If everything is related to everything, then the "choir of heaven and the furniture of earth," to use Bishop Berkeley's quaint phrase, reemerges as an imperative to "get it all together."

Ecology suggests that systematics must become ecumenics. The Gothic image and the Elizabethan chain put people and things in their proper places, but the ecological network is more concerned with mutuality and interdependency. Etymologically, "ecology" and "ecumenics" are rooted in the same familial or domestic notion of togetherness. This among other things is what Marshall McLuhan means by the "global village" which has been precipitated on our day by the electronic revolution.[13]

VII

Two major implications for theology seem to me to issue from this ecological consideration, one having to do with order (and its opposite disorder and chaos), and the other with nature (and its studied avoidance in most modern theology).

Chaos and order accompany each other as night follows day, but the basic question here has to do not with the temporary ambiguities and transitions of the day, which may go one way or the other, but with the *ultimate* convictions of faith. If this way of speaking seems hopelessly irrelevant for many today, it is instructive to be reminded of the ultimate ordering of ecology. This certainly does not mean to regard existing structures as inviolate, but it does mean that it is not enough to "cry havoc" without some ultimate, perhaps transcendent, reordering in mind.

Peter Berger has incorporated this "argument for ordering" as "a signal of transcendence" which comes to us apart from the religious or theological spheres. He regards this "signal" as supporting religious faith, in a time when transcendence appears to have evaporated, but it may not necessarily be related to religion at all.

Man's propensity for order is grounded in a faith or trust that ultimately, reality is "in order," "all right," "as it should be." Needless to say, there is no empirical method by which this faith can be tested. To assert it is itself an act of faith. But it is possible to proceed from the faith that is rooted in experience to the act of faith that transcends the empirical sphere, a procedure that could be called the *argument from ordering.*[14]

As an illustration, Berger uses the commonplace experience of a mother comforting her frightened child.

A child wakes up in the night, perhaps from a bad dream, and finds himself surrounded by darkness, alone, beset by nameless threats. At such a moment the contours of trusted reality are blurred or invisible, and in the terror of incipient chaos the child cries out for his mother. It is hardly an exaggeration to say that, at this moment, the mother is being invoked as a high priestess of protective order. It is she (and, in many cases, she alone) who has the power to banish the chaos and to restore the benign shape of the world. And, of course, any good mother will do just that. She will take the child and cradle him in the timeless gesture of the Magna Mater who became our Madonna. She will turn on a lamp, perhaps, which will encircle the scene with a warm glow of reassuring light. She will speak or sing to the child, and the content of this communication will invariably be the same—"Don't be afraid, everything is in order, everything is all right."[15]

It would be too simplistic to argue that the mother-child experience or similar signals of transcendence are persuasive reasons for believing in order as against disorder. But "inductive faith," as Berger calls it, tries to look beyond immediate disruption to ultimate patterns of reality. In our own time of dislocation, when traditional orders seem so dysfunctional, it may be necessary to be reminded of the human propensity for order and our vested ecological interest in redressing what imbalances there are.

A second ecological implication for theology, beyond affirming order in some fashion, is the necessity for coming to terms with nature itself. What is needed is a new natural theology. For the most part, modern theology has avoided taking seriously what amounts to a whole empirical dimension. The influence of the Barthian and neo-orthodox biblical emphasis on special as opposed to natural revelation now clearly seems a one-sided and misguided attempt to magnify the uniqueness of faith.

Some are now proposing that our western decimation of nature has been an outgrowth of biblical thought, particularly the account of creation with the divine command that human creatures, the consummation of creation, "be fruitful and multiply, and fill the earth and subdue it; and have dominion over the fish of the sea and over the birds of the air and over every living thing that moves upon the earth" (Gen. 1:28).

In a now classic discussion of this point of view, Lynn White nominates Francis of Assisi as a semiheretical patron saint for ecologists.

I am not suggesting that many contemporary Americans who are concerned about our ecologic crisis will be either able or willing to counsel with wolves or exhort birds [as Francis did]. However, the present increasing disruption of the global environment is the product of a dynamic technology and science which were originating in the western medieval world against which St. Francis was rebelling in so original a way. Their growth cannot be understood historically apart from distinctive attitudes toward nature which are deeply grounded in Christian dogma. The fact that most people do not think of these attitudes as Christian is irrelevant. No new set of basic values has been accepted in our society to displace those of Christianity. Hence we shall continue to have a worsening ecologic crisis until we reject the Christian axiom that nature has no reason for existence save to serve man.[16]

VIII

A crucial difference between the Gothic image and the Elizabethan chain-of-being, on the one hand, and contemporary ecosystems, on the other, has to do with the matter of stability and permanence. In former times, no doubt, the implicative systems were regarded as inviolable, enduring, tamper-proof. But today the problem of ecology is the disruption of the balances necessary for the maintenance of the system in some sort of workable equilibrium. If previous generations could invoke the harmony of the spheres as a signal of transcendence and supporting evidence for faith in the divine purpose, we today are compelled to observe that the ecological imbalance not only indicts us for our rapacity but presents us with an almost irreversible apocalyptic prospect.

The cynics and the stoics among us, perhaps calling themselves realists, will take what consolation they can from observing that we can hardly be expected to reverse a tide that has been running for centuries.[17] As James Reston once put it, the holocaust may come not because of atomic power but because of sex power. There are just too many reproducing humans, and the ecological disaster may have progressed beyond the point of no return.

Unless there is another alternative, a way to redress ecological imbalance and reorder the disorder of our times, hardly anything else seems worth talking about. And unless theology can participate constructively in such an alternative, who needs it?

NOTES

1. I venture to observe that unconventional approaches to ordinary things is one of Paul Lehmann's trademarks. I first heard him address a public audience in a chapel service following a seminary "day of prayer." He read from the Gospels about Jesus praying for his disciples and the subsequent betrayal by Judas, and then he began: "Imagine Judas Iscariot as the answer to prayer!"

2. The article "Cosmogony and Cosmology" in Hastings' *Encyclopaedia of Religion and Ethics*, Vol. IV, pp. 125–179, is written by several authors; a more recent discussion of cosmologies is Mircea Eliade's *Patterns in Comparative Religion* (Sheed & Ward, 1958).

3. Émile Mâle, *The Gothic Image* (Harper & Brothers, Harper Torchbook, 1958); translated from the third French edition of 1913, *L'Art religieux du XIII siècle en France.* Bernard Berenson said this work was "the most illuminating, the most informing, and the most penetrating book on the subject." The Gothic critical corpus is enormous, but that is not our focus here.

4. "The thirteenth century was the century of encyclopaedias. At no other period have so many works appeared bearing the titles of *Summa, Speculum* or *Imago Mundi,* " Mâle, *op. cit.,* p. 23. Cf.: "Like the High Scholastic *Summa,* the High Gothic cathedral aimed, first of all, at 'totality.' " Erwin Panofsky, *Gothic Architecture and Scholasticism* (World Publishing Co., 1963), p. 44.

5. The definitive study is Arthur O. Lovejoy's *The Great Chain of Being* (Harvard University Press, 1936); a later and more compact discussion is E. M. W. Tillyard, *The Elizabethan World Picture* (Macmillan, 1944).

6. Tillyard, *op. cit.,* pp. 26f.

7. *Ibid.,* pp. 27f.

8. The Elizabethan chain assumes that order in the state parallels order in the natural world; cf. the Church of England *Homily of Obedience* (1547), and Richard Hooker (1554–1600), *Laws of Ecclesiastical Polity.*

9. "The cosmology of the New Testament is essentially mythical in character. The world is viewed as a three-storied structure, with the earth in the centre, the heaven above, and the underworld beneath." Rudolf Bultmann, "New Testament and Mythology," in *Kerygma and Myth*, ed. by Hans Werner Bartsch (London: S.P.C.K., 1953), p. 1. A more recent discussion of some particulars of this

cosmology is Robert M. Grant's "Chains of Being in Early Christianity," in *Myths and Symbols*, ed. by Joseph M. Kitagawa and Charles H. Long (University of Chicago Press, 1969), pp. 279ff.

10. William Barrett, *Irrational Man: A Study in Existential Philosophy* (Doubleday, 1958); Martin Esslin, *The Theatre of the Absurd* (Doubleday, 1961); Hugh T. Kerr, *Mystery and Meaning in the Christian Faith* (Toronto: Ryerson Press, 1958); Harvey Cox, *The Secular City* (Macmillan, 1965), p. 36.

11. *Natural History*, Vol. LXXVII, No. 10 (Dec. 1968), pp. 8ff. The literature on ecology has grown enormously, especially since "Earth Day," April 22, 1970.

12. *The New York Times*, Nov. 1, 1970.

13. For the extensive use of *oikos* and derivatives in the New Testament, see the article by Otto Michel in Kittel's *Theological Dictionary of the New Testament*, Vol. V. "The new electronic interdependence recreates the world in the image of a global village." Marshall McLuhan, with Quentin Fiore, *The Medium Is the Massage* (Bantam Books, 1967), p. 67.

14. Peter L. Berger, *A Rumor of Angels: Modern Society and the Rediscovery of the Supernatural* (Doubleday, 1969), p. 67.

15. *Ibid.*, pp. 67f. Unless we are to say that the mother is lying to the child, says Berger, we must assume that "there is some truth in the religious interpretation of human existence." Another dimension of order-chaos tension is the psychological. See, e.g., William R. Rogers, "Order and Chaos in Psychotherapy and Ontology," in *The Dialogue Between Theology and Psychology* (University of Chicago Press, 1968), pp. 249ff.

16. Lynn White, Jr., "Historical Roots of Our Ecological Crisis," *Science*, Vol. 155 (March 10, 1967), p. 127.

17. Among those who question whether the ecological imbalance can be reversed are Paul R. and Anne H. Ehrlich (*Population, Resources, Environment: Issues in Human Ecology*, 1970). On the other side, John R. Sheaffer thinks that wastes, for example, can be recycled as valuable land nutrients and that even the Great Lakes have a future (cf. "Reviving the Great Lakes," *Saturday Review*, Nov. 7, 1970, pp. 62ff.).

Social Symbols
and Christian Faith

THE MUSEUM

Upon my recent return from nearly eight months in Europe, traveling and studying under a Guggenheim grant, some impressions and reactions may be permissible. Since my project had to do with "symbolism and religious ideas," I write not about political or ecclesiastical conditions as such but about certain (to the tourist) very obvious social and cultural patterns which (to the theologian) also have religious application.

Everywhere the traveler goes in Europe there is a museum. Some sophisticated tourists, with *Fielding's Guide to Europe* under their arm, may deliberately pass up the museums in search for the best place to eat and the best spot to shop. But if you would see anything at all of old Europe's treasures preserved from past days of glory, you must enter the museums. There are hundreds to choose from, for every city has one or two and often several. And in addition to museums of all kinds there are castles, palaces, villas, manor houses, former residences, and summer pavilions of kings, princes, dukes, popes, archbishops. There in brocaded splendor and glittering array the guided tour gapes and gawks at the furniture and bric-a-brac of an aristocracy that is no more.

Instructive as the museums and palaces may be, there is about most of them, especially in the gloomy grey light of winter, a haunting, nostalgic quality. For the museum is a

From "Theological Table-Talk," THEOLOGY TODAY, XVII (1960), 366–374.

repository for ancient riches. Some of these are still highly prized, but many more are only curiosities. Customs and tastes in art and architecture, in what we call today "gracious living," change swiftly. Perhaps this is the reason so many tourists hire an official guide to take them through the corridors of the past. A recent cartoon picturing two tourists outside the Louvre carried the dialogue: "What guide did you have?" "We went through without a guide!" "But how did you know what to admire?"

This line of reflection, for whatever reason, often led me to think of the church. Perhaps it was the disillusioning experience of walking through St. Peter's in Rome and the various Vatican adjuncts such as the Sistine Chapel. Here one inevitably wonders about the relation between church and culture. The interaction between medieval Christianity and Renaissance magnificence is everywhere exhibited. Yet the relation of essential Christian faith, of the teaching and the person of the Galilean, of the virtues of humility and meekness to the opulent extravagance of an institutionalized church of princes, secular and sacred—*this* is also very obvious and very disturbing.

When in my naïveté I asked what the schedule of services was in St. Peter's, thinking it would do a Protestant good to worship at the citadel of Roman Catholicism, I was told by the Chief of the Guides in Rome—"St. Peter's is no longer a church; it is a public museum."

Is this capable of further, more general extension? Has the church become a museum? That is a loaded question, but one of the sad and pathetic things about many of the great cathedrals and famous churches of Europe is that, for the most part, the only people who are inside are tourists. Notre Dame in Paris on Christmas Day was deserted, and there was no evidence of Christmas anywhere in the Cathedral. The Reformed theologian in me is tempted to say that all this is true of Romanism but that Protestantism, on the contrary, is alert and alive. I wish it were so. Has the church become a museum, a repository of interesting relics from the past, a maze of aisles through which tourists wander and wonder? Lest I be charged with faithless cynicism, let me say I am not ready to answer that question in the affirmative. To say "yes" to that is to say "no" to the gospel. But the question is there, and it cannot be evaded with pious phrases or proper theological propositions. To the Reformed among us comes again the unceasing summons to *be* reformed and to be *reforming*.

BREAD AND WINE

Every visitor to the Continent, especially in France and Italy, soon discovers that eating and drinking are highly ritualistic, even sacramental. No self-respecting Europeans would dream of gulping the breakfast coffee as they dashed for the office, snatching a sandwich at a drugstore for lunch, sitting down for dinner at 6 P.M. to a single main dish—even if it happened to be steak and french fries. The whole social—and perhaps religious—tradition is against such a vulgar attitude toward food and drink. At least the French or the Italians would think it vulgar to treat food as no more than fuel.

For one thing, food and drink have been hard to come by in Europe for centuries, and in many places and in many families they are far from plentiful even today. Bread is still bread, "the staff of life" and an inevitable and necessary feature of every meal. It is often home-baked, comes in endlessly variegated sizes and shapes, invariably encased in a crunchy crust, and eaten as often plain as with butter. To eat one's soup or spaghetti or fish or veal without gnawing constantly on a chunk of bread would be for the continental intolerable. Even the continental breakfast, which seems so skimpy to Americans and Britishers, is a well-rehearsed rite of rolls, croissants, brioches, butter and jam, as elaborate in its own way as griddle cakes and sausage.

The ritualistic attitude toward the drinking of wine is well known by all travelers, especially Americans, who laugh and joke about it and generously indulge themselves. But wine is not merely an alcoholic drink, it is (like bread) handmade, so to speak. It does not come from the corner "package store"; it comes from the little, local vineyards and is the careful and loving distillation of sun and rain, of hills and valleys, of spring and summer breezes, of the sky which fertilizes and the earth which receives the impregnated seed. To be sure, water (or at least so they say) can now be safely drunk in any large European city or town. But water, which has its own unique symbolism, is not the same as blood-red wine which reminds the continental of the elemental, coursing, slightly intoxicating processes of nature. As we should know from Pentecost, the effect of drinking too much new wine is apparently somewhat similar to being filled with the Holy Spirit.

But apart from such an ambiguous parallel, does all this have religious significance? It is no accident, I think, that the Eucharist, the sacrament of bread and wine, should have been interpreted so naturalistically or realistically in Latin European Catholicism. The dogma of transubstantiation, regardless of Aristotelian metaphysics, is easily acceptable to the French or the Italians whose every meal, every day, is a sort of ritualistic miracle of bread and wine, taken quietly, in leisure, in pleasant surroundings among family and friends.

Contrariwise, go to Protestant Germany, the Netherlands, or Great Britain and you immediately pass over into very different eating and drinking habits. Not only is the food different, generally heavier, but the mystique surrounding even the humblest restaurant in France or Italy is lacking. Not that food and drink are lacking; far from it. But northern Protestants eat their ragout, sauerkraut, roast beef, and boiled potatoes, and drink their lukewarm beer with a gusto that would horrify the French or Italians.

Is it more than coincidence, then, that the Protestant North in Europe, especially the conservative Calvinistic tradition, has not only had an uneasy conscience about food and drink but also about the sacraments of Christian faith? But such a question makes it look too simple. It is not really a matter of Catholic versus Protestant or of wine versus water. It is the old problem of nature and grace, of sacred and secular, and *that* issue—irrespective of how we eat or drink—requires fresh consideration in our day.

THE HIGH PLACES

Anyone driving a small foreign car over the well-traveled highways of Europe soon learns that the roads in the southern part of the Continent arc mostly up and down and around. Trains go through tunnels and planes fly over the highest Alps, but down-shifting the gears in a Volkswagen, whether to go up or to brake on a downgrade, is a tedious and sometimes painful introduction to the countryside. From Lyons in mid-France south into Provence, the storied and high-story towns of Nîmes, Orange, Avignon, and especially Les Baux begin to try the driver's skill while trying to enjoy the view. Along the French Riviera just behind the glittering resorts, hill towns like Grasse (perfume) and Vence (Matisse) stand back from the sea in security and loftiness. Monte Carlo is an escalator of villas and shops from sea to sky. The tiny principality of Monaco boasts three "corniche" roads: *Grande, Moyenne,* and *Inférieure* (but one is tempted to say that as roads they are all "inferior"). Switzerland's landscape is of course topsy-turvy and so are the roads. And except for the flat plain from Milan to Venice, Italy too is mostly vertical. The spectacular and dizzy Amalfi drive from Naples to Sorrento and around (and it is really around) to Positano, Ravello, and on to Salerno is a tingling experience, especially for the driver. In Sicily, if possible, the hills are higher and the roads are steeper. The Greeks, whose temples in wonderful preservation still adorn the island, built with a view for a view. The Greek theaters at Taormina and Syracuse, the stately ridge of structures at Agrigento, the jumbled heap of columns at Selinunte, and the magnificent aloofness of the temple at Segesta are silent but articulate witnesses to the age-old longing to go up to the high places, to look out on the surroundings from a lofty perch, and there to build a temple, a tabernacle, a fortress, or, in more modern times, a hotel or a restaurant.

The Bible speaks often of hills and mountains and high places. The Psalmist looks to the hills for divine help, and Jerusalem is a city "whither the tribes go up." Bultmann would suggest we demythologize Isaiah's spatial vision of the Lord who was "high and lifted up," but we may reflect briefly on the obvious implications of these and other high places.

For one thing, a high place promises an extension of vision. To go up is to be able to see further and better than down below. The exalted panorama is bigger, better, brighter. Another feature of the original high places was their security from outside threats. The hill towns of Assisi and Siena, for example, were virtually impregnable. Even today it is some trick to circumnavigate the hairpin curves up and over the mountain passes, and in Switzerland even with the best mechanized equipment many roads are tightly closed during the winter months.

Still another aspect of the high places is the sense of exhilaration and ecstasy which increases the higher you go up and the more the oxygen in the air decreases. Regardless of age or physical condition, climbing a steep hill makes the heart beat a little faster and the lungs breathe a little deeper, and perhaps the brain may swim a little freer. Mountain climbers have always known about this, and Jacques Cousteau tells us that there is a corresponding giddiness and intoxication for those who swim too deep or too long with an aqualung under the sea.

The higher up the more numinous is the experience, the nearer one is to the boundless sky above and to the heavens where Deity dwells. So Moses on Mount Sinai and Jesus on the Mount of Transfiguration. And whatever it was that infuriated the Old Testament prophets about the pagan high places, against which they thundered, Christian churches over the centuries have often been built upon the hills. The Conquistadores in Mexico erected their churches on top of Aztec pyramids; Europe is dotted with chapels on hill tops (a striking recent example is Le Corbusier's Notre Dame at Ronchamp);

the great high-reaching Gothic cathedrals like Strasbourg, Cologne, and Salisbury carry the worshiper's eye and soul up and up and up.

What does it mean that today the fascination of the old high places seems to have diminished? Once inaccessible and difficult to assault, the old securities and ivory tower euphoria have vanished. There is a curse on "modern Gothic"; "contemporary" church buildings like our ranch houses and suburban factories hug the ground, are low lying, and tend to move out rather than up. Or is it possible that a whole new experience of the high places is opening up before us in the as yet highly ambiguous but greatly exciting possibilities of space travel?

LET THERE BE DARKNESS

Electricity is no doubt more plentiful and cheaper in America than in Europe. But is that the only reason why shops and offices are so dark and lightless, windows so shuttered and barricaded, homes so walled off and secured against the outside world, museums and showplaces so dingy, dark, and dim? I am told that fluorescent lighting uses more electricity when it is switched on and off than when it is left burning. But in Europe, where there is lots of this kind of fixture, the lights are invariably out—until you enter the store as a prospective customer. I have watched cobblers mending shoes and women making embroidery as they huddled inside the dark recesses of their shops. Clerks in offices pore over their figures without lamps or lights. Paintings on art museum walls are sometimes so poorly illuminated, they can be studied better in prints. Even the Museum of Modern Art in Paris with acres of window space was so cold and grey, and the windows so streaked with grime and dirt, that it was no pleasure to visit. Almost never, in the south of Europe at least, do you see a private home set in an expanse of lawn. Homes are walled off and shut up; windows sometimes have several layers of blinds inside and out; gates are usually closed

and often locked; it is common to read a sign to the effect—
"Beware of the dog!"

This living in the dark was something I never could get used
to and coming from the United States where we have so much
light, picture windows, front lawns and backyard barbecues, I
found this contrast striking and unsettling. There are simple
economic and sociocultural reasons for this no doubt. But what
bothers me is whether the Europeans live in the dark because
they are afraid of the light; or is it because they know that life
is not all light and therefore they have learned to be at home
with the darkness. And for Americans, are we all sunshine and
neon lighting and glass windows and walls because we understand the light; or is it because we are really afraid of the
darkness and have never learned to make our peace with it?

It would be too didactic to pursue the darkness and light
contrast farther, whether in the Bible or as representing the
conscious and the unconscious, but here as in so many instances the age-old symbols have a way of reappearing and
provoking reflection in not only one dimension but in overlap-
ping planes of life and experience.

Loyalty and Freedom

One does not need to be a cynic, let alone a "fellow traveler," to doubt whether American democracy has yet devised ways and means for maintaining and preserving its freedom, on the one hand, and combating subversive and destructive forces, on the other. It would be disastrous to belittle or to wink at the actuality and potency of subversive elements in our political and national life. But the crucial question today is not so much *whether* such threats exist, but *how* they are to be confronted without forfeiting the freedoms we seek to perpetuate. As has been asserted so many times, the peril from *within* is as ominous as the peril from *without*, for democratic institutions can be throttled by inner fear and suspicion, and the frenzied search for freedom, loyalty, and security can stifle the very spirit which gives us breath and life.

Have we forgotten the gruesome consequences of "spectral evidence" in the Salem witch trials, an early instance of guilt by association in our own history? Have we forgotten the Inquisition? Does anyone read Milton's *Areopagitica* these days? Is Hitler so long dead that we forget what happened only yesterday to the forces of freedom in Germany?

What lies behind the opposition to a Presidential appointment because the person involved has questioned the role of private and parochial schools? Why is a black minister of the

From "Theological Table-Talk," THEOLOGY TODAY, X (1953), 105–106; these observations were occasioned by the wave of McCarthyism in the United States, and this alarming development was addressed again in "Fear and Freedom," a portion of "Theological Table-Talk," *ibid.*, XI (1954), 85–87.

gospel asked to turn in his passport after he has been speaking and lecturing on communism as he saw it on a trip to East Asia? What happens when a committee organized to discuss the question of civil rights is accused openly, but without the evidence being submitted openly, of being subversive? When a returned missionary speaks to a church-related college on "Communism and the Churches" and is flatly denounced as a communist by the local Roman Catholic priest—how do you deal with that sort of thing?

These are only a few samples of the inner peril we face. Let it be said again, since misunderstanding is part of the problem, that the question is not *whether* peril exists, but *how* it is to be met. In each of the instances mentioned above, nothing has come of the charges. The commissioner was approved, the minister was allowed to keep his passport, the committee referred to still functions, the Catholic priest later modified his accusation. But that only illustrates our panic and haphazard approach.

But in the meantime and perhaps for a long time to come the question of freedom, loyalty, security, and the creative possibilities of dissent will be at stake. If independent initiative and the free flow of ideas are hobbled, no amount of legislation, control, or security measures will avail. It is well that educators and teachers, scientists and artists, newspapers and press are deeply disturbed. For we need today voices not only that do not bypass the peril but that are raised on behalf of a positive and constructive freedom.

Such a voice was heard some time ago in the eloquent and much-quoted speech of Judge Learned Hand, who said, "I believe that that community is already in process of dissolution where each man begins to eye his neighbor as a possible enemy, where non-conformity with the accepted creed, political as well as religious, is a mark of disaffection; where denunciation, without specification or backing, takes the place of evidence; where orthodoxy chokes freedom of dissent; where faith in the eventual supremacy of reason has become so timid that we dare not enter our convictions in the open lists to win or lose. Such fears as these are a solvent which can eat out the cement that binds the stones together; they may in the end subject us to a despotism as evil as any that we dread; and they can be allayed only insofar as we refuse to proceed on suspicion, and trust one another until we have tangible ground for misgiving. The mutual confidence on which all else depends can be maintained only by an open mind and a brave reliance upon free discussion."

Need it be said—yes, it needs to be said—that the Christian church has a share and a responsibility in all this. For it is conceivable that the church, under the grace of God, may become in our day the last redoubt of freedom in the world.

The Fearful Distance

For most of us, the approach of the Bicentennial arouses mixed, ambivalent expectations. We certainly need to renew our national self-awareness, and we are desperately eager to recapture the innocent but potent ideals of our heritage. Yet, on the other hand, we are apprehensive that Bicentennial celebrations may prove a sham and show us up as a shallow, hollow people without vision or soul. It is one thing to light skyrockets in memory of the past; it is quite another thing to re-member the fragmented pieces of our torn and riven society.

I

In an address last May at the Boston Bicentennial Forum, Hannah Arendt italicized this mood of ominous anticipation. As a people, she said, we are deeply disturbed because we are "aware of the fearful distance that separates us from our extraordinary beginnings." The chronicle of our political and social confusion, especially in very recent years, is mournfully long, lugubrious, and humiliating. And the prospects for radical improvement are not bright. The Bicentennial coincides with a presidential election year, and as we try to celebrate our national unity, we observe at the same time a deeply divided people, a timid and leaderless Congress, and a mood of defeatism that would have grieved and astonished our colonial leaders.

THEOLOGY TODAY, XXXII (1976), 219–221.

As Hannah Arendt notes, a "fearful distance" separates this contemporary "disarray" from "our extraordinary beginnings." And how extraordinary they were! We need to be constantly reminded of at least three of the formative motivations behind our "beginnings."

First, the unity and federation of the new nation came about not by prior design but in consequence of a revolutionary emergency. As Daniel J. Boorstin puts it, the nation "could be born without ever having been conceived." The Declaration of Independence does not speak of a new Nation but of "the thirteen united [small case "u"] States of America." It was out of a sense of common purpose and simple survival that unity and independence were achieved. "We are in danger," says Boorstin, "of forgetting our oldest American tradition, that the nation exists for the sake of principles that can be shared" ("America: Our Byproduct Nation," *Time,* June 23, 1975, pp. 68–70).

Second, there is no mistaking the enthusiasm and exuberance of the early founders, as of the peoples everywhere, as new frontiers opened up, fresh prospects for freedom and liberty emerged, and opportunities for a new way of life were hailed and welcomed. In 1782, Jean de Crèvecoeur, a French-born farmer in upper New York, wrote: "What then is the American, this new man? . . . He is an American, who leaving behind him all his ancient prejudices and manners, receives new ones from the new mode of life he has embraced, the new government he obeys, and the new rank he holds. The American is a new man, who acts upon new principles. He must therefore entertain new ideas, and form new opinions." And in 1787, Benjamin Rush wrote: "The American war is over. But this is far from being the case with the American Revolution. On the contrary, nothing but the first act of the great drama is closed. It remains yet to establish and perfect our new forms of government, and to prepare the principles, morals, and manners of our citizens for these forms of government after they are established and brought to perfection."

Third, our "extraordinary beginnings" were underwritten

in the religious conviction that God has a purpose for this chosen people that could not be thwarted. "In God We Trust" was the motto engraven on our coins, and it was no mere pious pretension but a profound expression of gratitude for divine providence. When William Penn landed on the banks of the Delaware River, with his small, unpromising band of Quakers, he said: "Let us now see what love can do." And for Penn, as for so many, such lofty goals issued from faith in a holy God who covenanted with faithfulness, love, and justice.

II

A wonderful, but mostly unnoticed, emblem of these three founding principles can be seen on the reverse side of a U.S. one-dollar bill. If you have one handy, take a look. You will see two circles representing the two sides of what is known as "The Great Seal of the United States." On the same day the Continental Congress approved the Declaration of Independence, July 4, 1776, a committee to design a seal was appointed, consisting of Benjamin Franklin, John Adams, and Thomas Jefferson. After various revisions and changes, a seal (or, more accurately, a "device for an armorial atchievement and reverse") was accepted, and it has been in official use ever since.

Both sides of the seal are replete with heraldic, classical, and biblical symbolism. The unity of the new nation is designated by the "displayed" eagle holding together in its left *(sinister)* talons 13 arrows with the 13 colonies repeated above in the form of a constellation. In the eagle's beak is a scroll, reading *E Pluribus Unum.* The eagle's right *(dexter)* talons hold the olive branch of peace, to complement the 13 arrows of war. The reverse side of the seal figures an unfinished pyramid, suggesting that the firm foundation promises a more complete structure yet to be built. Above the pyramid, in a triangle, is the all-seeing eye of God, surrounded by a "glory." At the top and at the bottom, two adapted quotations from Virgil adorn the reverse of the seal: *Annuit Cœptis* ("He has prospered our undertakings"), and *Novus Ordo Seclorum* ("A new order of the ages").

Isn't it ironic that this official seal, with its comprehensive credo, passes through our hands almost daily, and yet it goes mostly unnoticed, and its symbolism probably remains obscure? What a perfect example of "the fearful distance that separates us from our extraordinary beginnings"!

III

Anniversaries, birthdays, and national holidays are times not only for reminiscing about the past but for recovering our ideals for the present. "History teaches" is, of course, a well-worn and thin aphorism. Can we really learn from our national past? A pertinent biblical precedent comes to mind.

In a time of great national division, political crisis, and moral and spiritual corruption (as recounted in I and II Kings), the reforms of Josiah came as a startling interruption to the general chronology of calamity. When Josiah's priest, Hilkiah, discovered "the book of the law" during repairs to the temple, the long-forgotten principles of the past (as contained in the book of Deuteronomy) came to light with fresh and urgent relevancy (II Kings, chs. 22–23). After consulting with Huldah "the prophetess," Josiah became convinced of "the fearful distance" that separated the monotonous corruption of his recent past from "the extraordinary beginnings" of God's chosen people.

Who knows? Maybe along with our required reading for the Bicentennial we should also read and ponder the Books of the Kings. For Josiah, the rediscovery of the ancient texts resulted in a new unity of the people, a rededication to the God of the covenant, and a reinvigorated moral conscience. If we will not only listen to but really hear the words of our illustrious and extraordinary founders, during these Bicentennial times of celebration, it is just possible, "under God" (as our children now say every school day when pledging allegiance to the flag), that as a people we may renew our vision and save our soul.

Treasures of Tutankhamun

The museum exhibit known as "Treasures of Tutankhamun" must be one of the most fascinating and exquisite
artistic treats of our time. The exhibit is of first-rate importance
from several angles of critical appreciation, but it solicits special attention, we think, because it is so pre-Christian and yet
so clearly religious.*

I

This exhibit of Egyptian antiquities is not large, as museum
exhibits go, consisting of only some 55 items, but it is of
breathtaking beauty capable of stirring the imagination and
lifting the human spirit. The narrative of the discovery of King
Tutankhamun's tomb in 1922 casts a romantic aura on the
recovered treasure trove. Exploring for more than ten years,
and mostly in vain, in the Valley of the Kings, the two moving
spirits, Howard Carter, the amateur archaeologist, and Lord
Carnarvon, the financial sponsor, suddenly stumbled on their
unique find just at the point of abandoning their whole project.
What they discovered was an almost intact depository of
hundreds of funerary objects associated with a young pharaoh

---

*The exhibit opened in Washington, D.C., in 1976 and was displayed for the next
two and a half years in five other major cities in the United States. It was organized
by the Director of the Metropolitan Museum of Art in New York, Thomas Hoving,
and supported through grants from the National Endowment for the Humanities, the
Robert Wood Johnson, Jr., Charitable Trust, and the Exxon Corporation.

THEOLOGY TODAY, XXXIV (1977), 1–8.

who died at the early age of nineteen and was buried in a relatively modest tomb about 1325 b.c. "King Tut," as the newspaper dispatches at the time familiarly referred to him, was by no means an outstanding Egyptian pharaoh, yet he could claim some distinction. For one thing, he was directly related to that superlative beauty, Queen Nefertiti, and also to Akhenaton, who not only consolidated upper and lower Egypt in an age of national unity and peace but initiated religious reforms in the direction of a kind of monotheism. The young king's name was composed of "Tut," his personal identification, plus "ankh," the symbol of life, plus "Amun," a divine title.

The "Treasures of Tutankhamun" makes an intriguing reflective exercise on the relation of religion and art. We now look upon these magnificent objects of gold, gems, ebony, and alabaster as singular examples of artistic skill, illustrating the highest standards of aesthetic achievement. And modern museum technology enhances the viewing of these ancient artifacts, for they are ingeniously displayed in walkaround plexiglass cabinets with hidden electric spotlights that make the long-ago treasures sparkle and glisten in dazzling brilliance.

But we must remember that all these treasures were never intended to be seen again. They were buried with the dead king in the dark of the tomb, and they were placed there not as artistic objects of great beauty to be admired. They were intended as necessary and practical accouterments for the pharaoh's long and mysterious voyage through the dark netherworld into the realm of eternal light and life. Almost everything retrieved from the ancient burial chambers symbolized the pervasive Egyptian passion for immortality in the midst of corruptibility. The art was not merely decorative addenda, but neither was it the main attraction, as if the ancient Egyptians were putting on a royal art show. *The reliquary was religious.* The art was the medium of the eschatological message. What for us may seem simply secular and beautiful was for Tutankhamun's contemporaries sacred and theological.

II

Writing some years ago about Egyptian art (in Hastings' *Encyclopaedia of Religion and Ethics*), Sir Flinders Petrie noted that "the religious aspect of art in Egypt includes almost all that is known of it." Two interlocking themes, light-darkness and life-death, dominated the religious and artistic world of the ancient Egyptians. But it would be a mistake to put such interacting pairs into some sort of existential formula, as if Tutankhamun and his sages were intellectually anxious about the paradox of meaning and meaninglessness.

What emerges clearly and unmistakably from the "treasures" is a sense of confidence, buoyancy of the human spirit, and vitality of form and expression. It is not so much a theology of hope that we witness as it is a religious and artistic style of life expressing vivacity, energy, assurance, and expectation. There is little evidence of gloom, depression, brooding, grief, skepticism, or nihilism. (The current theological fad that seeks to analyze and psychologize death and dying, with the help of biomedical ethics, must surely have seemed to Tutankhamun a lugubrious, detached, and mournful exercise.)

As the brilliant sun rises at dawn, marches majestically across the heavens, ominously dies and disappears at night, to be reborn mysteriously the next day, so life comes and goes but keeps renewing itself—like the sun itself, the Nile River, the grain in the field, and the progressive stages of human life. This is not really a doctrine or creed, as if spelled out in theological propositions. It is what the art objects, the "treasures," tell us.

The small (twelve inch) "sun-god on a lotus" (Fig. 1) says it all. A symbolic expression of the original creation, the infant emerges from a blue lotus on the river's edge and is reborn every day as the sun rises, hence immortal and eternal. But the figure is also a likeness of Tutankhamun himself, with the characteristic elongated head and the pierced ear lobes. Carved in wood and overlaid with painted gesso, the eyes and eyebrows are blue, matching the fecund lotus blossom.

Many different kinds of oil lamps and candles were found in

Tutankhamun's burial chambers. Here again the message is the same. Although the tomb is dark as death, there is a lamp to light the way through the darkness, flickering and delicate, but eerily translucent as a single piece of carved alabaster (Fig. 2).

"The King upon a leopard" (Fig. 3) symbolizes the light-dark theme. The leopard is painted black, the shade of night, death, and the underworld. But the pharaoh is clothed in gilded light and rides regally on the leopard's back. As the sun-god brought a brief ray of light to the underworld, as he passed through, so too will Tutankhamun traverse the darkness of death, emerging into the brightness of a new day.

The mirror case found in Tutankhamun's tomb (Fig. 4) suggests that even high and holy things can be treated lightly, even with a touch of frivolity. The design for the case, the "ankh," is the common hieroglyph for "life," but there is also a similar sign in Egyptian for mirror ("that which sees the face"). The artist presumably was making a play on words. But in the midst of the levity, there is a subtler implication. When we see ourselves as we are, as in a mirror, we are confronted with life. And if our mirror case is covered with thin sheets of gold and studded with gems, we may even think about the glories of eternal life. (The temptation to reflect on the parallel between the Egyptian "ankh" and the later Christian *crux ansata*, as well as on what Paul says about seeing through a glass —that is, a mirror—darkly, is almost irresistible.)

III

The individual items among the "Treasures of Tutankhamun," delightful and suggestive as they are, pale to virtual insignificance when compared with the reason for the existence of the exhibit—the mummified and decorated bodily remains of the pharaoh himself. The ancient Egyptians, thousands of years prior to modern chemical embalming processes, developed a rare skill in preserving mortal human flesh. Perhaps the dry, microbe-free climate had something to do with it. But even so, the most skilled practitioners of the art must have known that their best efforts were less than perfect. In any case, artisans covered the human face and head of Tutankhamun with an elaborately crafted gold mask (Fig. 5), certainly much more durable and handsome than the mummified corpse.

But the intent behind the process is perhaps more important, both religiously and artistically, than the actual results. All funerary customs, whether simple or contrived, no matter how sentimental or extravagant, are touching, poignant, and universal expressions of loving care for the deceased. More than that, they remind us that, in the midst of death and decay, human hope never quite dies. Artists through all the ages, in all the artistic media, have been preoccupied with this unquenchable flame of the human spirit. (As this is being written, a best-seller title on all current book lists is Raymond A. Moody's *Life After Life*, a physician's account of the "postmortem" experiences of persons declared clinically dead but who later survived.)

It has been widely assumed that belief in the resuscitation of the body is a distinctively Christian doctrine, based upon the resurrection of Jesus. But the religion of the ancient Egyptians, while knowing nothing of the Christ who was yet to appear, nevertheless approached the same faith and was at least as physical and literal minded about personal survival. Unlike ancient Greece and Rome, and for that matter much Christian piety, the Egyptians did not think of a radical division between soul and body so that while the body dies at death, the soul continues its immortal existence.

A peculiar, if somewhat grisly, aspect of the "Treasures of Tutankhamun," giving special emphasis to the Egyptian care for the very mortal remains of the dead, is the so-called "canopic" chest. This large, imposing structure contained the carefully preserved internal organs, including the intestines, of the king. Could anything be more corporeal, physical, or ephemeral? Yet this canopic chest is as ornamented and scrupulously crafted as Tutankhamun's golden headdress. In addition, the chest is guarded by four goddesses, facing toward the four walls with outstretched protecting arms. The figures are among the most striking of the "treasures," and the graceful form of "Selket" is surely the incomparable guardian of the four (Fig. 6). Standing about five feet tall and carved of wood laid over with gesso and gilt paint, Selket is an artistic masterpiece. With her heavily blackened eye shadow and her golden garb, Selket has achieved artistic immortality.

But Selket is not a beauty queen, standing royally aloof, blasé, disdainful. Remember, she stands guard over Tutankhamun's entrails, which are separated from his mummified body but nevertheless retained, preserved, and respected.

Selket's special signet, a scorpion, perches on the top of her head, for she was not only a canopic guardian but possessed magical powers to cure the dreaded, death-dealing scorpion sting. Selket, so solemn, so imperishably beautiful, has stood sentry for more than three thousand years over Tutankhamun's vital organs, as if to say in her own way, and for her own time, "O death, where is thy sting? O grave, where is thy victory?"

Figure 1 / *Sun-god on a lotus*

FIGURE 2 / *A triple lamp of translucent calcite*

FIGURE 3 / *Statuette of the King on a black leopard*

FIGURE 4 / *Mirror case*

FIGURE 5 / *Gold mask as found*

THE METROPOLITAN MUSEUM OF ART
PHOTOGRAPH BY HARRY BURTON
THE EGYPTIAN EXPEDITION

FIGURE 6 / *Selket, a guardian of the canopic chest*

What My Teachers Taught Me

Those of us in the teaching trade (and that includes not only teachers but preachers, pastors, counselors, deans, and administrators) have a vested interest in changing peoples' minds, ideals, and goals. This is a pedagogical and evangelical imperative of our profession. We are incurable do-gooders, with abounding confidence in the spoken and written word, in the influence of example (ours or others), and in the persuasive power of truth. We believe that teaching and preaching can change lives, and we strive to sharpen the tools of our trade.

But most of us are also very realistic about our didactic achievements. What we hope for is not what we always get; many people have a knack for resisting change of any kind; what is taught is not often caught; teaching and preaching can be frustrating, inconclusive, ambiguous. It is humiliating for teachers and preachers to reflect that what comes across to those being instructed, as most meaningful and enduring, are eccentric traits of character and casual methods of communication. Perhaps a personal retrospective on what my own teachers taught me will correspond with the reflections of others and, possibly, serve as helpful guidelines for beginners of all kinds.

I

From a long and almost endless educational servitude, I can select a half dozen teachers who influenced me in important

THEOLOGY TODAY, XXXV (1978), 247–253.

ways, shaped my own career, and really changed my life. Some are remembered because they were characters, some because of their methods, and some because they forced me into new areas of thought and life. I can group the six in pairs.

There are two teachers whom I remember because of their personal characteristics. Alfred C. Dickey was my mathematics teacher in secondary, preparatory school days. He didn't teach me anything about arithmetic, and I never mastered the subject in even an elementary sense. Time, rate, and distance problems were, for me, something like the riddle of the Sphinx, and plane geometry seemed like a practical joke dreamed up by Euclid to plague people who couldn't grasp the reasons for measuring angles or why the square of the hypotenuse was so important.

But Mr. Dickey was a character, an individualist, and the "Mr. Chips" of generations of students. He gave us all nicknames that had a way of sticking for life: Henry Cooper was "Hen Coop," Richard Burdick was "Dickie Bird," Newton Chapin was "Fig Newton," and I was dubbed "Thompy" (because I was called by my middle name, Thomson, usually misspelled as Thompson). Cheating in class was "rough stuff," and if anyone looked over on another's exam paper, the threat of "pink eye" (or conjunctivitis, to give it its proper medical designation) was directed at the unfortunate offender. In geometry class, we needed a pencil, a protractor, and a compass. If we forgot, Mr. Dickey could supply the missing instrument —but at a price. Five cents for a borrowed pencil, ten cents for a protractor, and a quarter for a compass. These coins were deposited in a special box and used eventually to buy something useful for the whole class—in my year, a small wall clock.

Mr. Dickey was a walker and hiker of great distances and speed, a devoted churchman, a gentleman of the old school, and an engaging and dedicated teacher. As a subject, mathematics eluded me, but I always enjoyed classes with Mr. Dickey, and hardly a day passed without a chuckle, a witticism, or a story to illustrate some abstract principle-—Poe's *Purloined*

Letter was a favorite. We all remembered the stories though few of us recalled the principles. One thing I learned from Mr. Dickey, that stayed with me all my life, was that even though the subject (logarithms, theology, etc.) might seem arcane to some, the classroom needn't be dull because it is full of human beings. If the teacher (preacher) also happens to be human, great and memorable exchanges can take place.

In college days, my favorite teacher was a Shakespearean scholar of wonderfully dramatic lecturing prowess. But J. Duncan Spaeth was not so much a scholar as an actor. A huge hulk of a man with a granite profile, he was a tweedy professor, reeking of tobacco, and always ready to posture or pontificate. His colleagues may have suspected him of showmanship, but students signed up for his courses in droves and sat spellbound during his lectures.

I took but one course from Spaeth (whom we all called "Drunken" behind his back). It was in the tragedies of Shakespeare. My choice was *Macbeth*, partly because I had already scanned it with my father, line by line, and partly because the Scottish locale was congenial. But Spaeth inclined toward *Hamlet* and *Lear*. He would lecture to us about plot structure and the Elizabethan theater, but what we all cherished most were his lengthy dramatic readings from the plays themselves. Moving from side to side and all around the lectern (and without public address amplification), he would take all the parts, including the women (in a high-pitched falsetto), while we sat captivated, hoping the bell would never ring. The lecture invariably concluded with spontaneous applause and much foot stomping. Our notebooks remained mostly empty, but we went away inspired, filled with images, and transported to a realm of wonder and delight.

Spaeth had one extracurricular enthusiasm—he was a voluntary, unpaid coach of collegiate crew. I suppose he had rowed as an undergraduate, but during his coaching years he would have sunk any shell. I can still see him, as we watched from the lake bank, paralleling the shells in his motor-driven launch, yelling instructions and encouragement through a hand-held megaphone. It seemed in character for such a character.

Did I learn about Shakespeare from Spaeth? Not much. But I learned a lot about one man's total dedication to a chosen field of literature. I don't suppose I ever said a dozen words to Professor Spaeth, nor he to me. But that big, throbbing lecture hall is still vivid in my mind. In a day when teachers and preachers downgrade the lecture as the least effective method of communication, it may be sobering to recall that this was not always so, and perhaps we are missing something in our more relaxed, discussive, and participatory age.

II

My next two teachers, Donald Mackenzie and Hugh R. Mackintosh, were both Scots and both in my academic theological days. Donald Mackenzie came from the Isle of Lewis in the Hebrides and was as dour and rough as a piece of Harris tweed. He had a fiercely flint-like face with a thick upper lip, black beetle brows, and a scowl that betrayed his human warmth and compassion. Before coming to Pittsburgh Seminary, he had written articles for the various Hastings' dictionaries (one on "Fornication"), and he later wrote a book on *The Paradox of God,* inspired by his reading of Kierkegaard (using his knowledge of German to decipher the Danish—long before there were translations). But he was not primarily a research scholar or a prolific author.

What Donald Mackenzie taught me was a love of words. The first day in class, he called the roll and came to the name "Trewolla." To the student's surprise, he said, "You must have a family background in Cornwall." "Why, yes; how did you know?" "Because of Sir Walter Scott's lines: 'By Tre, Pol, and Pen, You shall know the Cornish men . . .' "

Mackenzie was fascinated with the derivation of names and the roots of words in various languages. Our theology class was based on the Apostles' Creed, and our first assignment was to write out the Creed from memory in both Latin and Greek.

The Latin was hard going for some who had never studied the language (everyone in those days took Greek), but they were required to memorize the text anyway—with some odd results. One day, when Mackenzie asked a student to translate Virgil's epigram *Felix qui potuit rerum cognoscere causas,* he got the ingenious answer: "Felix was happy when he knew the reason for it." That is almost as clever as the translation of the French *Honi soit qui mal y pense*—"Honey, your silk stocking is hanging down."

Mackenzie expected great things from me because I had taken several years of languages (Latin 7, French 6, Greek 2, Hebrew 1—German was yet in the future). But I wasn't any good at languages, and it never occurred to me that a knowledge of words could illuminate ideas and thought. He put me on to Archbishop Richard C. Trench's *Synonyms of the New Testament* (1854). That summer I read the book like the Bible, marking the pages, looking up all the Greek and Latin, and devouring Trench's other books on language (I still have them in my ever-shrinking library). Mackenzie would have agreed with Swift's advice to a young cleric, "Proper words in proper places, make the true definition of a style." And he probably would have liked the comment of someone who predicted that nothing good would ever come of television because the word was half Greek and half Latin.

I didn't know, of course, when studying with Donald Mackenzie that I would ever become an editor of a theological journal, and I can't blame my scribbling on him. But I wish I could thank him for introducing me to word study and arranging a love affair that is still strong, true, and endlessly consuming.

H. R. Mackintosh was a very different sort of Scot. He was a handsome man with greying hair and a combed moustache worthy of a Highland drum major. He spoke in quiet, measured tones like the cultured gentleman he was, suave, urbane, but without a trace of guile or conceit. He had just finished his term as Moderator of the Church of Scotland when I first sat in his classes, and we all marveled at the way he combined his theological research with the practical matters of the parish minister. While he was lecturing to postgraduates on "Types of Modern Theology" (which issued in the much-used textbook), he was also giving a course on homiletics to undergraduates, which some of us took just for fun but with great edification. ("A sermon is like a pipe; it won't draw if too tightly packed. And it is usually too tight when you borrow from someone else's pouch.")

Mackintosh was my dissertation director. He urged me to choose a "big" topic and suggested Christology in the nineteenth century, as background for what was beginning to happen in Barth and the whole neo-orthodox movement. He sent me off for six months to Tübingen to work with Karl Heim. When I returned and asked what courses I should take, he said to my delight, "I think courses for you have ceased to be a means of grace." After approving my thesis (in consultation with Professor A. E. Garvie of London University, my outside reader), he startled me by suggesting that I should think of becoming a teacher of theology. It had never crossed my mind.

But what Mackintosh taught me was really something else. He developed a system of preparing a digest of his lectures, one single-spaced mimeographed sheet for each lecture, and these were handed out piecemeal the day before every next lecture. We always read these in advance and therefore knew more or less what to expect. Mackintosh's lectures were extended annotations to the printed sheets, but they were always carefully crafted and eloquently delivered. By the end of the course, we had a pile of printed sheets and pages of explanatory notes, an organized, incipient textbook for future reference.

This was a method I adopted much later in my own teaching, and I was encouraged to think that it was well received by many students. With the availability of electronic duplicating machines, I increased the number and volume of "handouts." It freed me from tedious class instruction about bibliography and other such matters, and in the process I learned to appreciate how much time and effort Mackintosh's mimeographed sheets represented. It is an excellent method for teachers (and preachers), but it's not for those who can't live by a disciplined schedule, and it's about ten times as much work as talking from notes.

Mackenzie and Mackintosh taught me much about many things, but I remember them today mostly for what they taught me about theological methodology. This is odd, for neither was particularly interested in methodology as are so many contemporary theologians. Word study and printed sheets were for them merely ways for expounding and interpreting classical Christian doctrines. Both Mackenzie and Mackintosh were committed to the "big" doctrines, and they would have scorned much of our current discussion about how to "do" theology. I think they would say, "The way to 'do' it is to do it."

III

Two more teachers, in this personal reminiscence, must be mentioned. One was a professor of chemistry and the other an analytical psychologist. They were not so much teachers in the classroom sense, but they were mentors who changed the direction of my life in midstream, as it were.

Chemistry was definitely not one of my favorite subjects, and I had a facility for dribbling hydrochloric acid on my shirt cuffs and trouser legs, as I still do when checking my car battery. Hubert N. Alyea was not only a distinguished professor of chemistry at Princeton University, he was everywhere known as the entrepreneur of a public demonstration, "Lucky Accidents, Great Discoveries, and the Prepared Mind." This fantastic sight and sound circus was usually scheduled for alumni day in June, early Saturday morning, in one of the big chemistry lecture labs. Every seat was always taken an hour before the start, and this performance was repeated year after year, and in many other places as well.

Alyea mixed chemicals with foaming and brilliant effect, dashing from one end of the long lab counter to the other, writing a formula on the blackboard, instructing everyone in elementary science, and now and then disappearing to a projection booth to flash a slide or a portion of film on an overhead screen. Children screamed with delight and older alumni, like me, wondered why in heaven we hadn't majored in chemistry with this genial genius.

But I wondered something else. My first viewing of Alyea's chemistry lesson came when I was in the middle of my teaching career, trying to teach theology to seminarians. They were teachable enough but not very confident that an instructor could make such a musty subject at all interesting. Alyea started me to rethink my own rather traditional approach. I figured that if he could make chemistry fascinating for a public audience, I should be able to stir the ashes of theological debate and generate some sparks of life in the old doctrines. After all, Alyea was restricted to his chemical formulas, whereas I could draw on everything in heaven and on earth.

Over the years, I experimented with every conceivable visual aid and prop, and I tried to use art, music, and dramatic sketches—not to put on a show but to suggest the multifaceted aspect of truth, the interconnectedness of one thing with another, and the wonderful excitement of theological improvising. Whether this approach was successful, I leave to others to decide, but I've always thought it amusing that a chemistry professor, whom I hardly knew, teaching a subject I disliked, steered my course in theology into new and, for me, refreshingly creative directions.

A final teacher on my list was a clinical psychologist who turned me in new inner directions as Alyea redirected my outward course. Dr. Ursula M. Knoll was born in Switzerland and had studied at the Jung Institute in Zurich before becoming associated as an analyst in an office of several others, including the chief psychiatrist on the medical staff of Princeton University. For reasons that now seem remote (and which later turned out to be more physical than psychological), I sought out Dr. Knoll's counsel, and we talked together one or two hours a week for a period of more than two years. This was not a couch type of analysis but more a conversation. While the time and money might seem excessive, that experience marked a radical turning point in perspective, and I look back on it with great pleasure and gratitude.

My mentor's initial assignment for me was Jung's big, sprawling book, *Psychology and Alchemy,* which I read from cover to cover. I didn't think about it at the time, but later it seemed curious that when Professor Alyea's chemistry lecture was sticking like a burr in my mind, another teacher was directing me to read about medieval alchemy. Professor Alyea's research involved him in the early development of atomic power; Dr. Knoll's tutelage exploded within my psyche. The two approaches complemented each other and later appeared to me as interlocked—one related to an *outside,* and the other to an *inside* dimension.

What I learned from Dr. Knoll, and by reading most of Jung's voluminous writings, the *Eranos* yearbooks, and a great deal of other material, was a new sense of the multilayered universe and the surprising ways in which outward symbols of reality correspond with inner psychic states. Professor Alyea pushed me toward a multimedia approach to theology; Dr. Knoll helped me see the many levels of personality.

Of even more crucial importance for me at this particular time was Jung's notion of the *anima,* the female side of the masculine self (or the *animus* for the feminine self). This seemed to me much more profound than Freud's tiresome Oedipus complex. If anyone has read this personal chronicle this far, it will be obvious that all my teachers and all my educational experience was almost exclusively masculinist. It was common enough in my day to go to an all-boys' secondary school and a men's college. Theological education in those days was almost completely male-oriented, and of course we've learned that the Bible and classic Christian theology are also overwhelmingly on the sex-exclusive side.

The feminine side of reality, outside and inside, came to me like a revelation—mediated through a woman teacher. We have learned in the meantime that most so-called masculine and feminine traits are culturally conditioned, and that anatomy is by no means destiny. But unless we understand what these sex differences were supposed to signify yesterday, we can hardly cope with contemporary sex-inclusive claims made upon us today. In any case, for me it was a liberating new insight that "there is a woman in every man," as Jung interpreted the creation of Eve out of Adam's rib. That seems to me as crucial for men as it is for women to realize that in Christ "there is neither male nor female."

IV

It is always dangerous to generalize about one's personal experiences. But allow three closing comments. *First,* as I look back on a long and continuous educational involvement, I see more clearly than ever that life is full of unexpected junctures, excursions, and detours. We rarely ever plan our pilgrimage from beginning to end; something new is always breaking in, turning us around in another direction. *Second,* it is essential, because of the foregoing, to adopt a teachable, tractable frame of mind. To expect the unexpected requires a receptive mood and a flexible perspective on life. And *third,* my personal testimony is that Christian faith implies belief in a God of providence. I remember my father telling me once that he had stopped praying for something that was dear to his desire, because he felt sure that his prayer had been answered, and that everything would be all right. Many today might think that a simplistic faith, and surely there are lots of unanswered prayers and misdirected journeys in everyone's life. But my own life's story seems to me, in retrospect, like a series of photographs and pictures, illustrating a textbook on the sovereign purposes of a gracious God.

All in All

If now the time seems out of joint, or skewed,
Glue comes unstuck, whirl's king, flux is, hope dims.
Not so! Disorder hides a plan pursued,
A chain of being joined in synonyms.
To wit: as up, so down; as then, so now;
As out, so in; as there, so here; all ways.
Most things entwine, conjoin, relate somehow.
The universe is one, if we but raise
Our eyes to scan reality's vast net.
As grass upon the field, so is the hair
Upon the head. Once sensed, we'll not forget
The storm outside, inside; they both cohere.
Each thing both great and small enjoys a place
Within the scheme of things; it is God's grace.

THEOLOGY TODAY, XXXIV (1977), 193.

Respondeo

When I first heard that my colleagues on THEOLOGY TODAY, James I. McCord and John M. Mulder, were proposing to publish a collection of my editorials and essays, the idea struck me as surprising and frightening. Editors don't usually think of their incessant scribbling as belonging in the category of immortal prose. It's true that I've been pushing my pen for thirty-five years and more, but almost everything I ever wrote for THEOLOGY TODAY carried an unmistakable *ad hoc,* dated, and evanescent quality. Like an animated conversation, I thought I was talking with someone about some important issue, and that our dialogue was being overheard. But how many conversations are worth preserving?

I

What really surprised me about this project was the suggestion that I was deserving of some sort of special praise for what I loved doing and always regarded as an extraordinary privilege. Even though it was a second full-time job, without salary and with an intrusive demand on every weekend and all vacations, it was something I willingly, even eagerly, accepted. It killed my free time for what I imagined might have been invested in writing those half dozen major theological tomes. I have a long list of unfinished writing projects, shelved because of the relentless pressure of every next editorial deadline. But I have absolutely no regrets. THEOLOGY TODAY has been so good to me, and for me, that I can't imagine why anyone thinks I'm due any kind of special attention.

Beyond all this, it frightens me to be singled out as some sort of mastermind for a publishing venture that has been built upon the faithful and creative writing of hundreds of authors and reviewers over a period of a full generation. Editors are nothing without their writers. For every author there must be hundreds of readers; for every quarterly issue of a journal there must be thousands of subscribers. Editors and authors are dependent upon each other, but they cannot indulge in a mutual congratulation society; they are both dependent upon readers, subscribers, and even future generations of scholars and researchers. To write for oneself alone is to live in a cocoon. THEOLOGY TODAY, so I believe, has never been a guild organ with theological specialists addressing other theorists. We think there is a big, eager, waiting readership out there, and, happily, it keeps on growing with the passing years. We bend every effort to write for them rather than for ourselves.

I am also surprised that anyone, especially those who are writers, should think an editor needs any praise beyond the minimum call of duty. Authors hate editors and regard them as insufferable interlopers. After all, editors are always cutting out purple prose passages, asking for impossible revisions, and questioning basic assumptions. Nowadays they may also irritate many writers by suggesting that less is more, that readers want to know what writers think themselves (and not what they think other thinkers think), and that sex-inclusive language, for example, is not only possible but prescribed.

II

Editors have always been a threatened species. It has been said that an editor is a person who knows precisely what is wanted—but isn't quite sure. Adlai Stevenson once defined a politician as a statesman who approaches every question with an open mouth, and, by analogy, an editor is a thinker who tackles every issue with pen and paper. As each successive volume of Gibbon's *Decline and Fall* appeared, the Duke of

Gloucester, who was responsible for presenting copies to the King, twitted the author, as many have wanted to say to their editors: "Always scribble, scribble, scribble! Eh! Mr. Gibbon?" As Chesterton once put it, editors and journalists are always announcing "Lord Jones Dead" for those who never knew Lord Jones was alive. When T. S. Eliot, who was an editor for many years in London, was asked if it weren't the case that most editors were failed writers, replied, "Perhaps, but so are most writers."

As Seward Hiltner, my colleague and an esteemed member of the Editorial Council of THEOLOGY TODAY, would say, "Enough of this mock modesty and editorial masochism."

III

THEOLOGY TODAY continues to reflect the imaginative and creative vision of John A. Mackay. It was providential, or what amounts to the same thing, a miracle, that a new theological quarterly took shape as it did, when it did. A handful of dedicated enthusiasts somehow carried it off. John Mackay conscripted people like H. Richard Niebuhr, Walter Lowrie, Theodore M. Greene, Nels Ferré, Joseph Haroutunian, F. W. Dillistone, and a dozen others to underwrite the project theologically, as the Trustees of Princeton Seminary agreed to sponsor it financially.

Others were working behind the scenes. Leonard J. Trinterud, then of The Westminster Press, did all the business and clerical work out of a bottom drawer of his desk at home; Kenneth S. Gapp, librarian and book review editor, imposed rigorous literary standards on reviewers; Bruce M. Metzger, the New Testament textual wizard, proofed and copy-edited the steady stream of manuscripts.

Somehow over the years we've been able to enlist the same kind of selfless, dedicated service. We are not able, mostly for financial reasons, to convene at one time all the members of the Editorial Council, much as we would like to do so. We do the next best thing, holding smaller conferences from time to time, and encouraging our Council members to write for us and otherwise help us to publicize our enterprise.

Our present working staff consists of John M. Mulder as Assistant Editor and promotion entrepreneur; Rose B. Rickert, our efficient and superlative Business Manager; James Irvine, assistant librarian who proofreads and does all kinds of reference work for us; James F. Armstrong, Registrar of the Seminary, who has served us in many capacities, most recently by programming for the computer our expanding and ever-changing list of subscribers. These and others contribute to an editor's peace of mind and assure an excellent product with each quarterly issue.

IV

Writing is a lonely profession, requiring long stretches of uninterrupted time and an unhurried disposition toward solitude and contemplation. But editing is a corporate, communal venture, demanding mutual respect, with a view to articulating for others the meaning of faith and life. It is within this cooperative context that I want to respond to those friends and associates who have prepared prefatory essays for this volume.

John A. Mackay is overly gracious, as ever, in deferring to the present editor the honor and praise so richly due him. His was the vision that made luminous a new chapter in theological journalism. He was himself a writer, a skilled craftsman of sentences, a constant reviser of what he had written, and a confident believer in the persuasive power of the written word.

But more than that, he always had something to say, for he wrestled with basic issues, always asserting his firm convictions about the authority of the Bible and the centrality of Jesus Christ. One of his favorite quotations, from his beloved Miguel de Unamuno, was: "Get a great idea, marry it, found a home with it, and raise a family."

In paying my respects to John Mackay, who has meant so much to me personally and professionally for so long, I am happy to recall that he, too, once published a collection of his editorials and essays in a volume aptly titled *Christianity on the Frontier* (Macmillan, 1950). He dedicated that volume "To my co-workers on Theology Today," as I would, if I could, dedicate this volume, appearing nearly thirty years later.

My dear friend, F. W. Dillistone, has prepared a typically acute and perceptive analysis of trends, moods, and accents during the long run of Theology Today. I'm emboldened to retain, and even parade, my diminutive nickname, when I remember that this distinguished Anglican Professor, Oxford Lecturer, and Dean of Liverpool Cathedral is known by everyone as "Dilly." He has a curious way of suddenly appearing at strategic intervals in my own pilgrimage.

We first met, I think, when he worked with John Mackay and others on the *Westminster Study Bible*, a cooperative reflection of the then-engrossing renewal of biblical theology. Later he surprised and embarrassed me by marching in the academic procession when I was inaugurated as the Benjamin B. Warfield Professor of Systematic Theology. Embarrassed, because my inaugural leaned heavily on something he had written earlier about the essence of the gospel. When I was first dabbling around in the miasmic swamps of primitive symbolism, Dilly's book on the subject showed me how a responsible and fruitful Christian perspective on symbols was possible. Now here he is again, this time with a remarkable overview of our journalistic stewardship. And why not? He's been a faithful reader since the beginning, an enthusiastic cheerleader for our efforts, and a valued contributor of articles and reviews. How delightful to meet Dilly again under such dulcet circumstances!

My two current associates, James I. McCord and John M. Mulder, are so much a part of the continuing progression of Theology Today that I would not know how to thank them for all they mean to the journal. Jim McCord, so he has told me and so I believe, is as proud of Theology Today as I could ever be. He says he finds it wherever he goes, and he goes almost everywhere. In libraries and pastors' studies, in theological seminaries and student rooms, in ecumenical centers and in the living rooms of church people—apparently, we are there.

These days presidents, deans, administrators, chief executive officers of all kinds come in for an unusually heavy dose of captious criticism. It is easy to blame them for our own frustrations and take out on them our feelings of inadequacy, petulance, and resentment. I don't buy that kind of cheap posturing and never did. When I was teaching, I always found Jim McCord disposed to discuss any reasonable request for support of what I was doing, and sometimes I was doing some way-out, innovative things. Usually, though not always, he approved. My impression is that he liked to be included in furthering educational experiments if they advanced the cause of learning and were in the best interests of the students. I found him similarly inclined when discussing faculty procedures and all the continuing policy decisions relating to THEOLOGY TODAY. But if an unannounced or unreasonable ultimatum were handed to him, he could dig in his heels, hold his ground, and stand fast.

Jim McCord has not only supported THEOLOGY TODAY as an instrument of intelligent Christian expression, but we have, I think, shared a common commitment about basic theological assumptions. I don't think we could work up an argument between us on the authority of the Bible, the meaning of Jesus Christ, or the fellowship of Christians in the church. I think we would stand together to affirm that there is, over all, a God who takes sovereign initiative in the whole process of creation and redemption, and whose purpose it is to make all things work together toward an ultimate consummation beyond our wildest dreams.

One should be reticent, no doubt, about ascribing faith affirmations for someone else, but I'm sure we are agreed about these matters, and others, and that they unite us in our common involvement in both the academic enterprise and the journalistic endeavors of THEOLOGY TODAY.

Lest this sound too saccharine or self-serving, let me add that within this orbit of compatibility we have our own differences of opinion and do not hesitate to make them known. It is just because we enjoy so much personal and theological congeniality that we also feel responsible to be honestly critical and corrective of each other.

John Mulder, my editorial associate, has been these past several years my right arm in programming and producing the quarterly issues of THEOLOGY TODAY. But more than that, he embodies, in my view, reason to hope for the future of a literate Christian world view, and nothing seems more crucial at the moment than that.

On the routine and necessary level of seeing each issue through the press, preparing publicity releases, and directing large mailing campaigns, John Mulder has done outstanding service. As senior editor, perhaps I take that too much for granted, but what intrigues me most about my younger partner is his ability to handle extra assignments, advise about future issues, suggest names, topics, books, and reviewers, and, all this time, he is carrying on a full schedule of teaching as a member of the Seminary faculty. As if that weren't enough, he is writing articles for other learned journals, and, this past year, he published two impressive books on American religious history.

V

It is urgent these days, so I believe, to emphasize the importance for younger scholars, teachers, preachers, and church administrators to become involved in the exacting and demanding craft of writing. We are a loquacious but illiterate generation. We talk a lot, but we haven't much to say, and don't know how to put it down on paper. Junior faculty members write, if at all, for themselves or each other, and most of them are bucking for promotion and tenure. Preachers who once upon a time published not only their sermons but decisive books on theology now seem curiously tongue-tied or reduced to self-help and inspirational how-to manuals.

It is easy, if not very instructive, to deplore a long and depressing decline in literate theological communication. Compared to the early days of THEOLOGY TODAY, when John Mackay, for example, enticed and persuaded us by the sheer impact of his verbal virtuosity, literary expression today seems dismal and dull. Perhaps it is an endemic disease of all writing today. Even the Sunday edition of *The New York Times* has been criticized for its vapid and empty prose, and I know for myself it is read more quickly and with less edification, as are the newsmagazines *Time* and *Newsweek*.

Whatever the reasons for the general decline in writing literate prose, the biggest problem we have today in editing THEOLOGY TODAY is finding authors who have something positive to say and who can say it with literary grace and style.

From my editorial experience of reading hundreds of manuscripts, most of which must be rejected, I would say that many would-be authors have three things going against them: (1) they are too derivative in their discussions, depending too much on what others have written; (2) they are too timid about coming straight out and asserting what they believe and why; and (3) they try to do too much, like many sermons with too many points.

The prophet Habakkuk, who along with the other "minor" prophets knew how to say a lot with a little, was given a divine assignment: "Write the vision; make it plain upon tablets, so he may run who reads it" (Hab. 2:2). The last phrase is not designed for commuters, hastily coming and going, but for those who want to understand readily and quickly what is written— "so they may read it at a glance, on the run, so to say."

That is still good advice, especially for younger writers who yearn and struggle, hoping that someday they will write that great, big, super book that will take the scholarly world by storm. Not only the minor prophets but most of the biblical writers knew how to write the vision so that it could be read easily.

I like Ambrose Bierce's definition that "good writing is clear thinking made visible." And that reminds me of Schleier-macher's definition that the essence of religion is not a knowing (philosophy) or a doing (ethics) but a feeling of absolute dependence on God (piety). But for religious and theological writers "seeing" suggests still another category. In the first place, we must "see" the vision, and then we must write it in such a way that it becomes a "visible" communication for the reader. So, believing is a seeing and, as the old expression has it, seeing is believing.

VI

There must be a personal equation somewhere that relates an editor's perspective to the themes being discussed and to the readership being addressed. Self-analysis at this point may not be very edifying, but something should be said about the point-of-viewing of an editor who has also been a teaching theologian.

Allow me, then, as a dwarf standing on the shoulders of giants, to invoke the names of Thomas Aquinas and Karl Barth. In the *Summa Theologica*, where each "article" to be examined is introduced by a question and argued pro and con, Aquinas eventually gets at his own resolution of the issue by way of a *Respondeo*, "I answer that . . ." Theologians, I do believe, must come clean and affirm their own considered opinions of faith and conviction. I am not so fearful these days of evangelical dogmatists, agnostic scoffers, humanist classicists, sentimental pietists, or liberal utopians; what frightens me are theologians and teachers of religious subjects who hide their beliefs, if any, behind their academic scholarship. I may be wrong, but I think I detect a growing wave of resentment everywhere against this kind of stylized objectivity.

Karl Barth, our modern *Summa* theologian, could hardly be accused of obscuring his own theological opinions. But he once startled some and delighted many when he commented, casually, that the contemporary theologian, preacher, or religion teacher should carry the Bible in one hand and the daily newspaper in the other. That just about perfectly defines what I regard as the responsibilities of an editor of a theological journal. (Perhaps in addition to the newspaper, an editor also needs a dictionary, an encyclopedia, a stack of pens and papers, and a fine typewriter, but that should go without saying.)

Let me try to make my own theological "response" in the spirit of the "Angelic Doctor" and according to the rubric laid down by King Karl. Like Aquinas, my own theological position, such as it may be, was—to use a medieval image—hammered out on the anvil of questions, objections, and contrary opinions. I nearly defected from a religious vocation during my first year at seminary simply because I felt a lack of intellectual curiosity on the part of many faculty members and students.

Authentic theological affirmations, I think, only emerge out of critical reflection, rigorous questioning, and continuing wrestling with the issues of truth and falsehood. I'm always suspicious of those who never want to query basic assumptions or who think Christian faith answers all the puzzling questions of life in a simplistic, obvious, or self-serving way. Reassuring faith, so it seems to me, comes as a God-given grace when all the questions and objections have been squarely confronted.

Moving from methodology to message, I'm convinced that "Bible and newspaper" provide a constructive clue for the vocation of any theologian, preacher, teacher, or religious editor. To me that means relating "what's happening" at any moment to the more enduring and classic tradition of Christian faith. It's disastrous, of course, to be blown about by every wind of doctrine, but it's equally tragic if no serious attention is paid at all to current events, even fads. As a theological editor, I make no apologies for exploiting shifting trends. I think one of the fine features of our editorial policy has always been to ventilate all kinds of religious moods, trends, and accents. As one of his former students told me not long ago, John Mackay used to say that he'd rather cool down a zealot than heat up a corpse. If anything's alive and kicking in the theological world, it merits some attention.

But there is a vast difference, in my view, between theological journalism and religious reporting. The difference is made by what is carried in the other hand. If, in the Barthian formula, one is also carrying around the Bible, and everything that the biblical revelation has meant for the Christian tradition, then a perspective on the news is provided, and a fulcrum for applying critical leverage is at hand. From the very beginning, THEOLOGY TODAY has had theological "aims" that undergirded and informed our journalistic enterprise. It could be that often enough the medium *is* the message, but I would prefer to say that the message makes possible interpretive analysis and critical evaluation of the medium.

So, what *is* the message? In my view, it is the gospel—the good news that God redeems us in Jesus Christ. *That* is what the Bible says; *that* is the voice of the Christian tradition; *that* is the testimony of convinced Christians in every century.

Anyone who carries the Bible in one hand and the daily newspaper in the other must, of necessity, be a generalist rather than a specialist. I would want to defend the specialist against attacks from populists, faddists, and simplifiers of all kinds. But those of us who try to articulate Christian truth must—so I think—be on the side of the generalists.

That, at least, has been my own conviction. The extensive and immodest bibliography included in this volume provides a continuing record of my stewardship. A minor item listed there really assumes major personal importance, namely, the annual edition since 1950 of *A Year with the Bible*. This little devotional manual has gone out to hundreds of thousands of church people over a period of nearly thirty years. I hope it has been of some service, but I know for myself that the yearly preparation of this booklet has been of inestimable value for me. It has forced me to read through the Bible, from cover to cover, every year for most of the years of my active theological and editorial apprenticeship.

One of the first things I did as a junior seminary instructor was to read through the whole corpus of the then-current "Moffatt New Testament Commentary." To be a generalist, so I persuaded myself, meant to dip into everything and be prepared to theologize on anything. Maybe the net was too big and cast too carelessly, but that random, comprehensive urge to cover the waterfront corresponds in many ways with my understanding of theology.

In this age of increasing specialization, I think it crucial to insist that theology includes everything—"the choir of heaven and furniture of earth," in Bishop Berkeley's wonderful phrase. There may be good reasons, academically, to divide the Bible, church history, and doctrinal theology into specialized compartments. But regardless of our specialties, I think all of us must necessarily be vitally involved in everything else. That is why I interpret "systematic theology" as an interlocking network of interdependent doctrines. This implicative system of Christian truth has become more meaningful and normative for me over the recent years. And, without having thought much about it, I suppose it has motivated my editorial supervision.

To balance the Bible (and the theological tradition), on the one hand, and the daily newspaper (and what's happening), on the other, seems to me the best possible way to be both really relevant and solidly rooted. I didn't deliberately plan it that way. But I'm enough of a "Reformed" theologian to believe in providence, grace, and forgiveness—regardless of our merit, or in spite of our demerit. Otherwise how could I have stuck at this dual task of theologizing and editorializing for so long?

VII

We began this rambling rejoinder by noting that editorial writing usually has an *ad hoc* quality. If that might threaten an editor's ego, there is consolation in the fact that the biblical redactors, who also wrote for their own times, are still very much with us. Even a quarterly journal such as THEOLOGY TODAY, I am persuaded to think, may achieve a kind of literary perpetuity on library shelves and in the research studies of future generations. So, even very transitory scribbling may partake of immortal prose. It's a staggering thought.

BIBLIOGRAPHY

The Writings of Hugh T. Kerr

Compiled by Elsie Anne McKee

DISSERTATIONS

The Search for a System of Ethics. Princeton University, A.B., 1931; awarded the "1869 Prize in Philosophy."

The Kingdom of God. Western (Pittsburgh) Theological Seminary, S.T.B., 1934.

The Plato of Diogenes Laertius. University of Pittsburgh, M.A., 1934.

The Person of Christ and the Principle of Redemption. University of Edinburgh, Ph.D., 1936.

BOOKS AND EDITED VOLUMES

A Compend of the Institutes of the Christian Religion by John Calvin, ed. by Hugh T. Kerr, Jr. Philadelphia: Presbyterian Board of Christian Education, 1939, 228 pp. Japanese translation. Tokyo: Shinkyo Shuppansha, 1958, 450 pp. Korean translation by Chong Sung Lee. Seoul: Christian Literature Society of Korea, 1961, 271 pp. Rev. ed., The Westminster Press, 1964, 228 pp. Also, London: Lutterworth Press, 1965, 228 pp.

A Compend of Luther's Theology, ed. by Hugh T. Kerr, Jr. The Westminster Press, 1943, 253 pp. Rev. ed., 1966, 253 pp.

Positive Protestantism: An Interpretation of the Gospel. The Westminster Press, 1950, 147 pp. Japanese translation. Tokyo: Shinkyo Shuppansha, 1954, 150 pp.

Mystery and Meaning in the Christian Faith. Toronto: Ryerson Press, 1958, 51 pp.

What Divides Protestants Today. Association Press, 1958, 127 pp.

By John Calvin: Introduction to the Writings of John Calvin. Selected and ed. by Hugh T. Kerr, Jr. Association Press, 1960, 124 pp.

Positive Protestantism: A Return to First Principles. Rev. ed., Prentice-Hall, 1963, 108 pp.

Sons of the Prophets, Leaders in Protestantism from Princeton Seminary. Ed. by Hugh T. Kerr, Jr. Princeton University Press, 1963, 227 pp.

Readings in Christian Thought. Ed. by Hugh T. Kerr, Jr. Abingdon Press, 1966, 382 pp.

Protestantism. Barron's Educational Series (Compact Studies of World Religions), 1978, 304 pp.

SYMPOSIA—ENCYCLOPAEDIAE

"John Calvin," *The World Book Encyclopedia,* 34th edition (1945).

"Arminius," "Atonement," "Blasphemy," "Catechism," "Conversion," *Collier's Encyclopedia* (1949).

"Docetism," "Pelagius," "Predestination," "Sabellians," *Collier's Encyclopedia* (1950).

"Holy, the Idea of the," *Twentieth Century Encyclopedia of Religious Knowledge.* Baker Book House, Vol. I, 1955, pp. 525–526.

"The Song of Songs" (Exposition), *The Interpreter's Bible,* Vol. V. Abingdon Press, 1956, pp. 102–148.

"Redemption," in *A Handbook of Christian Theology,* M. Halverson and A. A. Cohen, eds. Meridian Books, 1958, pp. 296–299.

"Emil Brunner," in *Ten Makers of Modern Protestant Thought,* George L. Hunt, ed. Association Press, 1958, pp. 69–77.

"John A. Mackay: An Appreciation," in *The Ecumenical Era in Church and Society,* Edward J. Jurji, ed. Macmillan, 1959, pp. 1–17.

"Protestantism," *The Encyclopedia Americana,* 1960 edition.

"Luther," "Protestantism," "Reformation," *The New Book of Knowledge.* Grolier, 1966.

"The Fate of the Will in Modern Theology: A Theological-Doctrinal Reflection," in *The Concept of Willing,* James N. Lapsley, ed. Abingdon Press, 1967, pp. 88–102.

"Technology and Tradition," in *The New Teachers,* Don M. Flournoy and Associates, eds. Jossey-Bass Publishers, 1972, pp. 50–60.

ARTICLES AND EDITORIALS

"Over-Seas Letter," *The Presbyterian Banner*, 121:17 (Oct. 25, 1934), 2, 9–10. "The Liverpool Cathedral; Edinburgh, Athens of the Modern World; Scottish Presbyterian Services; Launching the Queen Mary."

"Our Edinburgh Letter," *ibid.*, 121:21 (Nov. 22, 1934), 2, 8–9. "Parliament of Women; Faith in Man and God; Armistice Sunday; BBC and Religion; News from Germany; Unrest in Europe; A Royal Visit."

"Our Edinburgh Letter," *ibid.*, 121:26 (Dec. 27, 1934), 2, 9. "Moderator-Designate; The Church and War; Latin and Greek; Hints to Preachers; Learning to Fly; Science and Religion Again; The Labrador Doctor; Albert Schweitzer, Lecturer."

"Our Edinburgh Letter," *ibid.*, 121:30 (Jan. 24, 1935), 2, 9–10. "The New Year and the Church; The Brief Statement; Leisure Reading; Missions Crisis; Evidences of Revival."

"Our Edinburgh Letter," *ibid.*, 121:34 (Feb. 21, 1935), 2, 9–10. "Poet of Humanity; Sunday, Day of Rest and Work; A Fifth Gospel; Jubilee in Rome; Impressions of Ireland; Examination on the Bible."

"Our Edinburgh Letter," *ibid.*, 121:39 (March 28, 1935), 2, 7–8. "University Service; Karl Barth; Warrack Lectures; Letter Writing; Requiescat in Pace."

"Our Edinburgh Letter," *ibid.*, 121:43 (April 25, 1935), 2, 8–9. "Church and School; Suburban Church Methods; Epstein's Christ; The Motor Menace; Wishing Wells."

"Over-Seas Letter," *ibid.*, 121:48 (May 30, 1935), 2, 7–8. "From Scotland to Germany; May Day; Inflation Days; Groupers in Denmark; Church Service."

"A Letter from Germany," *ibid.*, 121:52 (June 27, 1935), 2, 8–9. "Anti-Jewish World League; Roman Catholic Smuggling; German Youth; We, the Young Generation; A New Marriage Service; The Monastery at Bebenhausen."

"A Letter from Germany," *ibid.*, 122:5 (Aug. 1, 1935), 2, 9–10. "The Augsburg Manifesto; Corpus Christi Day; Wurmlinger Kapelle; A Window and an Opera; Earthquake in Tübingen."

"A Letter from Geneva," *ibid.*, 122:10 (Sept. 5, 1935), 2, 9–11. "The Geneva Conference; Opening Chapel Service; Personalities; The

Church and the Churches; Reformation Monument; A Visit to the League."

"Over-Seas Letter," *ibid.*, 122:13 (Sept. 26, 1935), 2, 9–10. "Northern Italy; World War Landmarks; The City in the Sea; Milan and Monza; The Italian Lakes."

"Over-Seas Letter," *ibid.*, 122:19 (Nov. 7, 1935), 2, 8–9. "Life in Germany; Germany—Free, Unified, Respected; Will There Be Another Inflation?; The Levelling of Society; The Church's Struggle."

"Edinburgh Letter," *ibid.*, 122:23 (Dec. 5, 1935), 2, 7–9. "The Principal of New College; Sir George Adam Smith; Edinburgh Baptist Convention; The Bishop of Durham; The Moderator Designate; Rectoral Election; War Reactions."

"Our Edinburgh Letter," *ibid.*, 122:26 (Dec. 26, 1935), 2, 8–9. "Carnegie Centenary; Mr. Eden in Edinburgh; Dr. Schweitzer's Gifford Lectures; Dr. Black and the Groupers; Shakespeare and G.B.S.; The Christmas Spirit."

"Over-Seas Letter," *ibid.*, 122:31 (Jan. 30, 1936), 2, 8–10. "1935 Retrospect; Madame Tussaud's; Between the Old and New Testaments; The Salisbury Stonehenge; The Romance of Gretna Green; A Parable, a Prayer, and a Poem."

"Edinburgh Letter," *ibid.*, 122:36 (March 5, 1936), 2, 8–9. "George V of Happy Memory; Rudyard Kipling; Cunningham Lectures; Dr. Whyte's Centenary; German Voices; Front Page News."

"Edinburgh Letter," *ibid.*, 122:39 (March 26, 1936), 2, 9. "Our Knowledge of God; Scotland's Health; Palace in the Cowgate; Items Here and Abroad."

"Edinburgh Letter," *ibid.*, 122:43 (April 23, 1936), 2, 9. "Christian Pacifists; Naval Parsons; The Good Old Days; Religious Films; Fire Walkers."

"Over-Seas Letter," *ibid.*, 122:48 (May 28, 1936), 2, 12–13. "The Croall Lectures; Rectoral Address; General Assembly Plans; The Fool Hath Said; Professor Tillich."

"The Morning Cometh," *Pageant,* I:1 (1938), 3.

"Theological Existence Today." *The Register* (Louisville Presbyterian Theological Seminary), XXVII (1938), 7–12.

"An Interpretation of Karl Heim," *Religion in Life,* VII (1938), 128–139.

"Christian Education and Evangelism for Today," *Christian Observer* (Louisville, Ky.), 126:25 (1938), 5–6.

"Christian Principles in Sabbath Observance," *ibid.*, 127:11 (1939), 7.

"Religion: Experience or Doctrine," *The Presbyterian Tribune*, 58:5 (1943), 9–10.

"The Cross Is Crucial," *The Presbyterian*, CXIII:14 (1943), 3, 5.

"Peace and War," *Church Management*, XIX:10 (1943), 49.

"Semantics and Sermonics," *The Christian Century Pulpit*, XIV:11 (1943), 260.

"Our American Theological Heritage," *Christendom*, IX (1944), 344–353.

"Post-War Theology," *Religion in Life*, XIII (1944), 556–561.

"What It Means to Be a Presbyterian," *Presbyterian Youth*, Sept. 1944.

"The Human Problem in Contemporary Thought," *Theology Today*, I (1944), 158–172 (hereinafter cited as *TT*).

"The Church in the World," *TT*, I (1945), 541–544.

"A Decade of 'Pulpit' Texts," *The Pulpit*, XVI (1945), 164–165.

"Theological Table-Talk: My Country; The Sacraments and the Church's Witness; Chaplains in Mental Hospitals; In the Spirit of Saint Paul?; Ministerial Predicament; Not a Judas; New Religious Publishing," *TT*, II (1945), 113–117.

"Theological Table-Talk: Coventry Controversy; An Inter-Faith Picture Book; Kaj Munk, Martyr, Dramatist; Christianity, the Church, and the Creeds; Interdenominational Training for the Ministry; A Theological Chasm?," *TT*, II (1945), 248–254.

"The Gospel of Redemption," *TT*, II (1945), 294–299.

"Theological Table-Talk: Our Theological Vocabulary; Karl Barth on the Germans; Habits Worth Holding To; The Last Chapter of Job; We Shall Re-Build," *TT*, II (1946), 377–383.

"Some Living Issues," *TT*, II (1946), 435–440.

"Theological Table-Talk: What's in a Name?; Sholem Asch's Spiritual Credo; Humanism as Religion; The Christian Commando Campaigns; A Cut-Flower Morality," *TT* II (1946), 537–542.

"Book Helps for the Second Quarter, 1946," *Westminster Uniform Lesson Teacher*, LXIV:3 (1946), 58.

"The Present Theological Atmosphere," *TT*, III (1946), 10–15.

"Theological Table-Talk: Journalistic Ventures on the Continent; *The Gauntlet*—Scandal or Challenge?; The Theology of Patriotism; Evangelism—Where to Begin," *TT*, III (1946), 103–108.

"The Bible Today," *TT,* III (1946), 151–156.

"Theological Table-Talk: Books and the Book; The Theology of Ordination; Following or Leading?; Grammar and Christology," *TT,* III (1946), 247–252.

"The Reformation Testimony," *TT,* III (1946), 294–298.

"Theological Table-Talk: The Evangelical Alliance; The Minister's Motives; The Church in Search of a Theology; A Time to Laugh," *TT,* III (1946), 385–390.

"The Spirit Is Life," *TT,* III (1947), 439–443.

"Theological Table-Talk: The Preacher as Theologian; Youth's Dilemma and Christian Hope; The Problem of Contact; A Philosophical Poem; Books and Periodicals for Europe," *TT,* III (1947), 526–532.

"The Church in Search of a Theology," *The Presbyterian Record* (Canada), LXXII (1947), 11.

"Theology in Travail," *TT,* IV (1947), 11–16.

"Theological Table-Talk: Natural Theology; William Temple as Thinker; Growing Up in the Christian Faith; The Successful Minister; Attack on Book Reviews," *TT,* IV (1947), 114–121.

"Souls, Systems, and God," *TT,* IV (1947), 168–172.

"Theological Table-Talk: C. S. Lewis Pays a Debt; '. . . And Was Made Man'; The Teacher Problem; Puritan Architecture; The Chaplain as Counsellor," *TT,* IV (1947), 259–265.

"Theological Table-Talk: Theology Twenty-Five Years Ago; A Hymn Centenary; Barth on Baptism; Bridging the Gulf; Something to Sing About," *TT,* IV (1947), 400–406.

"Theological Table-Talk: The Ministry and Evangelism; The Christian Classics; Rufus Jones and a Faith for Today; An Index of Religious Periodicals; Religion and Education," *TT,* IV (1948), 534–542.

"The Preacher as Theologian," *The Pastor,* II:7 (1948), 2–4.

"The Queen of the Sciences," *ibid.,* II:8 (1948), 10–12.

"Protestantism and the Gospel," *ibid.,* II:9 (1948), 6–8.

"Our Uneasy Conscience and the Ecumenical Mood," *ibid.,* II:10 (1948), 16–18.

"Old Truths in New Words," *Presbyterian Life,* I:6 (1948), 23, 30.

"Concerning Culture and Religion," *TT,* V (1948), 8–12.

"Theological Table-Talk: A Humanist View of Death; A Suppressed Report on Spiritualism; Reprinting Religious Books; The Religion of Rembrandt; The Teacher as Apostle," *TT,* V (1948), 100–106.

"The Things That Cannot Be Shaken," *TT,* V (1948), 150–155.

"Theological Table-Talk: Alliance of Reformed Churches; The Message of the World Council; Taking the Long View; The Christian and the Jew; Reformed Churchmanship," *TT,* V (1948), 278–286.

"Faith and Civilization," *TT,* V (1948), 310–315.

"Theological Table-Talk: New Theological Journal; An Ancient Hymnary; Remember or Perish; Watts Bicentenary; The Holy Spirit and Church Unity; The Lord's Prayer and Thanksgiving," *TT,* V (1948), 406–414.

"Faith and the Sciences," *TT,* V (1949), 467–471.

"Theological Table-Talk: *The Ecumenical Review;* Conference of Christians and Jews; The Principle of Protest; The Confessional and Confessing Church; The Frontier Fellowship," *TT,* V (1949), 544–552.

"Keeping Up with Theological Trends," *The Pastor,* XXII:10 (1949), 11–13.

"Faith and History," *TT,* VI (1949), 5–9.

"Theological Table-Talk: *The Big Fisherman;* The Apostolic Credo; Young People and the Church; Biblical Scholarship and the Church; Prayer and the Lord's Prayer," *TT,* VI (1949), 92–102.

"Faith and Culture," *TT,* VI (1949), 150–156.

"Theological Table-Talk: The Barth-Niebuhr Colloquy; Christianity and Culture; Asking Them Questions; Catholic or Roman Catholic?; Orthodox Intentions; The Dynamism of Repentance," *TT,* VI (1949), 235–246.

"Phases and Facets of the Religious Situation," *TT,* VI (1949), 292–296.

"Theological Table-Talk: Withdrawal and Return; A Disturbing Religious Census; Theology in Finland; A Theological Classic; The Prayer Book and Ecumenicity," *TT,* VI (1949), 377–385.

"The Sense of Beyondness," *TT,* VI (1950), 438–443.

"Theological Table-Talk: The Silence of the Pulpit; Vocational Evangelism; The Making of the Minister; As Others See Us; Substituted Love; Women in the Ministry," *TT,* VI (1950), 531–540.

"For the Catechumen Class," *Monday Morning,* XV:10 (1950), 4–5.

"Love's Intention: The Motive of the Atonement," *Interpretation,* IV (1950), 131–142.

"Faith of Our Fathers," *The Princeton Seminary Bulletin*, XLIII (1950), 13–17; inaugural address as Benjamin B. Warfield Professor of Doctrinal Theology.

"The Church Declares Its Faith," (series of eight expositions on the Apostles' Creed), *Crossroads*, I:1 (1950), 25–34. Also *Westminster Teacher*, I:1 (1950), 77–88.

"Interpretations," *TT*, VII (1950), 9–12.

"Theological Table-Talk: Challenge to Democracy; The Pastor and the Theologian; Tax Exemption and the Churches; The Theology of the Last Decade; The City Church Takes a Stand," *TT*, VII (1950), 95–102.

"Concerning Religion and the Gospel," *TT*, VII (1950), 150–156.

"Theological Table-Talk: The Marks of a Good Sermon; Barth in English; The Puritan Challenge to Religious Literature; Calvin and the Trinity; Anniversary of French Review," *TT*, VII (1950), 237–244.

"Things Which Cannot Be Shaken," *TT*, VII (1950), 293–298.

"Theological Table-Talk: The Language of Reality; God, Immortality, and Statistics; Pamphlet Series; Brunner on Election; Science and Maturity; Approach to Assumption," *TT*, VII (1950), 376–385.

"The Churches and Our Times," *TT*, VII (1951), 436–441.

"Theological Table-Talk: Fact and Fancy; The Preacher as Teacher; Japanese Translations; The Christian Answer to Animism; Quakers and the Ministry; The New Testament Vocabulary," *TT*, VII (1951), 517–524.

"The Presbytery and the Seminary," *Monday Morning*, XVI:28 (1951), 3–4.

"Re-Presenting the Faith," *TT*, VIII (1951), 6–8.

"Theological Table-Talk: A Statement from Hromádka; The Case Against *The Miracle;* Reformed Ecumenicity; The Theology of Newton; On Making Religion Real; Christian Social Action; The New Testament Vocabulary (cont.)," *TT*, VIII (1951), 97–107.

"Expecting the Unexpected," *TT*, VIII (1951), 145–149.

"Theological Table-Talk: Schweitzer's Epilogue; Worship and the World; Prospects for Liberalism; Anglican Tensions; Three New Journals; Theological Orthography," *TT*, VIII (1951), 234–243.

"The Centrality of Christ," *TT*, VIII (1951), 294–299.

"Theological Table-Talk: An Inventory of Beliefs; The Genevan Psalter of 1551; The Structure of Thomistic Theology; Rural

Preaching; The Individual's Assumptive World," *TT*, VIII (1951), 380–389.

" 'Perplexed But Not Despairing,' " *TT*, VIII (1952), 434–439.

"Theological Table-Talk: Ivy League Conservative; Preparations for Lund; The Ministry of Teaching; The Point of Entry; Mixed Marriages: Fact and Fiction," *TT*, VIII (1952), 534–544.

"The Context of Christian Prayer," *The Princeton Seminary Bulletin*, XLV (1952), 5–10.

"Concerning Church and Mission," *TT*, IX (1952), 7–12.

"Theological Table-Talk: Buber on Religion and Philosophy; The Reformed Faith and Eastern Orthodoxy; Religion in the Colleges; Platonism as an Open System; Bach and the Bible; Minute Biographies," *TT*, IX (1952), 107–116.

"The Minister and the Ministry," *TT*, IX (1952), 158–162.

"Theological Table-Talk: The Taboo of Self-Criticism; Modern Miracle Play; Forgiveness and Legal Justice; Man-Woman Relationships; Authors Review Their Own Books; Harvard Divinity School; Christianity and Modern Man," *TT*, IX (1952), 223–233.

"Nature, Man, and God," *TT*, IX (1952), 298–303.

"Theological Table-Talk: The Old Gospel for the New Day; The Drama of Nicene Theology; The What and How of Communication; Chambers' *Witness;* New Theological Journals," *TT*, IX (1952), 376–386.

"The Church on the Spot," *TT*, IX (1953), 442–447.

"Theological Table-Talk: Enlightened Ignorance; The Town Hall of the World; A Reformation Tract; Ministry to Military Personnel; Estonian Theological Society," *TT*, IX (1953), 519–526.

"The Place and Status of Women," *Presbyterian Outlook*, CXXXV:11 (1953), 5–6.

"The Place and Status of Women in the Reformed Tradition," *The Presbyterian World*, XXII (1953), 101–109.

"The Word for Today," *TT*, X (1953), 11–16.

"Theological Table-Talk: Full-Time Christian Service; Theology and the Universe; Banderilla; Canadian Church Manual; A Lie Inside the Truth; New Journals; On Loyalty and Freedom," *TT*, X (1953), 96–106.

"Revelation and Relevancy," *TT*, X (1953), 143–149.

"Christ in Life and Thought," *TT*, X (1953), 149–153.

"Theological Table-Talk: American Theological Society; Demythologizing; The Twenty-Six Great Books; The Cleft Between Classroom and Chapel; For Those Who Have Had No Greek; Kierkegaard and the Bible," *TT,* X (1953), 240–248.

"A New and Living Hope," *TT,* X (1953), 304–309.

"Theological Table-Talk: The Christian Hope; A Synthesis of Knowledge; Lay Preaching; A Legal Question?; The Bible and Theology," *TT,* X (1953), 397–406.

"Theology as Queen and Servant," *TT,* X (1954), 456–461.

"Theological Table-Talk: Some Facts and Figures; Reprints, Translations, and Books; A Ten-Year Theological Index; The Structure of Theology," *TT,* X (1954), 525–532.

"Does the Gospel Say Something to Me?," *Crossroads,* V:1 (1954), 3–4.

"Touching the Untouchable," *TT,* XI (1954), 1–7.

"Theological Table-Talk: Fear and Freedom; Eschatology and History; Episcopal Faculty Mission; Lafayette College Survey; Servants of Christ the King; Mixed Company," *TT,* XI (1954), 85–95.

"Theological Table-Talk: 'In God We Trust'; Convincement and Concern; The Poetry and Prose of Faith; Jung in Translation," *TT,* XI (1954), 269–276.

"Making Old Things New," *TT,* XI (1954), 301–306.

"Theological Table-Talk: A Lesson in History; Negro Education and Religion; Theological Study Groups; A Theology of Stewardship; Reformed Alliance," *TT,* XI (1954), 385–391.

"Theological Table-Talk: A Comparative Catechism; Does Religion Beget Freedom?; Religion Through Scientific Study; Theological Education—What, How, Why?," *TT,* XI (1955), 528–533.

"Theological Table-Talk: The Non-Church Movement; Suffering as a Christian; Lutheranism and Culture; Theological Training—Asia and Africa; New Testament Society Journal," *TT,* XII (1955), 97–102.

"A Kierkegaard Centenary," *TT,* XII (1955), 291–294.

"Counting the Cost," *TT,* XII (1956), 425–429.

"The Christian Experience," *TT,* XII (1956), 430–433.

"Theological Table-Talk: Luther Translation; As Others See Us; New Reformed Hymnal; Negro Theological Education; Priesthood and Ministry," *TT,* XII (1956), 511–515.

"Strength Through Weakness," *British Weekly,* CXXXIX, 3659 (Dec. 27, 1956), 7; also *The Princeton Seminary Bulletin,* L (1957), 15–20; also *Crossroads,* VIII:2 (1958), 2–4.

"The Life of Man," *TT,* XIII (1956), 6–8.

"Theological Table-Talk: Intellectual Conversion; What About Baptism?; Greek and German; A Theology of Healing; Imperialism and Theology; Comic Book Life of Christ," *TT,* XIII (1956), 87–92.

"Tradition, Theology, and the Churches," *TT,* XIII (1956), 144–148.

"Theological Table-Talk: Theology in Russia; Two Dilemmas; Religion for Festive Occasions; Civil Defense and the Clergy; Signs and Symbols; Theology for Laymen," *TT,* XIII (1956), 232–239.

"A Colloquium on Barth," *TT,* XIII (1956), 294–297.

"Theological Table-Talk: The Curse of Conformity; Humanistic Communitarianism; Out-Dying the Pagan World; Campus Evangelism; Essentialism and Existentialism," *TT,* XIII (1956), 399–406.

"Hard or Soft Sell?," *TT,* XIII (1957), 437–442; also *Information Service,* National Council of Churches, May 11, 1957; also *New Christian Advocate,* II (1958), 41–43.

"Faith and Order in the Church," *TT,* XIII (1957), 442–446.

"Theological Table-Talk: Winds of Doctrine; The Sacrifice of Theology; Religion and the Arts; An Adaptable Altar; A Responsible Critique; Sunday Selling," TT, XIII (1957), 527–534.

"Past, Present, Future," *TT,* XIV (1957), 8–12.

"Theological Table-Talk: Sister Luke and Her Rule; Lent and Holy Week; A.A.T.S.; Latin in the Schools; A Czech Message to the Churches; Barth on Romans 5; Oiled Your Bible Lately?," *TT,* XIV (1957), 106–114.

"A Four Dimension Faith," *TT,* XIV (1957), 153–158.

"Evangel and Ethic," *TT,* XIV (1957), 158–161.

"Theological Table-Talk: Bultmann on Harnack; Religion and Life; Sin Without Salvation; Adam and Eve in Glass; A Birthday Celebration," *TT,* XIV (1957), 256–262.

"Fulfilling the Ministry," *TT,* XIV (1957), 314–318.

"Theological Table-Talk: Almost Persuaded; Drama in the Church; The Voice Above and the Knock Below; Theology and Mission; Gennadius Library; Library Theology," *TT,* XIV (1957), 401–408.

"Dead Dilemmas and Living Paradoxes," *TT,* XIV (1958), 449–454.

"The Individual Amid Social Upheaval," *TT,* XIV (1958), 454–457.

"Theological Table-Talk: Where Is the Church?; Edwards on the

Will; Words and Music; Graduate Studies; Agape and Eros," *TT*, XIV (1958), 527–534.

"Living on the Growing Edge," *TT*, XV (1958), 8–12.

"Theological Table-Talk: A Good Look at the World; Church Integration in Cleveland; Theology and Social Witness in Japan; Baptist History and Theology; Calvin and Channing," *TT*, XV (1958), 115–121.

"History and Meaning," *TT*, XV (1958), 160–164.

"Theological Table-Talk: Summer Doldrums; The Impatience of Job; The Vocation of Anglicanism; A Split-Level Church; For Crying Out Loud," *TT*, XV (1958), 246–254.

"In but Not of the World," *TT*, XV (1958), 293–298.

"Servant Lord and Servant People," *TT*, XV (1958), 298–301.

"Word and Worship," *TT*, XV (1959), 447–451.

"Theological Table-Talk: The Feel of the Word; Worship and the Arts; Dialogical Personalism; Protestant Phobias; The Here and the Hereafter," *TT*, XV (1959), 549–556.

"Theology and Imagination," *TT*, XVI (1959), 10–14.

"Theological Table-Talk: Sounding the Grace Note; Methodism's Lost Voice; Drive-In Congregation; Interseminary Seminar; The Worry-Go-Round; Revolutionary Ethics," *TT*, XVI (1959), 90–98.

"Christianity and Social Conscience," *TT*, XVI (1959), 148–152.

"Theological Table-Talk: The Ministry of the Laity; What Is Christianity?; A United Church Creed; Now You See It, Now You Don't; The Beginning and the End," *TT*, XVI (1959), 245–254.

"In Honor of John A. Mackay," *TT*, XVI (1959), 311–316.

"Competition or Conversation," *TT*, XVI (1960), 439–443.

"Theological Table-Talk: Birth, Death, Rebirth; Upgrading the Layman; Clerical Characters; Mennonite Focus; Synthetic Pentecost," *TT*, XVI (1960), 512–519.

"Theological Table-Talk: The Museum; Bread and Wine; The High Places; The Red Tape Worm; Let There Be Darkness," *TT*, XVII (1960), 366–374. Reprint of "Bread and Wine" in *Information Service*, XL:17 (Oct. 14, 1961) by WCC.

"New Occasions Teach New Duties," *TT*, XVII (1961), 417–423.

"Theological Table-Talk: The Light of the World; Plain Talk from a Bishop; Mary, Mother, Mediatrix; Religion in State Universities; Oedipus Re-Mythologized," *TT*, XVIII (1961), 87–93.

"Theological Table-Talk: Christendom and the Population Explosion; 'And There Was Light'; The New Agnosticism; The *N.E.B.*; Biblical Linguistics and Kerygmatic Theology," *TT*, XVIII (1961), 337–347.

"Theological Table-Talk: The Parish: Local and Ecumenical; Concern for Catholicity; Tomorrow's Education; Who Carries the Torch?; Religion and the History of Religion," *TT*, XVIII (1962), 482–492.

"The Christ-Life as Mythic and Psychic Symbol," *Numen*, IX (1962), 143–158; also in *The Princeton Seminary Bulletin*, LV (1962), 25–34.

"Theological Table-Talk: Sin, Sex, and the Soul; Migrant Theology; A Dimension of the Ineffable; Lecture Almanac," *TT*, XIX (1962), 90–97.

"Theological Table-Talk: Church Architecture Guild," *TT*, XIX (1962), 235–254.

"Building the Reformed Image," *Reformed Liturgics*, I (1963), 5–11. Reprinted in *The Reformed and Presbyterian World*, XXVII (1963), 304–310.

"Denominationalism," *Princeton Alumni Weekly*, LXIV (Oct. 1, 1963), 3.

"Theological Table-Talk: Christianity and Religion; Popcorn with Salt; Two Generations of Barth; Religion and the Arts; Bookstore Library; Dogma Obsolescence," *TT*, XX (1963), 87–94.

"Theological Table-Talk: Is God Up or Out or In?; Ecumenical Critique; Is Anatomy Destiny?; A Raw Slice of Life; Spirit Is Like the Wind," *TT*, XX (1963), 258–265.

"The Quick and the Dead," *TT*, XX (1963), 322–326.

"Time for a Critical Theology," *TT*, XX (1964), 461–466.

"Theological Table-Talk: Honesty as Theology; The Funeral, Death, and the Church; Last Stop—Silence; Pilgrim or Passenger?; Ministry Without Commitment," *TT*, XXI (1964), 86–94.

"What Do We Look for in a Church Building?" *AIA Journal*, XLII (1964), 62.

"Theological Table-Talk: How to Build a Church; Negro Christianity; Catholic-Protestant Reappraisal; Poetry and Preaching; Restructuring Church and Society," *TT*, XXI (1964), 342–351.

"Theological Table-Talk: The Ministry and the Seminaries; The Parochialism of the Present; Making the Holy Common," *TT*, XXI (1965), 485–490.

"The Open Option," *TT*, XXII (1966), 467–471.

"Theological Table-Talk: Tillich in Dialogue; Re-Mythologizing; Presence; Church And/In Society; Feedback," *TT,* XXIII (1966), 120–128.

"Theology as Encounter," *TT,* XXIII (1966), 175–180.

"Theology as Irritant," *TT,* XXIII (1967), 459–466.

"Theological Table-Talk: Turning the Corner; The Church at the Center; Tune In, Turn On, Drop Out; What's Happening?; American Religious Trends," *TT,* XXIV (1967), 56–63.

"Man and His World," *TT,* XXIV (1967), 276–279.

"Beyond the Crossroads," *TT,* XXV (1968), 8–9.

"Theological Table-Talk: What's an Institution For?; Professional Integrity; The Artist's Self-Image; To Pray Is to Play," *TT,* XXV (1968), 81–87.

"From People to Persons," *TT,* XXV (1968), 145–148.

"The Rhetoric of Theology," *TT,* XXV (1968), 291–294.

"For Twenty-Five Years—Doing Our Own Thing," *TT,* XXV (1969), 411–415.

"What Ever Happened to Dialogue?," *TT,* XXVI (1969), 1–4. Reprinted locally by Christian Board of Publication, St. Louis, Missouri.

"Change in (and by?) the Seminaries," *TT,* XXVI (1969), 107–110.

"Still Running," *TT,* XXVII (1971), 369–370.

"Education in General and Theological Education," *TT,* XXVII (1971), 434–452.

"Seminarians and Self-Directed Study," *The Princeton Seminary Bulletin,* LXIV (1971), 69–76.

"The Church and Change," *TT,* XXVIII (1971), 1–4.

"Lifelong Learning," *TT,* XXVIII (1971), 133–141.

"The Student as Person," *TT,* XXVIII (1972), 395–405.

"Who Is the Seminarian?," *The Princeton Seminary Bulletin,* LXV (1972), 100–107.

"A Paul Lehmann Festschrift," *TT,* XXIX (1972), 1–2.

"Ecosystems and Systematics," *TT,* XXIX (1972), 104–119.

"Classroom as Community," *TT,* XXIX (1973), 394–401.

"A Failure of Perception," *TT,* XXX (1973), 49–51.

"Time Out," *TT,* XXX (1973), 105–110.

"Wash Your Language," *TT,* XXX (1973), 211–217.

"This Point in Time," *TT,* XXX (1974), 328–330.

"Reflections on an Experiment," *Improving College and University Teaching,* XXII (1974), 195–197.

"What Use Is Religion?," *TT,* XXXI (1974), 1–5.

"The Stoic as Heroic," *TT,* XXXI (1974), 183–186.

"How to Write an Article," *TT,* XXXI (1975), 289–291.

"Seminarian, Meet Theologian," *The Christian Century,* 92:5 (Feb. 5–12, 1975), 105–107.

"Not like They Used To," *TT,* XXXII (1975), 1–9.

"What's the Story?," *TT,* XXXII (1975), 129–132.

"The Fearful Distance," *TT,* XXXII (1975), 219–221.

"Review of Reviews," *TT,* XXXII (1976), 419–423.

"This Issue," *TT,* XXXIII (1976), 3–4.

"Tomorrow via Yesterday," *TT,* XXXIII (1976), 196–197.

"Where Are the People?," *TT,* XXXIII (1976), 219–223.

"One Flew Over the Cuckoo's Nest: A Psycho-Symbolic Review" (with Lee Myers), *TT,* XXXIII (1976), 285–290.

"The Pastor and the Prophet," *TT,* XXXIII (1977), 325–328. Reprinted in *The Blind Theologian,* Louisville Theological Seminary. Also in *The New Pulpit Digest,* LVII (1977), 48–50.

"Treasures of Tutankhamun," *TT,* XXXIV (1977), 1–8.

"Theological Roots," *TT,* XXXIV (1977), 239–241.

"The Language of Prayer," *TT,* XXXIV (1978), 353–356.

"Prospects for Theology and the Church," *TT,* XXXIV (1978), 357.

"Apostles to the People," *TT,* XXXV (1978), 33–41.

"The Sacred, the Holy, and the Soul," *TT,* XXXV (1978), 135–138.

"Thinking Made Visible," *TT,* XXXV (1978), 393ff.

"What My Teachers Taught Me," II, XXXV (1978), 247–253.

"Who Teaches What to Whom?," *The Christian Century,* 95:4 (Feb. 1–8, 1978), 115–118.

REVIEWS

H. H. Farmer, *The World and God,* in *The Register,* XXV (1936), 18.

William Temple, *Christianity in Thought and Practice,* in *ibid.,* XXV (1936), 18.

A. G. Widgery, *Living Religions and Modern Thought,* in *ibid.,* XXV (1936), 18–19.

Edwin E. Aubrey, *Present Theological Tendencies,* in *ibid.,* XXV (1936), 18–19.

C. H. Dodd, *The Apostolic Preaching and Its Developments,* in *ibid.,* XXV (1936), 19.

Nicholas Berdyaev, *The Fate of Man in the Modern World,* in *ibid.,* XXV (1936), 19.

Karl Barth, *The Church and the Churches,* and Nicholas Arseniev, *We Beheld His Glory,* in *ibid.,* XXV (1936), 19.

Karl Barth, *God in Action: Theological Addresses,* in *ibid.,* XXV (1936), 19–20.

Harris F. Rall, *A Faith for Today,* in *ibid.,* XXV (1936), 19–20.

E. G. Homrighausen, *Christianity in America: A Crisis,* in *ibid.,* XXV (1936), 20.

E. C. Moore, *The Nature of Religion,* in *ibid.,* XXV (1936), 20.

Karl Heim, *The Church of Christ and the Problems of the Day,* in *ibid.,* XXV (1936), 20.

Emil Brunner, *Our Faith,* in *ibid.,* XXV (1936), 20.

Albert Schweitzer, *Indian Thought and Its Development,* in *ibid.,* XXV (1936), 20.

Shailer Mathews, *New Faith for Old: An Autobiography,* in *ibid.,* XXV (1936), 20–21.

Nathaniel Micklem, *What Is the Faith?,* in *ibid.,* XXVI (1937), 16–19.

H. V. White, *A Theology for Christian Missions,* in *ibid.,* XXVI (1937), 16–19.

Sergius Bulgakov, *The Orthodox Church,* in *ibid.,* XXVI (1937), 16–19.

Frank Gavin, *Some Aspects of Contemporary Greek Orthodox Thought,* in *ibid.,* XXVI (1937), 16–19.

F. S. Downs, *The Heart of the Christian Faith,* in *ibid.,* XXVI (1937), 16–19.

R. J. Clinchy, *A Reasonable Faith,* in *ibid.,* XXVI (1937), 16–19.

C. S. Macfarland, *Trends of Christian Thinking,* in *ibid.,* XXVI (1937), 16–19.

A. R. Wentz, *A New Strategy for Theological Education,* in *ibid.,* XXVI (1937), 16–19.

H. R. Mackintosh, *Types of Modern Theology,* in *ibid.,* XXVI (1937), 33–36.

Sydney Cave, *The Doctrine of the Work of Christ,* in *ibid.,* XXVI (1937), 33–36.

William Ernest Hocking, *Thoughts on Death and Life,* in *ibid.,* XXVI (1937), 33–36.

C. R. Skinner, *Liberalism Faces the Future,* in *ibid.,* XXVI (1937), 33–36.

Reinhold Niebuhr, *Beyond Tragedy,* in *ibid.,* XXVI (1937), 33–36.

Edgar S. Brightman, *The Future of Christianity,* in *ibid.,* XXVI (1937), 33–36.

E. F. Scott, *The Validity of the Gospel Record,* in *ibid.,* XXVII (1938), 12.

Rufus M. Jones, *The Eternal Gospel,* in *ibid.,* XXVII (1938), 13; also in *Pageant,* I:8 (1938), 27.

D. S. Cairns, *The Riddle of the World,* in *The Register,* XXVII (1938), 13.

Hornell Hart, *Skeptic's Quest,* in *ibid.,* XXVII (1938), 13–14; also in *Pageant,* I:7 (1938), 27.

John S. Whale, *What Is a Living Church?,* in *ibid.,* XXVII (1938), 14.

H. A. Jones, *Evangelism and the Laity,* in *ibid.,* XXVII (1938), 14.

Oliver C. Quick, *Doctrines of the Creed,* in *ibid.,* XXVII (1938), 16–17; also in *Pageant,* I:12 (1938), 25.

J. S. Whale, *The Right to Believe,* in *The Register,* XXVII (1938), 16–17; also in *Pageant,* I:12 (1938), 25.

John Haynes Holmes, *Rethinking Religion,* in *The Register,* XXVII (1938), 16–17; also in *Pageant,* I:12 (1938), 25.

Hall Caine, *Life of Christ,* in *The Register,* XXVII (1938), 16–17; also in *Pageant,* I:12 (1938), 25.

H. G. Wood, *Did Christ Really Live?,* in *The Register,* XXVII (1938), 16–17; also in *Pageant,* I:12 (1938), 25.

Hans Lietzmann, *The Founding of the Church Universal,* in *The Register,* XXVII (1938), 16–17; also in *Pageant,* I:12 (1938), 25.

James Moffatt, *The First Five Centuries of the Church,* in *The Register,* XXVII (1938), 16–17; also in *Pageant,* I:12 (1938), 25.

Karl Barth, *Trouble and Promise in the Struggle of the Church in Germany,* in *The Register,* XXVII (1938), 19.

Hendrik Kraemer, *The Christian Message in a Non-Christian World,* in *ibid.,* XXVII (1938), 20; also in *Pageant,* I:7 (1938), 27.

Richard C. Cabot, *Honesty,* in *The Register,* XXVII (1938), 20; also in *Pageant,* I:7 (1938), 27.

W. L. Sperry, *We Prophesy in Part,* in *The Register,* XXVII (1938), 20–21; also in *Pageant,* I:8 (1938), 27.

George Stewart, *The Church,* in *The Register,* XXVII (1938), 21.

W. R. Inge, *Freedom, Love and Truth,* in *Pageant,* I:7 (1938), 27.

R. H. Walker, *The Modern Message of the Psalms*, in *ibid.*, I:9 (1938), 27.

Howard H. Brinton, *Children of Light*, in *ibid.*, I:9 (1938), 27.

G. W. Richards, *Creative Controversies in Christianity*, in *ibid.*, I:10 (1938), 27.

S. A. Cook, *The Truth of the Bible*, in *ibid.*, I:10 (1938), 27–28.

Louis Golding, *In the Steps of Moses the Law Giver*, in *ibid.*, I:10 (1938), 28.

R. J. Barker, *It Began in Galilee*, in *ibid.*, I:11 (1938), 27.

Fred Eastman, *Men of Power*, in *ibid.*, I:11 (1938), 27.

G. R. Jordan, *Adventures in Radiant Living*, in *ibid.*, I:11 (1938), 27.

Elbert Russell, *More Chapel Talks*, in *ibid.*, I:11 (1938), 27.

Mrs. Crosby (Juliette Graves) Adams, *Studies in Hymnology*, in *ibid.*, I:11 (1938), 27.

Edward Chiera, *They Wrote on Clay*, in *ibid.*, I:11 (1938), 27.

K. E. Kirk, *The Study of Theology*, in *The Register*, XXVIII (1940), 27.

Karl Barth, *The Knowledge of God and the Service of God*, in *ibid.*, XXVIII (1940), 27–28.

Nels F. S. Ferré, *Swedish Contributions to Modern Theology*, in *ibid.*, XXVIII (1940), 28.

Samuel Angus, *Essential Christianity*, in *ibid.*, XXVIII (1940), 28–29.

Robert E. Speer, *When Christianity Was New*, in *ibid.*, XXVIII (1940), 29.

Karl Barth, *The Church and the Political Problems of Our Day*, in *ibid.*, XXVIII (1940), 29–30.

E. E. Aubrey, *Living the Christian Faith*, in *ibid.*, XXVIII (1940), 30.

Reinhold Niebuhr, *The Nature and Destiny of Man*, in *The Princeton Seminary Bulletin*, XXXV (1941), 55–56.

Joseph Haroutunian, *Wisdom and Folly in Religion*, in *ibid.*, XXXV (1941), 56–57.

Henry P. Van Dusen, *Reality and Religion*, in *ibid.*, XXXV (1941), 57.

J. S. Whale, *Christian Doctrine*, in *ibid.*, XXXV (1942), 44–45.

Michael Coleman, *Faith Under Fire*, in *ibid.*, XXXVI (1942), 61.

John Wright Buckham, *The Inner World*, in *ibid.*, XXXVI (1942), 62.

D. C. Macintosh, *Personal Religion*, in *ibid.*, XXXVI (1943), 49.

Walter Marshall Horton, *Our Eternal Contemporary*, in *ibid.*, XXXVI (1943), 49–50.

Edgar Sheffield Brightman, *The Spiritual Life*, in *ibid.*, XXXVI (1943), 50–51.

Emil Brunner, *The Divine-Human Encounter*, in *ibid.*, XXXVII (1943), 57–58.

C. S. Lewis, *The Case for Christianity*, in *ibid.*, XXXVII (1943), 58.

Nels F. S. Ferré, *Return to Christianity*, in *ibid.*, XXXVII (1943), 58.

C. S. Lewis, *Out of the Silent Planet* and *Perelandra*, in *ibid.*, XXXVIII (1944), 60–61.

James D. Smart, *What a Man Can Believe*, in *ibid.*, XXXVIII (1944), 61.

Edwin Grant Conklin, *Man: Real and Ideal*, in *TT*, I (1944), 132–133.

W. K. Anderson, *Protestantism*, in *TT*, I (1945), 556–558.

D. T. Jenkins, *The Nature of Catholicity*, and A. G. Hebert, *The Form of the Church*, in *TT*, II (1945), 138–140.

O. T. Allis, *Prophecy and the Church*, in *TT*, II (1945), 420–422.

F. C. Grant, *Can We Still Believe in Immortality?*, in *The Princeton Seminary Bulletin*, XXXVIII (1945), 41–42.

W. L. Sperry, ed., *Religion and Our Divided Denominations*, in *ibid.*, XXXIX (1945), 48.

J. N. Neve, *Churches and Sects of Christendom*, in *ibid.*, XXXIX (1945), 48–49.

Zofia Kossak, *Blessed Are the Meek*, in *The Presbyterian*, CXV:2 (1945), 22–23.

Albert Hyma, *The Life of John Calvin*, in *ibid.*, CXV:2 (1945), 22–23.

Gladys I. Wade, *Thomas Traherne*, in *ibid.*, CXV:2 (1945), 22–23.

Walter Lowrie, *A Short Life of Kierkegaard*, in *ibid.*, CXV:2 (1945), 22–23.

Nicolas Zernov, *Three Russian Prophets*, in *ibid.*, CXV:2 (1945), 22–23.

Leo Auerbach, *The Babylonian Talmud*, in *ibid.*, CXV:12 (1945), 22–24.

St. Augustine, *The Soliloquies of Saint Augustine*, in *ibid.*, CXV:12 (1945), 22–24.

Jan van Ruysbroeck, *Jan van Ruysbroeck's The Seven Steps of the*

Ladder of Spiritual Love, in *ibid.*, CXV:12 (1945), 22–24.

Philip Melanchthon, *The Loci Communes of Philip Melanchthon*, in *ibid.*, CXV:12 (1945), 22–24.

Herbert of Cherbury, *Lord Herbert of Cherbury's De Religione Laici*, in *ibid.*, CXV:12 (1945), 22–24.

J. H. Newman, *A Newman Treasury*, ed. by C. F. Harrold, in *ibid.*, CXV:12 (1945), 22–24.

Daniel A. Poling, *A Treasury of Great Sermons*, in *ibid.*, CXV:24 (1945), 22–23.

G. Paul Butler, ed., *Best Sermons, 1944 Selection*, in *ibid.*, CXV:24 (1945), 22–23.

The American Pulpit Series, 8 vols., in *ibid.*, CXV:24 (1945), 22–23.

H. A. Bosley, *The Philosophical Heritage of the Christian Faith*, in *The Westminster Bookman*, IV:4 (1945), 6–7.

R. B. Perry, *The Hope of Immortality*, in *ibid.*, IV:5 (1945), 17.

L. D. Weatherhead, *The Will of God*, in *ibid.*, V:1 (1945), 19.

H. H. Stroup, *The Jehovah's Witnesses*, in *ibid.*, V:1 (1945), 27–28.

St. Athanasius, *The Incarnation of the Word of God*, in *The Princeton Seminary Bulletin*, XXXIX (1946), 49–50.

Walter M. Horton, *Our Christian Faith*, in *ibid.*, XXXIX (1946), 50.

C. S. Lewis, *The Great Divorce*, in *ibid.*, XXXIX (1946), 50–51.

William R. Cannon, *The Theology of John Wesley*, in *ibid.*, XL (1946) 47–48; also in *Christendom*, XII (1947), 250–252.

Willard L. Sperry, *Religion in America*, in *The Princeton Seminary Bulletin*, XL (1946), 48.

George A. Buttrick, *Christ and Man's Dilemma*, in *The Westminster Bookman*, VI:1 (1946) 13–15.

Arthur Dakin, *Calvinism*, in *ibid.*, VI:1 (1946), 26–27.

Wilbur M. Smith, *Therefore Stand*, in *Christendom*, XI (1946), 107–108.

Emil Brunner, *Revelation and Reason*, in *The Presbyterian*, 117:18 (1947), 14.

K. S. Latourette, ed., *The Gospel, the Church, and the World*, in *The Westminster Bookman*, VII:1 (1947), 13–14.

Emil Brunner, *The Mediator*, in *Monday Morning*, XII:36 (1947), 15.

O. W. Heick, *History of Protestant Theology*, in *Interpretation*, I (1947), 512–513.

Heinrich Boehmer, *Road to Reformation*, in *The Princeton Seminary Bulletin*, XLI (1947), 47–48.

Robert M. Grant, *The Bible in the Church: A Short History of Interpretation*, in *ibid.*, XLI (1948), 51–52.

R. J. Clinchy, *Faith and Freedom*, in *Christendom*, XIII (1948), 96–97.

J. J. Gavigan, *Writings of St. Augustine*, in *Presbyterian Life*, I:11 (1948), 26.

G. Aulén, *Church, Law, and Society*, in *Monday Morning*, XIII:28 (1948), 16.

Gerald Heard, *Is God Evident?*, in *The Westminster Bookman*, VIII:1 (1948), 9–10.

C. S. Lewis, *Miracles*, in *The Princeton Seminary Bulletin*, XLII (1949), 63–64.

Alan Richardson, *Christian Apologetics*, in *ibid.*, XLII (1949), 64–65.

Vergilius Ferm, *What Can We Believe?*, in *Presbyterian Life*, II:5 (1949), 31.

Donald Baillie, *God Was in Christ*, in *TT*, VI (1949), 121–123.

J. E. Dirks, *The Critical Theology of Theodore Parker*, in *Interpretation*, III (1949), 370.

E. M. Carlson, *The Reinterpretation of Luther*, in *Religion in Life*, XVIII (1949), 456–457.

John Calvin, *Instruction in Faith*, ed. by P. T. Fuhrmann, in *Presbyterian Life*, II:22 (1949), 25; also in *TT*, VII (1950), 270–271.

D. D. Williams, *God's Grace and Man's Hope*, in *The Westminster Bookman*, IX:2 (1949), 13–14.

Joseph Haroutunian, *Lust for Power*, in *The Pastor*, XIII:7 (1950), 38.

Benjamin B. Warfield, *The Person and Work of Christ*, ed. by Samuel G. Craig, in *The Princeton Seminary Bulletin*, XLIV (1950), 46.

Emil Brunner, *The Christian Doctrine of God*, in *ibid.*, XLIV (1950), 56–58.

Oscar Cullmann, *Christ and Time*, in *ibid.*, XLIV (1951), 60–61.

W. Norman Pittenger, *The Historic Faith and a Changing World*, in *Interpretation*, V (1951), 105.

H. Richard Niebuhr, *Christ and Culture*, in *The Presbyterian Tribune*, LXVI:12 (1951), 21.

Edward A. Dowey, *The Knowledge of God in Calvin's Theology*, in *Interpretation*, VI (1952), 376–377.

Herbert Schneider, *Religion in Twentieth-Century America,* in *The Princeton Seminary Bulletin,* XLVII (1953), 63.

Charles W. Kegley and Robert W. Bretall, eds., *The Theology of Paul Tillich,* in *ibid.,* XLVII (1953), 63–64.

Daniel D. Williams, *What Present-Day Theologians Are Thinking,* in *The Pastor,* XVI:6 (1953), 38–39; also in *The Westminster Bookman,* XII:1 (1953), 8–10.

Emil Brunner, *The Christian Doctrine of Creation and Redemption,* in *Interpretation,* VII (1953), 351–353.

John T. McNeill, *The History and Character of Calvinism,* in *The Christian Century,* LXXXI (1954), 924–925.

Edgar P. Dickie, *God Is Light,* in *The Westminster Bookman,* XIII:4 (1954), 13–14.

Otto Weber, *Karl Barth's Church Dogmatics,* in *The Princeton Seminary Bulletin,* XLVIII (1955), 48–49.

C. W. Kegley and R. W. Bretall, eds., *Reinhold Niebuhr: His Religious, Social, and Political Thought,* in *ibid.,* XLIX (1956), 58–59.

Paul Tillich, *Biblical Religion and the Search for Ultimate Reality,* in *ibid.,* XLIX (1956), 59.

Donald M. Baillie, *To Whom Shall We Go?,* in *The Westminster Bookman,* XV:3 (1956), 28–29.

D. R. G. Owen, *Body and Soul,* in *The Princeton Seminary Bulletin,* L (1957), 65–66.

Carl Michalson, ed., *Christianity and the Existentialists,* in *ibid.,* L (1957), 66–67.

Wilhelm Niesel, *The Theology of Calvin,* in *ibid.,* L (1957), 67–68.

Alexander C. Zabriskie, ed., *Dr. Lowrie of Princeton and Rome: Nine Essays in Acknowledgement of a Debt,* in *ibid.,* LI (1957), 54–55.

John T. McNeill, ed., *Calvin: Institutes of the Christian Religion,* in *The Westminster Bookman,* XX:1 (1961), 1–3.

Edward F. Gallahue, *Edward's Odyssey: An Autobiography,* in *TT,* XXVII (1971), 497–499.

The Baltimore Museum of Art; The M. H. De Young Memorial Museum, San Francisco; The Brooklyn Museum, *Vincent van Gogh: Paintings and Drawings,* in *TT,* XXVIII (1972), 263–265.

Hedy B. Landman, ed., *European and American Art: From Princeton Alumni Collections,* in *TT,* XXIX (1973), 334–336.

MISCELLANY

Translation from the French of Victor Monod, "The Relation Between Travel and Conversion," *The Expository Times*, L (1939), 183–187.

An Outline of the Christian Faith (revised edition of the "Intermediate Catechism," with Earl L. Douglass *et al.*). The Westminster Press, 1948, 16 pp.

A Year with the Bible. The Westminster Press, 1950, 24 pp. Published annually since 1950.

The First Systematic Theologian: Origen of Alexandria. Number eleven of Princeton Pamphlet Series. Princeton Theological Seminary, 1958, 43 pp.

"In Memoriam," Faculty minute for Dean Edward H. Roberts, *The Princeton Seminary Bulletin*, XLVIII (1955), 30–32.

"If You Have Been Raised with Christ," Vesper Meditation, April 20, 1958. Princeton Theological Seminary Speech Studio Library, 1958.

Vesper Meditation on Matt. 9:10 (Nov. 16, 1958). Princeton Theological Seminary Speech Studio Library, 1958.

"Who's Teaching Whom What?," *The Seminarian* (Princeton Theological Seminary), X:8 (Nov. 20, 1959), 1, 4.

"Theological Education Needs New Courage to Question," *ibid.*, XI:12 (Dec. 30, 1960), 1–2.

"Modern Art Reflects Existing Patterns and New Agnosticism," *ibid.*, XI:21 (Feb. 24, 1961), 3, 4.

"Modern Artist Depicts World's Chaos," *ibid.*, XII:4 (Oct. 20, 1961), 3.

"Review of Lectures: Paul L. Lehmann," *ibid.*, XIII:9 (Nov. 30, 1962), 3.

"The Pilgrim and the Passenger," Gallahue Conference, April 20, 1963. Princeton Theological Seminary Speech Studio Library, 1963.

"Kenneth S. Gapp, 1905–1966" (obituary), *TT*, XXIII (1966), 335–338.

"In Memoriam," Faculty minute for Kenneth Sperber Gapp, 1905–1966 (with B. M. Metzger), *The Princeton Seminary Bulletin*, LX (1966), 69–71.

"Faculty Report on the Funeral," Princeton Theological Seminary Faculty Minutes, 1967, 36 pp.

"Hints for Writing Term Papers," *The Wineskin* (Princeton Theological Seminary), VI (March 24, 1967), 1.

"A Note on the Tune 'Amberson,'" *TT*, XXIV (1967), 8–10.

"Memorial Tribute: Donald H. Wheeler" (with W. J. Beeners, E. G. Homrighausen), *The Princeton Seminary Bulletin*, LXI (1968), 92–93.

"Conference Summary," Gallahue Conference, April 21, 1968. Princeton Theological Seminary Speech Studio Library, 1968.

"Response to a Letter from the Vietnam Moratorium Committee," faculty section, *Viewpoint* (Princeton Theological Seminary), VII:4 (Dec. 5, 1969), 4.

"Karl Barth: 1886–1968" (obituary), *TT*, XXV (1969), 418.

"Nels F. S. Ferré, 1908–1971" (obituary), *TT*, XXVIII (1971), 5.

"Reinhold Niebuhr, 1892–1971" (obituary), *TT*, XXVIII (1971), 141.

"Chapel Service," Feb. 18, 1971. Princeton Theological Seminary Speech Studio Library, 1971.

"Teaching Religion with the Short Film." Abstracted for the American Academy of Religion, Atlanta, Ga. (Oct. 27, 1971).

"The Life of Jesus," class lectures, Feb. 17 and 24, 1972. Princeton Theological Seminary Speech Studio Library, 1972.

"Critic's Corner: Editor's Note on Symposia: Morality and Foreign Affairs," *TT*, XXVIII (1972), 486.

"A Tribute to Abraham J. Heschel," *TT*, XXX (1973), 266.

The Symbolism of Water and the Sacrament of Baptism. Pittsburgh: Thesis Theological Cassettes, 1974.

"John W. Meister, 1916–1974" (obituary), *TT*, XXXI (1974), 103.

"A Service of Remembrance" (June 3, 1974). Princeton Theological Seminary Speech Studio Library, 1974.

"Rossellini's 'Socrates'—A Colloquy," *TT*, XXXI (1974), 199, 203–204.

"Plato," *TT*, XXXI (1974), 205.

Here Is My Method (Tools for the Teaching Trade). Abstracted for the American Academy of Religion, Washington, D.C. (Oct. 25, 1974).

"A Select List of 50+ Short Films." Presented at the American Academy of Religion, Washington, D.C. (Oct. 25, 1974), 9 pp.

"An Interview with Dr. Hugh T. Kerr," *Viewpoint*, II (Nov. 1974), 1–4.

"Live and Learn," *Princeton Alumni Weekly,* LXXV (Nov. 12, 1974), 5.

Spirit '76: A Multi-Media Bicentennial Celebration (with Alan R. Blatecky and John M. Mulder). Princeton Theological Seminary Speech Studio Library, 1975.

"From a Marburg Sermon by Rudolf Bultmann, 1884–1976," *TT,* XXXIII (1976), 341.

"Symposium on Biblical Criticism," *TT,* XXXIII (1976), 354–355.

"All in All," *TT,* XXXIV (1977), 193.

"Meditation for Maundy Thursday," *TT,* XXXIII (1977), 368.

"Books That Shape Lives," *The Christian Century,* XCIV (Oct. 5, 1977), 888.

"Tim," *Princeton Theological Seminary Alumni News,* XVIII:1 (1977), 3–7.

"Bible Picture Stories," *TT,* XXXIV (1977), 52.

"Women and the Pastorate," *TT,* XXXIV (1978), 422.